Jean de Saintré

THE MIDDLE AGES SERIES

Ruth Mazo Karras, Series Editor
Edward Peters, Founding Editor

A complete list of books in the series
is available from the publisher.

Jean de Saintré

A Late Medieval Education
in Love and Chivalry

Antoine de La Sale

TRANSLATED BY

Roberta L. Krueger and Jane H. M. Taylor

PENN

UNIVERSITY OF PENNSYLVANIA PRESS

PHILADELPHIA

Published by
University of Pennsylvania Press
Philadelphia, Pennsylvania 19104-4112
www.upenn.edu/pennpress

Printed in the United States of America on acid-free paper
10 9 8 7 6 5 4 3 2 1

Library of Congress Cataloging-in-Publication Data

La Sale, Antoine de, 1385?–1461?
  [Hystoyre et plaisante cronicque. English.]
  Jean de Saintré : a late medieval education in love and
chivalry / Antoine de La Sale ; translated by Roberta L.
Krueger and Jane H. M. Taylor.—1st ed.
      p.   cm.— (The Middle Ages series)
  Includes bibliographical references and index.
  ISBN 978–0-8122–4586–8 (hardcover : alk. paper)
  1. Saintré, Jehan de, approximately 1320–1368—Fiction.
  I. Krueger, Roberta L.   II. Taylor, Jane H. M.
  III. Title.   IV. Series: Middle Ages series.
  PQ1567.H3K78   2014
  843′.2—dc23
                                          2013042038

CONTENTS

INTRODUCTION

Antoine de La Sale's *Le Petit Jehan de Saintré,* or *Jean de Saintré* is one of the most important works of prose fiction of the later Middle Ages. It has been hailed as one of the first historical novels for its account of what purports to be the chivalric biography of a historical knight, the fourteenth-century Jean of Saintré (1320–68), who was seneschal of Anjou and Maine. But, as we shall see, La Sale's account of the glorious exploits of a knight who lived a hundred years prior to the book's composition bears often only a tenuous relationship to historical events: the author's agenda extends well beyond providing an accurate account of the past. Written in the last days of the flowering of chivalry, poised on the threshold of the print revolution, *Saintré* can also be rightly considered one of the last great medieval compilations. Among the many materials incorporated within the fictional love story that will be described below, *Saintré* includes a treatise on the seven deadly sins; tracts on the Beatitudes and the seven virtues; advice about personal grooming; numerous detailed descriptions of clothing and armor; lengthy set pieces recounting ceremonial tournaments and other combats; as well as a conclusion strongly evocative of a fabliau. This fascinating blend of sacred and profane, fictional and historical, serious and comic modes has long intrigued critics and has earned *Saintré* a place in the French canon as a precursor to Rabelais, Madame de La Fayette, and Laclos.

Written in 1456 for Jean, Duke of Calabria, son of King René of Anjou, *Jean de Saintré* has long been prized for its accounts of chivalric exploits, heraldic blazons, and lavish costumes and for its sharp observation of social relations in a pseudo-historical court. The romance has also delighted readers with its seeming upending of courtly conventions in the last part of the romance, when a lusty monk cavorts with the earnest young knight's lady love and makes a laughingstock of self-proclaimed chivalric heroes, before being painfully punished by the hero for his wicked tongue. The splendid scenes at court, the comic undercutting of the hero, and the ironic twists and turns of the plot recounting a youth's social ascension from lowly page to one of the finest knights in the realm have ensured *Jean de Saintré* a place in the pantheon of late medieval French romances.

Nonetheless, certain aspects of *Saintré* have given readers pause. The romance includes lengthy didactic passages and citations from church doctrine that would seem more appropriate for a devotional treatise than a romance. La Sale's ample descriptions of clothing and livery, weaponry, heraldry, and chivalric protocol sometimes overwhelm the narrative thread. Indeed, as one critic has calculated, the love story that frames and supports the romance—the tale of Jean, Madame, and Lord Abbot—occupies less than a quarter of the text.[1] Readers interested primarily in the amorous intrigue may feel annoyed by what have been described as "ponderous moral, philosophical, or religious digressions that add nothing to the story being told" and as rather "laborious reports" of knightly processions and combats.[2] Yet it is precisely *Saintré*'s mosaic of discursive registers and its blended interlace of literary genres—courtly romance, didactic treatise, chivalric biography, heraldic handbook, fabliau—that make it such an intriguing example of a late medieval didactic romance.[3] Furthermore, this same amalgam of diverse styles, multiple voices, and different registers has earned *Saintré* recognition as a harbinger of modernity from Julia Kristeva.[4] Whatever one may think of this assessment (since the qualities that make *Saintré* the first prose novel for Kristeva are features of many late medieval narratives), *Saintré*'s hybrid textuality enhances rather than diminishes its character as a transitional text, a late medieval didactic compilation in a fictional frame that foreshadows in different ways both the encyclopedic narratives of Rabelais and the dramatic frame story of Marguerite de Navarre's *Heptaméron*, a collection of *nouvelles*.

Lest we doubt that Antoine de La Sale and his medieval readers valued the material that modern readers might find tedious—which is to say, the extensive parts of the romance that are not directly related to the love triangle—we have only to consider the romance in its manuscript context. One of the ten extant *Saintré* manuscripts, Bibliothèque nationale de France [BnF] MS nouv. acq. fr. 10057, is considered an author's manuscript, a copy on which La Sale made editorial corrections and additions, perhaps in his own hand.[5] The *mise en page* (layout) of folio after folio of this manuscript (fig. 1) shows that the author had no intention of minimizing the didactic citations or condensing the passages devoted to heraldry and tournaments. These sections are heavily rubricated, punctuated with larger capital letters, and generously laid out, with ample spaces between items. Each of the Ten Commandments, for example, appears on its own line. The processions of knights take place over many pages; rubricated letters penned with flourishes often introduce each knight. The hand of the editor (the author himself?) frequently indicates which citations or passages should be underlined in red, which in black. Although BnF MS nouv. acq. fr. 10057 is not illustrated, it is far from drab.[6] Its rubricated, pen-flourished initials, prominent *pieds-de-mouche* (paragraph markers), and elegant *mise en page* provide a decorative, vibrant frame that animates and enhances its contents. La Sale presents his patron with a handsome course pack of texts that would have been considered useful for a medieval courtly audience; moral lessons and practical advice are cleverly enfolded within an engaging love story whose racy dénouement keeps one reading to the end.

Antoine de La Sale's Life and Works: An Overview

Antoine de La Sale was born around 1385, the illegitimate son of the Gascon mercenary swordsman Bernardon de La Sale, whose martial skills served first for the English on French soil during the Hundred Years' War (1337–1453); then for popes based in Avignon during the Great Schism; and finally for Louis II of Anjou, putative heir to the throne of Sicily through his aunt Jeanne of Naples, descendant of Saint Louis's brother.[7] At the age of fourteen, Antoine became a page in Louis of Anjou's court. La Sale would remain in service to French noble families for the rest of his life, initially as page and squire to Louis II of Anjou (d. 1417), then as squire for Louis III (d. 1434) and preceptor for Jean of Anjou, son of King René (from around 1435 to 1448). His last assignment was as tutor for the three sons of Louis of Luxemburg, whom he served until his death in 1460. This varied experience included extensive travels: as we learn from autobiographical fragments within his writings, La Sale accompanied his benefactors and patrons throughout France, Italy, England, and the Mediterranean basin. He recounts several stories of journeys in Italy: into a mountain cave in the Apennines; on the Lipari Islands; and in the hills of Pozzuoli.[8] He describes a military expedition to Ceuta in North Africa in 1415;[9] he mentions tournaments and *pas d'armes** in Brussels, Ghent, Nancy, and Saumur (which we discuss further below). He accompanied René's daughter Marguerite to

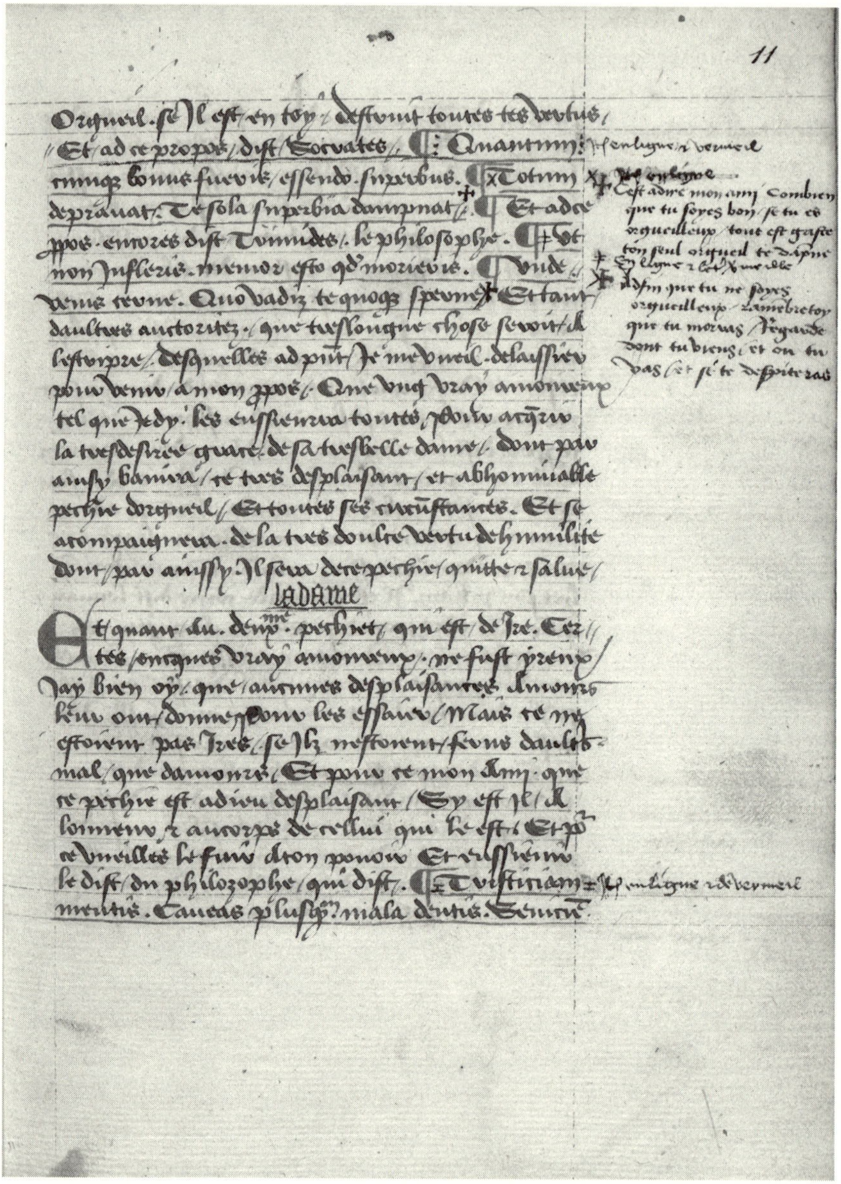

FIG. 1. Paris, BnF, MS nouv. acq. fr. 10057, f. 11r: showing La Sale's emendations.

Reproduced by permission of the Bibliothèque nationale de France.

London to marry King Henry VI.[10] It was perhaps these travels that gave him an international perspective[11] from which to observe the rich textures of court life and perceive firsthand both the protocol and the physical realities of chivalry. His experience as a tutor also gave him, no doubt, a predilection for moralizing discourse, much of it culled from classical authors and Christian doctrine, and stemming from the many years in which he was charged with the moral education of noble youth.

La Sale's first pedagogic tome was written in 1442–44 for Jean de Calabre, who had married Marie de Bourbon in 1437 at the age of eleven. Aptly named *La Salade,* an obvious play on the author's name, the book claims to be a textual mixed salad composed of "plusieurs bones herbes" (several good herbs) for Jean's instruction; it includes eight "grains of wisdom" from Cicero, along with numerous exempla from Frontinus and Valerius Maximus focusing on political tactics and military strategies. La Sale's principal source for the latter is not the Latin original but a fourteenth-century Middle French translation by Simon de Hesdin.[12] *La Salade* also presents a genealogy of the kingdom of Sicily that supports King René's and his son Jean de Calabre's claim to the throne; a royal edict by Philip the Fair regulating judicial duels, parts of which recur in *Saintré,*[13] as well as rules for the making of emperors in the Holy Roman Empire, and rules of chivalric engagement from Vegetius; La Sale concludes with several folios of a coronation ceremony in Latin, and a fragment from the epic poem *Aliscans,* in which the hero, weeping over adversity, is consoled by his wife. *La Salade* offers a recommended reading list of classical authors on various subjects for La Sale's young charge that is borrowed from Simon de Hesdin and closely resembles one that Madame des Belles Cousines will offer the young hero in *Saintré.*[14] La Sale's first didactic anthology seems tailored to the needs of an Angevin prince aspiring to the throne of Naples.

However, *La Salade* has a ludic element as well. In the midst of this rather ponderous tome of moral exempla and military strategies, La Sale offers two stories "pour rire et pour passer le temps" (to laugh and pass the time).[15] One is an eyewitness account of an expedition he took up Mount Sibilla near Pilate's Lake in the Marche to what was said to be the mouth of the Sibyl's grotto—a story that he composed some three years earlier (c. 1437 or 1438) for Marie de Bourbon's mother, Agnès. He retells the local legend of a German knight and his squire who disappeared forever within the Sibyl's cave, an apparent courtly "paradise" that is in fact a demonic lure. *Le Paradis de la Reine Sibylle,* as the story is known, mixes "realistic" geographic details with fantastical folklore.

The second tale, *The Voyage to the Lipari Islands,* also recounts an adventure from La Sale's youthful travels—a failed attempt with his companions to ascend Mount Vulcano and a strange encounter with a rather diabolic messenger who offers dubious and potentially dangerous advice about their moorings. The story, which claims to be truthful, leaves the reader with questions about the boundary between reality and fiction in La Sale's narration.[16] The fantastic tales of the Sibyl and the mysterious messenger both enliven the didactic compilation of *La Salade* and perhaps expressly complicate its moral lessons. One can see in *La Salade*'s playful blend of moral wisdom and fictional detour the seeds of *Saintré.*

If *La Salade* is an expressly haphazard "mix" of nutritious ingredients, a second pedagogic tome, *La Sale,* written in 1451, places its 167 exempla, or short moral tales, largely copied from Simon de Hesdin's translation of Valerius Maximus,[17] in a much more orderly frame. The compendium is organized as an allegorical "salle," or great room, in which the chapters stand as architectural elements that represent the moral virtues. If *La Salade* lacks a coherent theme, *La Sale* has been criticized as being "indigestible"[18] and excessively pedantic at best and, at worst, a work of plagiarism, sloppy scholarship, a "caricature" of his sources.[19] It is true that as many as two-thirds of the exempla are drawn from Simon de Hesdin. But to dismiss the work as mere plagiarism fails to take account of the pedagogical nature of the project; the book was written for the edification of Louis of Luxemburg's three sons. La Sale certainly makes no claim to originality—he says that he draws his work from "several holy authorities and other historians," making a selection because no one but God can know all that has been written.[20] Yet La Sale marks the collection as his own, not only through the title, but also at the beginning of each chapter, which he begins with his device, "Il convient . . ." (It occurs / it is appropriate), thus consciously framing the collection from first chapter to last; as Sylvie Lefèvre has shown, La Sale conspicuously signs his works as his own.[21] Among the sometimes tedious succession of salutary exempla and derivative stories are a few pieces that reflect La Sale's own travels. He includes both historical exempla—about Roman military heroes, for example—and stories that are explicitly fabulous—such as marvels from Ovid's *Metamorphoses* or from Ulysses's voyages. He incorporates a story that will be retold almost verbatim in *Saintré*—that of the widow who had survived twenty-two husbands but was survived by the man who had taken twenty wives—the exemplum and commentary both culled from Simon de Hesdin.[22]

Finally, and most extraordinarily, La Sale situates the work as the outcome of a personal crisis, a state of "très deplaisant merencolie" (very unpleasant melancholy) that overcame him as he left the house of Anjou, at the age
of sixty-three, in his forty-ninth year of service.[23] We know nothing about
the circumstances that led to his separation from King René's entourage; his
former pupil, Jean de Calabre, was certainly no longer a child. As the editor
of the manuscript has noted, however, in the ensuing pages La Sale intones a
half-dozen times against ingratitude;[24] perhaps the author has experienced
rejection and lack of rewards firsthand. By the time he pens *Saintré*, at the
age of seventy, not only has La Sale acquired vast experience as a teacher and
observer, he has also had occasion to reflect on human foibles and on the
social tensions and pressures involved in maintaining a high standing at court.

Jean de Saintré

Viewed against La Sale's earlier didactic tomes, *Jean de Saintré* can be
seen as a summa of his career as writer and teacher. *Saintré*, like *La Salade*
and *La Sale*, is among other things an anthology of instructional materials
largely derived from other sources. As we've seen, *Saintré* includes an exemplum and a reading list already incorporated into earlier work; numerous
lessons from Christian doctrine; and lengthy descriptions of coats of arms
and battle cries, as well as detailed accounts of chivalric protocol and ritualized feats of arms. Quotations from classical authors, from the Old and New
Testament, and from the Church Fathers abound.

Although the biblical citations and some of the classical dicta can be
matched to an original source, in most cases it is impossible to know what
particular medieval texts might have served as Antoine de La Sale's direct
inspiration, since many of the passages he cites appear in similar forms in
many other works. Tracts warning against the deadly sins, written originally
for monastic use, became common features of medieval literature, appearing
in penitential manuals for priests but also in conduct books for laypeople,
often changing the ordering of the sins and the description of their effects
according to the audience. Ramon Llull's *Livre de l'enseignement des enfants*,
ostensibly written for youths, lists gluttony as the first sin; the fourteenth-
century *Ménagier de Paris*, addressed to a Parisian bourgeois housewife, warns
first against pride and envy; for *Saintré*, the first sin is pride, followed by
anger and envy. Biblical and classical quotations and proverbs may have come

from a variety of sources, including florilegia, books of collected sayings, organized by theme or problem.[25]

Among the many didactic works that La Sale may have known are chivalric manuals such as Raoul de Houdenc's *Roman des eles,* Ramon Llull's *Book of the Order of Chivalry,* Geoffroi de Charny's *Book of Chivalry,* and Christine de Pizan's *Book of Deeds of Arms and of Chivalry* (which draws heavily on Vegetius), and didactic works such as the above-mentioned *Livre de l'enseignement des enfants,* the *Distichs of Cato,* and *Le Livre du Chevalier de la Tour Landry pour l'enseignement de ses filles.* La Sale may also have been inspired by one of numerous treatises on table manners that circulated in the later Middle Ages.[26] He and his audience might have known any number of other medieval conduct books, which instructed young men and women in proper comportment and imparted moral and religious values.[27] Conduct manuals were transmitted in a great variety of forms and formats during the Middle Ages; the broadest definition of the genre would include all the works mentioned in this paragraph. Often, as in *Saintré,* these books included a mix of didactic discourse and fiction.

An indisputable source for a few of *Saintré*'s didactic passages is *Saintré* itself. Most remarkably, at the dramatic moment that the aggrieved Saintré restrains himself from killing the Abbot (p. 199), he recalls almost verbatim the biblical passages that Madame had recited to him earlier (p. 30). By incorporating citations from the lady that had themselves been taken from another source, La Sale reveals his mastery of the art of strategic citation. Here and elsewhere, he recasts well-known words of wisdom to illuminate a particular moral action, here with the added irony that it is Madame's treachery that has provoked Saintré's need for spiritual guidance to curb his wrath.

Yet even as La Sale draws from the wellspring of numerous literary traditions, he goes much further than in his earlier work to present his borrowed materials in a clever, personalized frame. Moral teachings and Christian doctrine are voiced by Madame des Belles Cousines, a widow whose name suggests that she was one of the royal cousins. Madame's *enseignements* (teachings) are central to her campaign to groom a handsome, charming youth to become a valiant knight in her service. La Sale not only recasts the convention of numerous *chastoiements* (instructions) where older relatives or authorities teach young boys or girls, from the *Enseignements* of the historical Saint Louis for his son and daughter, to the fictional advice-giving of mothers to would-be knights in Chrétien's *Perceval* or Robert de Blois's *Beaudous.*[28]

He also draws explicitly and more broadly on a long, rich tradition of courtly romances in which a knight tests his mettle and proves his valor for love for a lady. When the lady chides Saintré that he can never hope to be a knight as fine as Lancelot, Tristan, or Ponthus and a host of others if he does not have a ladylove (p. 8), she evokes the legacy of Arthurian romances and their avatars in verse and prose, hundreds of tales that circulated from the twelfth to the fifteenth-century, in a diversity of manuscripts—from plain, service-able copies for well-to-do households to lavishly illustrated books for royal courts.[29] Madame's unfavorable comparison of Saintré to a well-known type of literary hero highlights an ironic gap between La Sale's representation of the pseudo-historical Saintré and his fictional sources. When Saintré suc-ceeds, he does so, as Michelle Szkilnik has argued,[30] less in the mold of an Arthurian hero than as the embodiment of a new kind of knight, one who fights more for personal advancement at court than to uphold a chivalric ideal.

La Sale and his audience were also familiar with chivalric biographies, such as the fifteenth-century biography of the historical Jean le Meingre, called Boucicaut,[31] who figures in a cameo in *Saintré,* and the life stories of fictional knights such as Jehan d'Avennes and Ponthus, whom La Sale cites explicitly.[32] It has been suggested that La Sale's inspiration for the figure of Saintré was less the historical Saintré himself (who lived a hundred years before the book's creation) than the contemporary Jacques de Lalaing, who died in 1453, and whose life eventually inspired a biography that postdates *Saintré* and seems in part to have drawn directly from it.[33]

Yet *Saintré* cannot be neatly summed up simply as either a conduct book, a courtly romance, or a straightforward chivalric biography. The last third of *Saintré* takes a new turn, into the realm of the recently minted *nouvelle,* a short narrative, often humorous, based on purported "true" contemporary events.[34] The *nouvelle* sometimes replays elements of the fabliau, a genre dating from the thirteenth century in which the principal players hail from a decidedly profane world and are ruled by base self-interest and carnal passions rather than lofty ideals of chivalry and courtly love. When, at the end of the romance, the lady who has preached scrupulous avoidance of the seven deadly sins has an affair with a hairy abbot during a series of copious Lenten meals in order to avenge herself on Saintré for his alleged betrayal of their love, she allows herself to be swayed by pride, anger, gluttony, and lust. Do we read this conclusion as an exemplum *in malo,* warning against the wiles of women, as the narrator at one point advises?[35] If so, are the previous teachings of Madame invalidated, since she has proved to be such a notoriously untrustworthy character?

La Sale gives didactic, courtly, and chivalric conventions a unique twist by intertwining them so cleverly together in his narrative thread that the book is impossible to classify generically. Is the text a courtly romance with a sometimes ponderous didactic bent; a didactic compendium within an amusing courtly framework; a chivalric biography that announces a new kind of knight, more courtier than warrior; a handbook of chivalric practices and lavish ceremonies that have fallen sadly out of use; or a bit of all of the above? Perhaps, with its ironic conclusion, *Saintré* sends up all these literary traditions and social practices. Perhaps the book functions above all as a celebration of the writer's skill in manipulating didactic, heraldic, and chivalric discourse at the same time that he critiques courtly values. One of La Sale's aims in writing such a complex story, with so many possible moral valences, may have been to encourage mature readers to engage with the material and draw their own conclusions. We invite our readers to do likewise.

To judge from his final works, La Sale continued to be deeply engaged in courtly culture. *Le Réconfort de Madame de Fresnes*, completed in 1457, offers two moving, short narratives about noble women who lost their sons in acts of war. In *Le Traité des anciens et des nouveaux tournois* (1459), written for Jacques of Luxemburg,[36] La Sale revives chivalric and heraldic traditions, which he claims are on the wane, by offering a digest of chivalric protocol.

Expert in Chivalry

In the summer of 1446, King René of Anjou, La Sale's patron and employer, organized a sumptuous *pas d'armes* at his castle of Saumur, in the Loire Valley. The conceit was highly theatrical: in a pavilion pitched on a dais in the tournament field was a damsel guarded by two lions. At her side was a dwarf, in charge of a shield; in the pavilion was a knight; any combatant who wished to—king, duke, count, baron, says the account—could strike the shield with his sword and demand combat with the damsel's knight-guardian.[37] It was, however, important to supervise the combats, and seven noblemen of the highest rank, with the wisdom brought by long experience (*sens amassé*), were ushered into a stand to act as judges (*juger en raison*). Among the seven judges was . . . Antoine de La Sale.[38]

His position of authority at such a prestigious royal event is significant, and speaks to the esteem in which he was held by René. La Sale had been attached for more than forty years to a court universally acknowledged, in the fifteenth century and at a time when such events were magnificent as never before, as the epicenter of the tournament and the *pas d'armes*; he had made a point of frequenting the kings of arms and heralds who were the repositories of chivalric knowledge; he seems to have taken part personally, in his youth, in at least two tournaments, in Brussels in 1409 and in Ghent in 1416. By 1456, as the author of *La Salade* and *La Sale*, he must have been recognized as knowledgeable and discerning—and indeed, only three years later, in 1459, he was to write the authoritative *Traité des anciens et des nouveaux tournois*,[39] dedicated to a new patron, Jacques of Luxemburg, which René himself drew on, in the 1460s, for his own magnificently illustrated *Livre des tournois*.[40] Once again, it is a tribute to La Sale's reputation that he should be asked to set out both a history of tournaments and the regulations that should govern them: he is, he says, a repository of knowledge drawn not only from his own experience but from extensive consultation and reading: he has a unique understanding of the finer points of tournament organization, heraldry, nobility. And it is difficult not to believe that his fictional *Jean de Saintré*, with its careful fictional portrayals of every variety of chivalric experience—tournament, *mêlée*, joust, *pas d'armes*, pitched battle, combats with lances, swords, daggers, poleaxes*—and its meticulous blazoning, is not, similarly, designed as a compendium of chivalry for his then patron, Jean de Calabre.

What emerges from *Saintré*, as well as from La Sale's *Traité*, is the ubiquity and seriousness of the tournament and the *pas d'armes* in the fifteenth century:[41] chroniclers of the late Middle Ages—Froissart, Olivier de La Marche—stud their histories with such occasions celebrating betrothals, marriages, peace negotiations. They are, largely, royal occasions, meticulously planned, choreographed, and executed, a showcase for the knight's skills, and, of course, a training ground for war. Geoffroi de Charny's manual of knighthood (c. 1350) reminds readers that a tournament may carry *peril de mort*.[42] Jousting, and the tournament, demanded sheer brute force, even brutality, and it is important to see that violence is a necessary component,[43] as in the case of Loisselench's damaged hand (p. 111). La Sale's *Saintré*, like his *Traité*, is written for an expert readership: entry to the lists is heavily regulated (both as to birth and as to record, hence, as *Saintré* has it, participants must be noble and *sans reproche* [p. 117; the *Traité* devotes several clauses to issues of rank and potential disqualification]); weapons are prescribed and carefully calibrated (see pp. 78, 105); the phases of each encounter are drawn up in detail (see p. 56), as are the permitted moves, and the criteria for judging success: how many courses* must be run, how many lances must be splintered, and how (pp. 56, 57). This latter point brings out how important the tournament and the joust are in terms of aesthetic experience: just as a modern sports devotee will appreciate, in the United States, the cunning of a forward pass, or in the United Kingdom the elegance of a cover drive, so the enthusiast reading La Sale's tournaments will understand, for instance (p. 81), that to strike the opponent's lames,* or his gardbrace,* is less meritorious than a direct strike on his breastplate. Appreciation of these niceties is, of course, difficult in the sort of *mêlée*, or mock battle,[44] that is Saintré's first venture into chivalry (see p. 61)—hence, perhaps, the preference for the sort of ritualized single combats that he was more generally to undertake: the jousts, the *pas d'armes*, or the *emprises*,* of the sort that René had organized at Saumur.

   Jean de Saintré includes a number of such exercises: did La Sale think that they best expressed chivalric mentalities in a princely court? They involved a theatricality[45] that even contemporary chroniclers and historians recognized: Olivier de La Marche, for instance, calls the famous "Pas de la Fontaine des Pleurs," held in 1449–50 under the auspices of the court of Burgundy, a *mistere*.[46] The hero of this latter notorious event was Jacques de Lalaing, whose life story may in part have inspired La Sale's *Jean de Saintré*; the account of Lalaing's career, written later, in c. 1468, draws, in part, on *Saintré*, as we have seen.[47] Lalaing—Alice Planche calls him "un homme-orchestre"—had a magnificent pavilion erected at a fountain; beside it sat a weeping lady with a unicorn. A herald in attendance would carry notice of any challengers to Lalaing, who would emerge from his lodgings in nearby Châlon-sur-Saône and offer combat, as prescribed in the *chapitres*, the articles, of the event, with different weapons: lance, sword, poleaxe, dagger. Opponents might present themselves anonymously, or in costume ("mesconnu")—the analogies with romance are powerful, and often, as with another Burgundian extravaganza, the "Pas de l'Arbre d'Or" (1468), perfectly explicit.[48] Saintré's *emprises* and *pas d'armes*, orchestrated by Madame des Belles Cousines, run very much the gamut of fifteenth-century chivalric display[49]—and it is worth noticing how far these are pan-European: a challenge issued to the Iberian courts eventually taken up in Barcelona by Messire Enguerrand; a challenge from a visiting Polish champion, the Seigneur de Loisselench; another from touring champions from Lombardy freshly arrived in Paris from Germany; a challenge issued, by Saintré, to all comers, for a joint enterprise against English knights from Calais. In all cases, and as with the historically attested *pas d'armes* we mentioned, the regulations governing the event are stipulated with a precision that shows how elaborate the forms of combat had become by the 1450s: the ranks and reputations that the combatants are to possess; the weapons to be used and in which sequence; the duration and rhythm of the event; the successes that will constitute victory; the prizes to be awarded. These latter are largely tokens: the exchange of magnificent jewels, as with Enguerrand, for instance (pp. 81–82), has analogies with the award of gold medals. But an adept jouster—like Boucicaut, who figures in the romance (pp. 95–124), like Jacques de Lalaing, or like Saintré himself—might expect to make a respectable living from the rich gifts (see pp. 90–92) donated by the courts at which the combats took place: money, jewels, sumptuous armor, magnificent fabrics, thoroughbred horses, even pottery or silverware. Lalaing, for instance, built an outstandingly successful career, and a fortune, largely out of his expertise in such exercises.

That said, participation in tournaments, *emprises,* and *pas d'armes* demanded major financial outlay—which is, of course, where Madame's generosity to Saintré means that she has, to a large degree, "made" him. It is she who prescribes, in minute detail, Saintré's equipment and dress, his retinues, his horses, and his weapons: they are models of conspicuous consumption. Luxury cloths and ornaments, heraldic achievements,[50] a whole apparatus of courtly display, is deployed at the service, with *Saintré*, of personal and chivalric reputation: self-adornment (p. 50) brings notice from the court and a coveted position as the King's *varlet-tranchant*;* gift giving (pp. 45, 50) is prescribed by Madame as a way to buy influence; chivalric ceremony— magnificently, ritually staged—confers prestige on Saintré himself, but also, of course, on the court where such glorious extravagances were practiced. Which explains the outlays that provided the material infrastructure for the tournament: La Sale describes, with some complacency (p. 118), the construction of the lists, the building of viewing stands for noble spectators and even houses for the competitors, the provision of liveries, the employment of kings of arms, heralds, minstrels, trumpeters.[51] Nor should we see these events as merely decorative—although La Sale might lead us to do so: on the contrary, tournaments and *emprises* are representations of the nature of power, and the hierarchies of court society were enacted and reinforced by such spectacles. Jacques of Luxemburg, presumably anxious to provide authentic ceremonial, was later to commission La Sale to lay out for him "comment les tournoiz en armes et en tymbres se font";[52] by fictionalizing such occasions, in *Jean de Saintré*, La Sale mitigates the transience of events and manufactures something like an official account—as his contemporaries did with careful, detailed verse accounts of René's authentic *pas d'armes*.[53]

But a tournament or a *pas d'armes*, as the last paragraph suggests, is of course also a visual spectacle: it is one of the important ways in which a court articulates an iconography for itself, in part, and most important, by means of the heraldry on which La Sale insists so meticulously.[54] As a tournament judge, and no doubt also by inclination, he had a vested interest in the art of blazon: on the tournament field, the armorial device served not only to mark out the individual, and to identify him as a member of an exclusive military elite, but also to provide a visual record of pedigree, and of familial and social ties. A coat of arms painted on a shield or on a banner, or embroidered on a surcoat, gave the wearer a chance to secure honor and prestige through deeds of arms, and heralds, and judges like La Sale, would be expected to identify, even in the confusion of the *mêlée*, those whose deeds had been most honorable—although realistically, in the *mêlée*, different means might be employed to make sure that the wearer was identifiable—hence the use of devices and helmet crests (Saintré's intertwined initials, Loisselench's silver bull), simple designs or badges intended to be easily recognizable, above the throng and at a distance. La Sale manipulates these complexities with practiced ease: although he may well have exploited existing sources,[55] he is visibly familiar with the formal, highly disciplined language of heraldry, which has its own vocabulary and syntax (whose intricacies we have tried to match in our translations of his blazons). And his luxuriant panoramas of the tournament field and the joust—translated into luscious color and detail by the British Library manuscript (see cover)—demonstrate, perhaps, how expert is the readership that he intended: what might seem to us an interminable list of champions and blazons (pp. 127–135), which in all probability he will have transcribed from an existing roll of arms,[56] were presumably pored over by an audience delighted to decipher identities and meanings from what to a present-day reader seems sadly hermetic.

Tournaments and *pas d'armes* may seem to take the lion's share of La Sale's attention—but there is an event which, clearly, overrides them: Saintré, we are told (pp. 123, 144), in spite of his prowess and his growing reputation, has refused flattering offers, from the King and others, to dub him knight because he prefers to achieve that honor on the battlefield—where, says Charny, deeds of arms are most honorable[57]—and ideally, says Madame, in a battle "contre les Sarrazins." The opportunity is provided by a military expedition to Prussia[58]—which readers may be surprised to see described as pagan, "Saracen," territory and ripe for a crusade. Briefly, one of the great orders of crusading knighthood, the so-called Teutonic Knights, established their headquarters in the thirteenth century in Marienburg (now in Poland), from where they pitted themselves, from about 1263 to 1386, largely against the powerful state of Lithuania until it accepted Christianity at the latter date.[59] In the fourteenth century, every winter, "crusaders" from all over Europe, in greater or lesser numbers, ventured north on what was seen as a prestigious expedition, success in which allowed the victors to display their coats of arms in Marienburg Castle; the expeditions, in reality, involved relatively small raiding parties that usually confined their efforts to destroying an enemy castle or, more reprehensibly, to plunder. Saintré's holy expedition to Prussia (p. 126) is imagined on a far greater scale than any authentic Prussian crusade, and involves adversaries—Turkey, Persia, Mesopotamia—quite beyond the imaginings of history: is La Sale compensating for what, by the mid-fifteenth century, amounted to the failure of the crusading movement, by amalgamating the Prussian crusades with the Nicopolis crusade, the disastrous expedition of 1396 where a huge crusading army was routed by Sultan Bayazid?[60] It is surely significant that the standard-bearer for the fictional Christian army is a "Gadiffer de La Sale" (c. 1350–c. 1422; see p. 144), a figure highly regarded in chivalric circles who did indeed take part in expeditions to Prussia in 1378 and 1390;[61] La Sale, it seems, is basking in the reflected glory of a namesake (and family member). But more important is the mere fact that it is here that Saintré has himself dubbed knight, and at the hand, specifically, of the near-blind John of Luxemburg, King of Bohemia, who had indeed crusaded in Prussia, who in 1346 died with spectacular gallantry at the Battle of Crécy, and who was regarded by contemporaries as a paragon of perfect chivalry.[62] Saintré's expedition is described in hyperbolic and idealized terms: the exhaustive list of participants, from France but also from the Empire,[63] the impressiveness of the "Saracens," the precision of Saintré's tactics, the ringing—and by 1456 deeply implausible—victory, Saintré's own unlikely triumph over the Grand Turk himself: these successes especially must have had particular resonance given that in 1453, only three years earlier, Mehmed II, with a huge besieging army, had taken Constantinople (Istanbul), and must have seemed a very present threat to Europe more generally. La Sale's portrait of a victorious Christian West, with Europe united in a common cause, is self-glorifying, and misleading: by 1456, a crusade to Jerusalem was largely a pious hope, although in July 1456 in Hungary—was La Sale conscious of it?—a small Christian army had repulsed a much larger Turkish one.[64] The romance seems nevertheless to assume that a knight wishing, like Gadiffer de La Salle, like our fictional Saintré, to make his own reputation, needed to enlist in a crusade.

La Sale's glorious aestheticization of chivalry is essentially nostalgic: even though the details of armor and deeds of arms, purportedly fourteenth-century, belong irreducibly to his own time, the romance plays out in the distance between the author's present and an imagined past of chivalrous encounters and gallant warriors. It is also, of course, distinctly literary: just as later medieval tournaments, like René's at Saumur, made their events theatrical,[65] so La Sale makes the "real" Saintré of the Hundred Years' War a performer, essentially the creator of his own romance.[66] This nostalgia, this literariness, must have made Madame's treachery and the Abbot's sneers all the more disruptive. Raymond Kilgour and Johann Huizinga make *Saintré* prime evidence for the "decline of chivalry";[67] on the contrary, perhaps for La Sale the romance is a glorification of a true chivalry that can, with the help of an enthusiast like La Sale, an authority like René d'Anjou, be reborn.

Saintré Editions and Translations

Jean de Saintré is by far La Sale's most celebrated work. There are ten medieval manuscripts, including one known as the "author's manuscript," containing editorial corrections that may have been penned by La Sale himself; two of these manuscripts were illustrated,[68] in very different fashions: the more ornate one in London, British Library MS. Cotton Nero D IX, in glorious jewel colors, by one of the most outstanding fifteenth-century illuminators, known as the Chief Associate of Maître François, who had worked extensively for royal patrons; and the second in Brussels, Bibliothèque Royale MS. 9457, in a series of rapid cartoons in black and white, done by an artist from what is known as the School of the Wavrin Master, whose figures are angular sketches against rudimentary backgrounds, and who specialized in densely illustrated manuscripts.

Four printed editions were produced in the sixteenth century (Michel Le Noir, 1517; Philippe Le Noir, 1523; Trepperel, n.d.; Bonfons, 1553). A full-text version edited by Thomas Gueulette, printed in 1724, inspired a whimsical adaptation, sharply condensed, without didactic tracts or heraldry, by the Comte de Tressan in 1780. Tressan's *Saintré*—a sentimental romance with chivalric highlights, bearing little resemblance to the original medieval compilation, was reprinted numerous times, in a variety of formats, throughout the eighteenth and nineteenth centuries.[69] This popular but distinctly inauthentic version of *Saintré* gave rise to a vaudeville production (by Dumersan et Brazier, performed in 1817) and even a comic opera (by Jules Barbier et al., 1893).

Le Petit Jehan de Saintré was restored to its integrity as a medieval romance in a succession of nineteenth- and twentieth-century editions that returned to manuscript sources.[70] Recent editions and translations into modern French, as well as a spate of books and articles, have brought *Saintré* into the critical limelight in French studies. *Saintré*'s generic complexity, La Sale's authorial self-consciousness, his clever framing devices, and his narrator's evident relish for telling a good tale in a splendid setting all ensure that the romance continues to fascinate students and scholars of European literature. With this translation, we hope to bring the pleasures and challenges of reading *Saintré* to a broader audience.

Saintré has been twice translated in full into English.[71] Both editions are out of print and stylistically dated. Our translation is based on the 1978 edition by Jean Misrahi and Charles A. Knudson; bracketed numbers in the text refer to pages in the Misrahi and Knudson edition. This one-volume text transcribes the Vatican manuscript, Bibl. Vaticana, Reg. Lat. 896, which Misrahi and Knudson feel best preserves the corrections that the author began in the "author's manuscript," BnF MS nouv. acq. fr. 10057, and then carried through to the end in three other manuscripts. Among the author's additions are the *didascalies*, or stage directions, that indicate who should be speaking—the Author, The Lady, or, more rarely, Saintré. This feature, which Misrahi and Knudson maintain, reinforces the sense that the narrator presents a dynamic amalgam of different discourses and narrative registers. Although we cannot of course reproduce the distinctive rubrics, flourishes, and *mise en page* of the manuscripts in which *Saintré* circulated during the Middle Ages, our retention of the designation of the Author, Madame, and

Saintré encourages readers to remember that *Saintré* was conceived as a multiplicity of voices and registers.

Our translation provides students and nonspecialized readers an entrée into the romance; medieval scholars should of course work directly with the original Middle French editions, not only Misrahi and Knudson but also Otaka, Eusebi, and Blanchard (which offers a translation into modern French by Quereuil). Scholars seeking more detailed information about La Sale's sources should consult the detailed notes in Otaka, as well as in Dubuis's translation, which provides perceptive, useful annotations. In preparing our translation, primarily from Misrahi and Knudson, we have benefited at various points from other editions and translations, to confirm a doubtful passage or to provide insights into a term. When our reading of a particular passage has been influenced by another translator, or when readers may find the notes of another edition particularly illuminating, we have indicated this in our notes.

Our aim here is above all an engaging narrative that moves the reader along through the different registers of the text—and so we have attempted to reproduce La Sale's different tones: didactic moralizing, heraldic pomp, chivalric heroism, ironic innuendo, comic reversal, while revising, as appropriate, the author's occasional repetitions, errors, and lapses. We have occasionally broken up more convoluted sentences and attempted to clarify awkward passages—and ironed out some syntactic awkwardnesses (like tenses, for instance, where La Sale often shifts from present to past and back again). La Sale's "translations" from the Latin are usually rough paraphrases or renderings of similar aphorisms in colloquial Middle French; there are frequent errors of transcription or grammar. We have remained faithful to the Middle French as it stands, and do not usually attempt to correct either the original Latin or the translation, unless the language is truly opaque. We have replicated for English, as accurately as possible and with the help particularly of the specialists we thank in the Acknowledgements, the particular terms that La Sale uses for foods, fabrics, dress, furnishings, weaponry, heraldry,[72] courtly ceremony; many are obscure, and hence are explained in the Glossary, with an asterisk in each case at the first occurrence. Proper names can be tricky: a romance like this, purporting to be historical, has a very large historical cast list—and since many of the players come from all over Europe but La Sale's knowledge of other languages and geographies is dubious, he gives them Middle French spellings. Only when the "correct" form is unmistakable do we translate (so the *conte de Bouquincan*, from

England, becomes the Duke of Buckingham, whereas the *seigneur d'Engorde*, also, but unidentifiably, from England, remains Lord Engorde). The result will not always be an easy ride, but we hope to have found a mode of translation that will be intriguing and will convey La Sale's pleasure in the variety of his story, the richness of his exempla, and the sheer opulence of the court culture in which he moves with such assurance.

Jean de Saintré

[1]¹ To you, most excellent and all-powerful prince, Monseigneur Jean d'Anjou, Duke of Calabria and of Lorraine, marcher lord and Marquis du Pont, my most honorable lord:² following my most humble and obedient commendations, in answer to your prayers, which are my total commands, I have the pleasure of offering you four beautiful treatises, arranged in two volumes so that they may be more easily carried. The first treatise tells about a lady of Belles Cousines from France, without identifying her by any other name or surname, and the most valiant knight, the Seigneur de Saintré. The second recounts the most loyal love and pitiable end of my lord Floridan, a knight, and of the most beautiful, gracious demoiselle Elvide, whom the book, which has been translated from Latin into French, does not name further, as it follows the story word for word. And the third will be a work that I've culled from the *Chronicles of Flanders*, which is a thing of wonder.³

First: The story of the lady whom
we shall call Belles Cousines and Saintré

At the time of King John of France, eldest son of King Philip of Valois,⁴ [2] there was in his court the Seigneur de Pouilly in Touraine, in whose entourage there was a most well-born and gracious youth named Jean, oldest son of the lord of Saintré, which was also located in Touraine.⁵ The youth's good manners found favor with the King, who determined to retain him and who ordered that he be made his page—for he was still quite young—and that he ride directly behind the King, and even further that he serve in the great hall as did his other nobly born young page boys. This Jean de Saintré excelled over all the other pages in serving each member of the court at table more diligently and industriously than did any of the others, and especially in providing the ladies, as best he could, with all the attentions and services that they ordered. Furthermore, for his thirteen years, he was a very clever, daring young lad, whether he was riding a very strong courser* or singing and dancing, or playing tennis,* running, jumping, or engaging in all the other exercises and activities that he saw men enjoying. He attempted to do everything joyously; in spite of the fact that his physique was then and remained slim and slight, his heart was of steel and surpassed all others. For his considerable talents, sweet demeanor, numerous courtesies, and gracious behavior, he was so beloved and praised by the King and Queen, by the lords and ladies, and by all others that everyone maintained and believed that if he lived he would be considered one of the most renowned gentlemen in France. And this turned out to be the case, for when he departed from the world he was esteemed as being among the most valiant of knights, as the following story, which recounts just a part of his many deeds, will tell.

THE AUTHOR: At that time, at the court of Queen Bonne of Bohemia,[6] wife of the aforementioned John, there was a rather young widow who was one of the royal cousins; [3] the story says nothing of her name or her lineage, for reasons that you will soon understand. Ever since the death of her honorable late husband, this lady had refused to remarry for any reason, perhaps wishing to resemble the real widows of ancient times of which Roman histories (which are the most excellent stories) make such glorious mention; I will skip over these histories to shorten my tale and come to the story of this particular lady who refused to remarry after her husband's death. It seems to me that Madame des Belles Cousines wanted above all to follow the example of the venerable widows from the past, as the histories tell it: which is to say that the Romans had the admirable custom of greatly praising and honoring those widows who resolved to remain unmarried after the death of their first husbands, and who chose to remain faithful and entirely chaste out of the very great and faithful love that they felt for them.[7] The Apostle Paul in his first epistle to Timothy, etc., speaks of this in the fifth chapter, "Honor the widows."[8]

Widows cannot be truly considered honorably so if they remain unmarried because they cannot find a husband to satisfy either their passion or their material interest or for any other reason; such women remain unmarried not for the love of God or for the love they bore their husbands. The truly honorable widows are those who refuse to remarry anyone at all, for either better or worse, as Virgil says in the fourth book of the *Aeneid*. Aeneas would have died for love of Dido, but Dido took no account of his love, for she had so loved and still loved her deceased husband that she was unable to forget him. When her sister, Anna, spoke to her about marriage, [4] Dido uttered the following words:

Ille meos, primus qui me junxit, amores
Abstulit; ille habeat secum servetque sepulcro.[9]

Which verse can be translated as: "The one who first joined me to himself, alas, has carried away my true love and taken it with him to his grave, where I want it to remain."

Just as the Romans honored with crowns those who had performed the most valiant deeds in arms (crowning anyone who led the way across the moat or the palisade of an enemy stronghold with the crown of valor, and bestowing on the one who first climbed up the ladders and scaled the walls of a city during a siege a mural crown) and similarly rewarded other acts of valor in the customary ways, by the same token they crowned widows who never intended to remarry and wished faithfully to maintain their chastity with the crown of chastity. These women were honored more than all the other widows were.

Saint Jerome writes about this in his second book, speaking to Jovinian about these widows, offering fine examples of several women who refused to take second husbands, such as Marcia, daughter of Cato, who ceaselessly mourned her dead spouse.[10] As her friends consoled her, they would question her and say, "Alas, when will your sorrows cease?" And she would answer them, "Not until the end of my life." Jerome speaks also of another widow, named Lucia, who wept continually day and night as she remembered her dear, departed husband; [5] to console her, her father spoke to her about a new husband. "Alas, my lord," she said, "for the love of God, say no more about this." And when her father rebuked her for remaining a widow at such a young age, she finally replied to him, "My lord, I loved my husband so much that I could never love another man even a little. And if in my confused state, I took another husband who was good to me, my heart could never feel any joy, for fear of losing him. And if another man should be proud or harsh with me, my sorrowful life would surely be brief." Thus she intended to remain an unmarried widow as long as she lived.

Blessed Saint Jerome offers many other fine examples that I will not mention, since anyone who wishes to can consult them. Among these examples of marriage, he mentions one that is amusing, in the ninety-sixth book of his *Letters*.[11] This concerns a Roman woman who was not one of these perfect widows, for she had been married to twenty-two husbands. It just so happened that she found a man in the city who had married twenty wives, whom she married amid great laughter and festivity to the great delight and amusement of the Romans, who were eager to see which of the two would survive. As it happened, the woman died first. At which point, all the young gallants of Rome came forth to bestow laurel branches on the husband as a salute to his victory over the woman who had finished off twenty-two husbands. So with great glee they crowned him with a garland of green leaves and led him so bedecked through the city to the sound of drums and trumpets, crying throughout: "Long live Palmo! Long live Palmo, who has overcome the woman with twenty-two husbands!" I shall give no further examples, so that we can return to the story of Madame and young Saintré. [6]

THE AUTHOR: Although she had vowed never to marry again under any circumstances, this lady harbored many contradictory thoughts in her heart, including the idea (which she often entertained) that she might transform a young knight or squire from the court into a gentleman of great renown, and she finally made the decision to do just that. She spent many days observing the conduct and behavior of all the young gentlemen and boys at court, intending to select the one who pleased her most, and in the end she settled on young Saintré.[12] She spoke to him about various matters many times in public in order to assess his demeanor and his speech; the more she spoke to him, the more he pleased her. But she did not dare—nor did she intend—to speak of anything at all related to love.

So it came to pass, as Fortune and Love would have it, that one day after Madame had assisted with the Queen's bedtime rituals and was passing through the galleries toward her chambers followed by a retinue of squires, ladies, and damsels, she came upon little Saintré, who was watching a tennis game in the courtyard below. As he saw Madame's squires pass, he immediately fell respectfully to his knees.

Delighted to see the young man, Madame said as she swept by him, "Saintré, what are you doing here? Is this the proper way for a squire to behave, not escorting the ladies? Now go along, master Saintré; run ahead and place yourself in front of us."

Little Saintré was mortified. His face red with embarrassment, he bowed and took his place in front of the others. When Madame saw him run ahead, she strolled along laughing with her ladies and saying, [7] "Just wait until we get to my room; we'll really be able to laugh."

"About what, Madame?" said Lady Jeanne.

"About what? As soon as we get there, you'll see the battle between little Saintré and me."

"Alas, Madame," said Lady Katherine, "what has he done wrong? He's such a good boy."

No sooner had she uttered these words than Madame entered her room and announced to everyone there, "Now all you gentlemen go away, and leave us alone here."

At these words, the men all hurried out, and little Saintré knelt to take his leave. When Madame saw him kneeling before her, she said, "You will stay here, young man, you aren't included among the gentlemen. I want a word with you here." Then the door was closed.

Madame, seated at the foot of the little bed, made him sit with her and her ladies; she then made him promise to answer all her questions truthfully. Yet as he gave his word, the poor lad—who did not understand Madame's motives—thought to himself, "Alas! What have I done wrong? What's going to happen to me?"

While he was racking his brains, Madame, smiling at her ladies, said, "Now, master, by the faith that you've promised me, tell me first of all: how long has it been since you have seen your ladylove?"

Saintré had never thought of any such thing, so when he heard talk of a ladylove, his eyes filled with tears, his heart trembled, and his face turned pale; he could not utter a word.

Then Madame said, "What's this, master? Whatever do you mean by this behavior?"

And the other ladies, who were sitting around him laughing, said, "Saintré, dear friend, why won't you let Madame know how long it has been since you've seen your lady? It's scarcely an onerous request, or something you ought to conceal [8] since you promised to tell the truth."

They pressed him so hard that he finally said, "Madame, I don't have a ladylove."

"You've no one?" asked Madame. "Well, who would be the lucky lady to have you as a lover? Perhaps you have no one; that I can believe. But how about the one whom you love above all others and *wish* would be your lady: how long has it been since you've seen *her*?"

Little Saintré, who had yet to feel or enjoy any amorous desires, as has been said, lost all his composure during this questioning; all he could do was to twist the tassel of his belt between his fingers, wordless for quite some time.

When Madame saw that he was not answering, she said, "All right, good sir, what does this behavior mean? Have you nothing to say at all? When I ask you how long it has been since you have seen your lady, I'm doing you no harm."

Then Lady Jeanne, Lady Katherine, Isabel, and the others, who were laughing at all this, took pity on him, and said to Madame: "He's not ready to answer such a question today, but if you forgive him this time, he'll bring you an answer tomorrow."

"Tomorrow?" asked Madame. "I want an answer before he leaves this room."

Then the ladies crowded around him, calling him "my son" or "my friend" or "young Saintré." "Tell Madame precisely when it was that you last saw your ladylove, or she won't let you go."

Completely overwhelmed by the ladies' attention, Saintré finally said, "What do you expect me to say, when I don't have a ladylove? If I had one, I would gladly tell you!"

They replied, "Tell us, without further ado, whom you love the most."

"The one I love the most is my mother," he answered, "and after that my sister Jacqueline." [9]

To which Madame retorted, "Young man, I don't want to hear about your mother and your sister; love for mothers, sisters, and parents is completely different from the love one feels for a ladylove. I'm asking about women who are no relation to you."

"Truly, my lady, I don't love any lady like that."

"There's no woman at all?" Madame inquired. "Ha! That's disgraceful for a gentleman—and you insist that you have no ladylove at all? I can tell from this statement that you'll never amount to anything. Oh, cowardly heart that you have, where do you think all the great acts of valor come from—those great feats of arms and chivalrous deeds of Lancelot, Gauvain, Tristan, Guiron le Courtois, and the other worthy knights of the Round Table? What about the valor of Pontus and of so many other worthy knights and squires from the kingdom of France—and so many others I can't count them, whom I'd name if I had the time—where would any of these knights be if it weren't for their love service and their efforts to remain in the favor of their dearly beloved ladies? I even know some gentlemen whose efforts to be true lovers and to serve their ladies loyally have earned them such high honors that their fine reputations will live forever. And if they hadn't been in love, no one would have taken any more account of them than of an ordinary man. And you, my lord, you're saying that you've never loved a lady, nor ever desired to have one? Since this is the case, you should leave immediately, as the most wretched of human failures!"

Since Madame smiled as she pronounced these words, the ladies realized that she was only joking.. But when poor Saintré heard Madame bid him leave so cruelly, alas! he thought at the very least that he was completely disgraced, and he began to weep bitterly. [10] Then Lady Jeanne, Lady Katherine, Isabel, and the other ladies took pity on him; they knelt down laughing before Madame, begging her to deign to pardon him this one time and promising on his behalf that he would appear within two days, having chosen a lady whom he would serve.

"Certainly not," replied Madame. "You're deluding yourselves if you think that a cowardly heart can ever accomplish anything of merit." "Yes he will, my lady," they said.

"What do you say, my lord?" inquired Madame. "You're half asleep! Will you ever be as worthy as they claim?" Then the poor unfortunate lad summoned up his courage and said, "Yes, my lady, if it should please you."

"Do you promise me that?"

"Yes, Madame, by my faith," he replied.

"Well then, be off now; and whatever happens, make sure that tomorrow you appear in the galleries at the same time that I found you there today, and that I find you there again, or otherwise you may consider yourself dismissed."

The poor prisoner, thus freed, knelt to take leave of Madame and the others and left the room. As he bade farewell to the ladies, they told him, "Remember your promise, for we've pledged our honor against your actions."

As soon as Saintré left the room, he bolted and ran as if chased by a pack of wolves. Madame and her other ladies, who were retiring for an afternoon nap, could not stop laughing and discussing the fright that Saintré had shown in her chambers; they kept laughing until vespers rang, and they had to get up without having slept at all.

When Saintré encountered the rest of his young companions, God knows that he told them about these new adventures! [11] But then, overcome by relief at having escaped, he gradually forgot his promise, except at those moments when he fled at the sight of Madame and her other ladies, which made them laugh in glee. But once, at dinner, two of Madame's ladies were seated at table watching him move back and forth as usual, serving all the other ladies and maidens except them; they called him before them and scolded him. "So, good lord Saintré, what game have we lost you in? You used to serve us along with the others, but now you're avoiding us."

"My ladies," he replied, lowering his eyes in humiliation, "with your permission . . . ," running off as he spoke. The two ladies fell into fits of laughing.

It so happened that Madame, who was seated at the foot of the King and Queen's table, caught sight of little Saintré as he stood before the ladies and noticed how they laughed at him; she asked them, once the tables were removed, what Saintré had said to them to make them laugh so hard. The ladies told Madame how Saintré had served all the ladies but them, and how he had replied to their request as he hurried past them.

"Now let me handle this," said Madame. "But let's wait until Madame the Queen has retired to her chambers, so that we'll laugh even more."

When it came time for the parting cup,* Madame, who observed little Saintré bringing a cup to serve them, made him come to her side, saying, "Saintré, go to the galleries and wait for me there, whatever happens, for I wish to send you to town to do me a favor; I'll be much obliged if you do."

Little Saintré was delighted to hear Madame speak so kindly; he thought that she had completely forgotten his promise, [12] so he said, "I shall be very pleased to do it, Madame."

After the King and Queen retired, young Saintré took himself off to the galleries. It wasn't long before the King fell asleep and Madame headed to her bedchamber, where she found little Saintré just as she had instructed him, and she said, "Go on ahead with the others."

When she arrived in her room, she sat at the foot of the little bed and ordered all her squires and the other men to leave. Then she called little Saintré over and said, "Now, sir, I have you here with me. Where is your good faith, which you have twice promised me? You've been avoiding me for the past four days! What vengeance and what punishment should one impose on a man who has broken his promise?"

Hearing these hard, cruel words, Saintré wished he were dead; he fell to his knees with his hands clasped before him, begging Madame for mercy, saying that he had really been very busy. Madame, who saw her ladies laughing behind his back, controlled herself as best she could, and told him, "Very well, young sir, let's suppose that it's just as you say: in these four days, have you chosen a lady?"

When he heard these words, he wished he were dead; his eyes flooded with tears, his face grew pale and began to sweat, for he had forgotten everything: he no longer knew what to say or how to make excuses for himself.

Seeing him in such straits, Madame then said, laughing softly to her ladies, "What do you have to say about a failure of a squire, who has twice given his word to a lady, as you know, and failed at such a small task: [13] what punishment should he have? You, Lady Jeanne, I ask you first."

When the poor, well-born youth heard himself so bitterly reproached by Madame, he could only think that all was lost at one blow and that he would be forever disgraced. So with hands clasped, still on his knees, he entreated Madame once again, for God's sake, for mercy and then turned toward the other ladies, begging for their help.

Madame was delighted by all this, all the more so when she saw how humble and innocent he was. Thinking that she could cleverly enlist him in her service and that she would put him in her thrall, she found him all the more lovable. Yet she still wanted Lady Jeanne and the others to answer her question.

Lady Jeanne, moved to pity, not realizing—any more than did any of the others—what Madame was intending to do, said, "Alas! My lady, if he's failed in his promise, you've heard him offer the excuse that he has been so very busy. He implores your mercy so humbly on bended knees with his hands clasped, just as we all do on his behalf."

"And you, Lady Katherine, what do you think?"

"Alas, my lady, I don't know what to say, except that he is repentant and that you'll find him so: so I beg you to have mercy on him."

"And you, Isabel, who are the eldest, what's your opinion?"

"My lady, I agree with the others; and, furthermore, you know that the poor prisoner has confessed truthfully that he has not chosen a lady to serve; I find that more convincing than anything else he might say. My lady, pardon me for saying this, but there is much to think about if you haven't been inspired to love anyone yet and if you're a new lover determined to love and serve loyally, as he is. [14] You have to make a good choice, and be able to submit yourself completely to the commands of a lady; but in all honesty, my lady, I think that he has never seen Love and that Love has never spoken to him."

"Isn't that true, my son?" Isabel inquired of Saintré.

"By my faith, mother Isabel, I swear that I've never spoken with Love nor seen him."

"Now look, my lady, at this poor supplicant who has not seen Love, or known Love, or spoken with him. How could he possibly have chosen a lady so quickly? For even those who are acquainted with Love, fearing a refusal, often spend a good deal of time reflecting on these matters. That's why, my lady, I really think that just this time he deserves to be pardoned."

"And what do you think, Marguerite, Alice, and all you other ladies? I want each of you to have your say."

Then all the others expressed the same opinion as Isabel, who was the eldest and who had seen and heard the most.

MADAME: "Now I've heard what everyone thinks, and you're of one voice about his broken word and the pardon he deserves. As for me, out of love for you all, I'll forgive him this one time. But I'm warning you that he has failed to name his lady, as he was supposed to have done."

"Ha, my lady," they said, laughing, "he has indeed done so."

"No, he hasn't," insisted Madame.

"Well! Don't you think, my lady, that he has spent the past four days choosing the lady whom he intends to serve?"

"No, I don't," replied Madame.

"But he has," they answered. "We guarantee that he's done so." And then they asked him, "Isn't this true, my son?"

The poor lad, completely frightened and tormented by the ladies' question, [15] was obliged to say yes, and Madame said, "Well, then, you seem to be a man of your word, as long as this is the case. Do tell us who she is, and you'll truly be my friend."

At these words, Jean felt forced to name someone; he began to weep and his face lost all color, as if he were someone who had never done such a thing before.

Then Madame addressed her ladies, "Didn't I tell you so? If he said he had a lady, it was only in order to escape us."

"Alas," the ladies all said. "Saintré, you must tell Madame truthfully. And you, Madame, draw him aside. Do you think that a true lover would announce in public the name of a lady he loves so much?"

So Madame said to him, "Then come over here with me," and then whispered, "Saintré, my friend, right now, only you and I can hear what you're going to say: now tell me truthfully who it is."

When poor Saintré saw that there was no way no way out, he said, "Alas, my lady, forgive me. And since you want so much to know . . ." As he reflected on whom he would name, since hearts that resemble one another have a natural affinity, he decided to name a young girl at court who was ten years old; and so he told her, "My lady, it is Matheline de Courcy."

When Madame heard him name Matheline de Courcy, she realized that childhood love and ignorance were at work; nonetheless, even more than before she pretended to be deeply scandalized. "Now I see that you really are a poor excuse for a squire for having chosen to serve Matheline. I'm not saying that Matheline is not a very pretty girl, from a good family, one that's even better than your own, young man. [16] But what possible benefit, profit, honor, support, advantage, comfort, aid, or counsel can you hope to gain from this choice that would make you a worthy gentleman? What are the benefits that you can expect to have from Matheline, who is still no more than a child? My boy, you ought to select a lady of high, noble blood, who is wise and has the wherewithal to help you and meet your needs; you ought to serve such a lady and love her loyally, so that whatever pains you may suffer, she'll easily recognize that you bear her a perfect, sincere love. Don't believe for a minute that if you select the right woman she won't eventually acknowledge it, and have pity, mercy and compassion for you, or that she won't be extremely grateful—unless she is the cruelest woman I've ever heard of. Remember that this is how you can be sure to become a man of worth. And if you don't do this, I wouldn't give you or your deeds the slightest chance of success, just as the Master says in his ballade, which goes like this:

> The Master
> Firstly, man must love loyally,
> And on one lady set his heart;
> Any who does so differently,
> Will never do his noble part:
> He will forget the chivalric art.
> For if he gives himself free rein,
> And to all ladies gives his heart,
> He'll always make but little gain. [17]

> What gain he'll have comes wretchedly,
> And comes from sources of bad part;
> Nor can it yet be differently.
> And then when so he gives his heart,
> And recognizes his own heart.
> He'll see, God knows, how far in vain

He's wasted all riches of the heart,
And always make but little gain.

The gain he has is niggardly,
When so many have taken their part;
And Love refuses vehemently,
To have such, men beloved at heart.
By all such, men are torn apart.
For if he gives himself free rein,
And to all ladies gives his heart,
He'll always make but little gain."

THE LADY: "Still on this subject, I'm informing you that he who seeks to serve such a lady loyally can be saved body and soul, and I'll tell you why. Concerning the soul, we should know that anyone who refrains from mortal sin is saved, for other venial sins are remitted by true confession and annulled through minor penance. Therefore, if someone keeps himself from mortal sin—if he loves loyally as I shall explain—he will be saved.

"First, about the sin of Pride: if the lover wishes to obtain the longed-for grace of his lady, he must strive to be agreeable, humble, courteous and gracious, so that no dishonorable words might be uttered about him. This is according to the saying of the wise Thales of Miletus,[13] who said: *Si tibi copia, si sapiencia formaque detur, sola superbia destruit omnia si commitetur.* That is to say, my friend: [18] 'Even if you abound in riches, even if you have wisdom, nobility, and every bodily perfection, Pride alone, if it be in you, destroys all your virtues.' And with respect to this, Socrates says: *Quantumcunque bonus fueris, essendo superbus, totum depravat, te sola superbia dampnat.* Which is to say, my friend: 'However good you may be, if you are proud, everything is corrupted: your pride alone condemns you.' Along these lines again the philosopher Trimides says: *Ut non infleris, memor esto quod morieris; unde venis cerne, quo vadis, te quoque sperne.* 'Lest you be proud, remember that you will die; observe where you have come from and where you will go, so hold yourself in contempt.' So many other authorities have written about this that it would take a very long time to list them all. So I'll drop this matter at present to return to my subject, which is that a true lover, the kind I'm talking about, will follow all this advice in order to obtain the longed-for grace of his very beautiful lady, for the sake of whom he will banish this most unpleasant and abominable sin of Pride and all its features. He will adopt the very sweet virtue of Humility, by which he will be spared and saved from sin."

THE LADY: "As for the second sin, which is Anger, certainly no true lover was ever angry. I've heard that love has sometimes inflicted unpleasant situations on some people, to test them, but the effect produced by this cannot be considered anger if it was caused by nothing other than love. Because this sin displeases God, Anger strikes the honor and the heart of the one who displays it. For this reason, you should do all that you can to avoid it, following the saying of the Philosopher,[14] who says, *Tristiciam mentis caveas plusquam mala dentis; seniciem fugias, numquam piger ad bona fias.* [19] Which is to say, my friend: 'Flee dark thoughts more than a toothache; beware also of laziness, to rid your heart of sorrow, and strive always to do well.' And along these lines, Pittacus of Mytilene says: *Effugias yram, ne pestem det tibi diram: iuris delira nutrix est scismatis yra.* Which means, my friend: 'Flee Anger and Ire, so that you are not stricken by their fearful malady; for these states will lead you astray from the right path; they nurture all schisms and divisions.'

"And the Gospel has this to say: *Non odias aliquem, sed eum pocius tibi placa: quisquis odit fratrem censetur ab hoc omicida.*[15] Which means, my friend, that you should bear neither anger nor hatred, but rather should live in peace with all; for whoever hates his brother is a murderer, as the Gospel says. And about this Saint Augustine says, in one of his Letters, that just as bad wine spoils and ruins the vessel in which it is stored, if it remains there for a long time, so Anger spoils and corrupts the heart where it is held. And on this the Apostle agrees, who says: *Sol non occidat super yracondiam vestram.*[16] Which means, my friend, that the sun should not set on your anger or ire.

"And in the same vein, Cato says: *Impedit ira animum, ne possit cernere verum.*[17] In other words, my friend: 'Ire and Anger so obstruct and blind the heart of a person that he cannot see the truth.' Which is why, my friend, the true lover I speak of is always joyous, and should always be so, with the hope that by serving loyally and well he will be rewarded by love and by his most beloved ladylove. [20] Therefore, he sings, dances, and makes merry, following the sayings of Solomon, who at the end of his last book concludes by saying, *Bene vivere et letari.* Which means: 'Live well and joyously.' But such good living implies not simply eating delicious meats, drinking good wines, sleeping late in the morning in a comfortable bed and enjoying all the other delights of love; rather, it means living well with God, maintaining oneself honestly, truthfully, and taking joy in doing so. Therefore I say that all true lovers wishing to bask in the good graces of their very beautiful ladies should do everything in their power to avoid the sin of Anger, which is despised by God and by the world, and should keep company instead with the most loving virtue of Patience, so that they may be exempt from the unpleasant, bothersome sin of Anger.

"As for the third sin, which is Envy, the true lover I speak of will never feel envious of anyone; if his lady found out about it, he would lose her forever. For a lady of honor could never love an envious man, unless he be envious of good virtues: to be the best person, to be the most devout at church, the one who eats most courteously at table, who is the most gracious and agreeable in the company of ladies, the most valiant in military arms or in courtly jousts, and who desires to do the very best of all, and is envious in no other sense. Seneca has this to say about it: *Quid auro melius? Jaspis. Quid jaspide? Sensus. Quid sensu? Racio. Quid racione? Modus. Omnibus adde modum; modus est pulcherrima virtus.* Which means, my son and friend: 'What is better than gold? Jasper. What is better than jasper? Sense.[18] What is better than sense? Reason. [21] What is better than Reason? Manner.[19] Manner is the crown of all virtues.'

"The Philosopher has more to say on the subject: *Filius ancille morosus plus valet ille quam regis natus, si non sit moriginatus.* Which is to say, my friend, that the well-instructed son of a chambermaid is more worthy than the badly brought up son of a king. And furthermore, on the subject of good morals, my friend, I report that the wise Solon of Athens has this to say: *Per vinum miser, per talos et mulieres: hec tria, si sequeris, semper egenus eris.* Which means, dear friend, that if you keep company with wine, dice, and loose women, you will always be poor, mean, and miserable, and hated by all good men. And again about the base sin of Envy, Plato says: *Invidiam fugere studeas et amore carere, que reddit siccum corpus faciens cor iniquum.* 'Strive to flee Envy, for Envy is without love and dries up the body and makes the heart evil and cruel.' Therefore, my friend, flee all vices and all vicious people, for Love itself and all ladies of honor command all true lovers to follow the wisdom of the Philosopher, who says, *Malo mori fame quam nomen perdere fame.*[20] Which means, my friend: 'I would rather die of hunger than lose the name of a good reputation.' So to conclude, dear friend, remember the saying: 'I would prefer to die of hunger than be willing to lose my good reputation.' And speaking further about these words of the Philosopher, the wise Chilon of Lacedaemonia says: *Nobilis es genere, debes nobilis magis esse: nobilitas morum plus est quam progenitorum: nobilitas generis mortem superare nequibit.*

Which is to say, my friend: 'If you are of noble birth you must be even more noble in your virtues, [22] for nobility of good conduct is worth more than nobility of birth, and noble birth, no matter how great or powerful it may be, will never be able to overcome death.' Therefore, in order to be the very true lover of whom I speak, you must avoid the extremely unworthy sin of Envy. And if you keep company with the most glorious virtue of Charity, who is a daughter of God, and which we have previously commended to you, you will be clean, pure, and saved with respect to this sin."

THE LADY: "And as for the fourth sin, which is Avarice, certainly Avarice and true Love can never dwell in the same heart. If a miser falls in love, for whatever reason, there is no reason to believe that it won't be with a miserable, base creature, so that he won't have to spend anything on her. But the true, loyal lover will have no greater ambition than to serve Love and his lady honorably with the greatest liberality, by being well dressed and mounted on a fine horse, along with his entire retinue, although always in a manner appropriate to his rank. And anyone who spends beyond his means will be foolish and unhappy, for Love and honorable ladies do not love extravagant lovers of this sort but rather love those who maintain themselves according to their estate; that is to say, those who outfit themselves in arms for battle, tournaments, jousts, and all manner of noble assembly as honorably as they are able to without foolish expenditures, and who willingly give of their wealth for the sake of God to those most in need, following the Gospel, which says, *Beati misericordes quoniam ipsi misericordiam consequentur* (*Mathei, quinto capitulo*).[21] Which means, my friend: 'Blessed are those who are merciful, for they will find mercy.' So also says Periander of Corinth: *Ut sis preclarus, non sis cupidus nec avarus, vix ut illi carus cupidus cunctis fit avarus.* [23] Which is to say, my friend: 'So that you may be considered superior, be neither covetous nor avaricious, and possess only sufficient wealth, for a man who lives by avarice will be loved by no one, but rather hated by all.'

"The Philosopher agrees with this, saying: *Furtum, rappina, fenus, fraudem, simoniam causat avaricia, ludum, periuria, bella: radix cunctorum fit nempe cupido malorum.* That is to say, my friend: that Avarice is the cause of theft, rapine, usury, fraud, deception, simony, perjury, war, and, to sum up, is the root of all evil. Bias of Priene agrees with this, saying, *Plus flet perdendo cupidus quam gaudet habendo: et magis est servus cum plus sibi crescit acervus.* Which means, dear friend: 'The covetous man cries more over what he loses than he enjoys what he has; and the more he hoards, the more he becomes a miserable slave to his possessions.' On this subject, Saint Augustine says that the heart of a miser is similar to Hell, for Hell does not know how to say of the hearts it swallows up, 'That's enough,' and so it is with the miser, for even if all the wealth in the world were in his possession, he would still never have enough. On which subject, the Gospel says, *Insaciabilis oculus cupidi in partem iniquitatis non saciabitur (Ecclesiastici xiiii^e capitulo).*[22] Which means, my friend: 'The miser's eye is insatiable: he will not be satisfied by any amount of iniquity.' And there are so many other authorities, my friend, who have so much to say on the subject that I must leave them and this subject now. Therefore, for all these reasons, in order to acquire the highly desired favors of his very beautiful lady, the true lover, as I have defined him, will accomplish all these good things and will shun the most unpleasant sin of Avarice, keeping company instead with the sweetest, most amiable virtue of generosity, [24] which is beloved by God and honored by the world. And in this manner he will be saved.'

THE LADY: "Concerning the fifth sin, which is Sloth, indeed my friend no true lover can be slothful, for the sweetest and most loving thoughts that he harbors day and night about how to earn the desired favors of his most beautiful lady would never allow this. For whether in singing or in dancing, above all others he will be the most diligent and enthusiastic: he will rise early in the morning, will say his Hours,[23] will piously attend Mass, and will take off to hunt game while lazier lovers are still sleeping; that's how he will avoid the sin of Sloth, following the words of the philosopher Epicurus, who says, *Ocia, vina, dapes caveas ne sit tibi labes; vix homo sit castus requiescens et bene pastus.* Which is to say, my friend: 'Avoid Sloth and excessive wine and food, lest you be sullied by lust; for he who is idle and has overindulged at the table will have a hard time remaining chaste.' Saint Bernard has more to say about the dreadful sin of Sloth: *Vidi stultos se excusantes sub fortuna: vix autem diligenciam cum infortunio sociabis; sed minus infortunium a pigricia separabis.* Which means, my friend: 'I have seen many fools blame their condition on bad fortune: you will be hard pressed to find a diligent man who is unfortunate, whereas you will see many for whom Sloth and bad fortune go hand in hand.' And Saint Bernard has this further to say about that: *Revidere que sua sunt, quomodo sunt, summa prudencia est.* Which is to say, my friend: 'To keep things constantly under review and to see them as they are and for what they are is the height of prudence.' And by 'revidere' he doesn't mean simply to 'see' things but to 're-view' them: and by 'review,' he means that no one can look too often.

[25] "And the poet Atheus has more to say about this, when he says: *Ocia sunt juvenum menti plerumque venenum est juvenum pausa viciorum maxima causa.* Which means, my friend, that idleness is often the venom that poisons the thoughts of young people, for the idleness of youth is a particularly insidious cause of vice. And on this subject, Seneca says: *Accidiam linque que dat mala tedia vite: tedia virtutis fuge nam sunt dampna salutis.* That is to say, my friend, you should avoid idleness, which engenders evil affliction in life; flee the enemies of all virtuous qualities. And because the lovers of whom I have been speaking are spared by such virtues, they abandon the vilest and most unfortunate sin of Sloth to keep company rather with the most splendid virtue of diligence, therefore I entreat you to be like these virtuous lovers, and thus you will be saved from the unfortunate sin of Sloth."

THE LADY: "And as for the sixth sin, which is overeating[24] or Gluttony, indeed the true lover has not even a bit of this quality, for he eats and drinks soberly and only in order to sustain himself, following the Philosopher, who says that one must eat and drink to live and not live to eat and drink, as do swinish people. The wise Thales of Miletus has this to say on the subject: *Pone gule frenum ne sumas inde venenum: Nam mal digestus, cibus exta sepe molestus.* That is to say, my friend: 'You must curb your appetite so that you don't ingest venom, for an abundance of badly digested food is a very harmful poison for the body.' And the wise Solon of Athens has more to say about this: *Ne confunderis numquam vino replearis; vili diceris nisi vino te modereris.* That is to say, my friend, you should never drink your fill of wine, [26] lest you become drunk; for you will earn the reputation of a lout if you are not moderate in your drinking. And on the subject of Gluttony, Saint Gregory says in his commentary on the Book of Job that whenever the vice of Gluttony takes hold of someone, that person loses all the good that he has ever accomplished. When the stomach is not restrained by the rightful order of abstinence, all virtues are drowned in him. As Saint Paul says, *Quorum finis interitus: quorum Deus venter est; et gloria in confusione eorum qui terrena sapiunt (Ad Philippenses, iiii* capitulo).*[25] Which is to say, my friend, that the end of those who savor earthly pleasures is death, as it is for those who worship their bellies as if they were God; and the glory that they derive will be the ruin of their ambitions in arms, in love, and in the body. So I pray that you not be one of these people, but that in order to avoid such a fate you rather live according to the sayings of Avicenna, who says: *Sic semper comedas ut surgas esuriendo; sic eciam sumas moderate vina bibendo.* That is to say, my friend: 'Eat always in such manner that when you rise from the table your appetite is not sated, and also drink in moderation.' By these means you will naturally live a very long life, and you will be in God's grace with respect to this sin, as well as in the good graces of Love and of your lady. Thus you will have avoided the shameful, disgraceful sin of Gluttony, and you will keep company with the sweet virtue of Abstinence, flower of all virtues; you will therefore be clean of this sin and saved. And thus I come to the end of the salvation of true, loyal lovers with respect to the sixth deadly sin, which is Gluttony.'

THE LADY: "As for the seventh sin, which is Lust, truly, my friend, [27] this sin is completely extinguished in the heart of the true lover, for he is in such great fear that he may thereby lose his lady and that she may be displeased that even a single base thought resides in him: therefore he follows the maxim of Saint Augustine, who preaches: *Luxuriam fugito, en vili nomine fias; carni non credas, ne Christum crimine ledas.* That is to say, my friend: 'Flee Lust, that you not be held in ill repute; furthermore, avoid the flesh, lest you offend Christ with your sin.' Saint Peter the Apostle offers more on this subject, in his first Epistle, where he says: *Obsecro vos, tanquam advenas et peregrinos, abstinere vos a carnalibus desideriis quae militant adversus animam (Prima Petri, iiii* capitulo).*[26] That is to say, my friend, 'I entreat you as strangers and travelers that you abstain from carnal pleasures, for they wage war night and day on the soul.'

"And the Philosopher has more to say about this: *Sex perdunt vere homines in muliere: Animam, ingenium, mores, vim, lumina, voces.*[27] Which means, my friend, that the man who frequents loose women loses six things: the first thing he loses is his soul, the second his wit, the third his good morals, the fourth his strength, the fifth his sight, the sixth his voice. And therefore, my friend, you should flee this sin in all its different forms. Furthermore, it is said, Cassiodorus in his commentary on the Psalms says that Vanity turned the angels into devils and brought death to the first man, taking away all the bliss that had been given to him, and that Vanity is the nursemaid of all evil, the wellspring of all vice, the path of iniquity, the sin that casts man out from the grace of God. [28]

"On this matter, David says in the Psalms, speaking to God: *Odisti observantes vanitates supervacue (Psalmus xxx).*[28] That is, my friend: 'You, my only God, have hated and hate all those who defend vanities.' And so many other authorities have written on this matter, not only the holy fathers of Holy Church, but also philosophers, poets and other wise pagans who did not yet possess the true knowledge of the most holy, loving grace of our true

God the Holy Spirit—so many who have so strongly condemned this sin that it would be too long to recount all their writings, which I intend to skip over, to get to the rest of the story. I will cite only Boethius, who says, *Luxuria est ardor in accessu, fector in recessu, brevis delectacio corporis, et anime destructio.* Which is to say, dear friend, 'Lust brings ardor in union, stench at separation, brief enjoyment to the body, and destruction to the soul.'

"And so, my friend, because this sin is so vile, the true lover, as I've said, fearing his lady's displeasure and longing to bask in her favor, will do all that he can to avoid it. And if ever, under the pressure of love, he should fall into this sin, so great are the agonies and dangers that he might suffer through the great perils that might ensue, the perils that the agonized hearts of loyal lovers must endure, that this should not be counted as a mortal sin. If ever such a sin were to occur, it would surely be quenched by the thought of the great pains I've mentioned that these lovers will have to endure. Therefore, I can honestly say that the true lover whom I've described will be clean of this deadly sin and all the others—he will be free of all these sins, and saved." [29]

THE LADY: "And as for the salvation of the body: I said earlier that the true lover can be saved by these means in body and soul: after salvation from the seven deadly sins that concern the soul, I will now turn to the salvation of the body. This will come about in several ways, of which the first is the state of Love. The true loyal lover, who is of noble birth, is healthy and clean in mind and body. Day and night he engages in the loving quest for the favors of his very beautiful lady, and this in seven ways that are the very opposite of the seven deadly sins, as I've said. This lady will surpass all others in honor (and here I mean all the ladies, for all women are ladies when they are in love). Even if she had no desire to feel love for him or for any other man, nonetheless, nature, justice, and reason will compel her to love, honor, and esteem him all the more. She should be overjoyed by his honor and his advancement, and on the other hand, she should be sorry for his misfortunes, whatever kind of lady she may be. Whatever his rank or nobility may be, as I've said, she will never fail to come to his aid, if necessary, with her goods and possessions, otherwise she should be considered base, ungracious, fit to be cast out from the worthy and then thrown body and soul into the wide, putrid abyss of the sin of Ingratitude—although I have never heard of a single lady like that. And by these means the true lover who is saved in his soul may also be saved in his body."

THE LADY: "And as for the rest, concerning other ways the body may be saved, the truly noble lover who has no inclination or directive to do so, need

not study the virtuous, holy sciences of theology, canon law, or other fields
of law. [30] All that he need learn is the most noble and illustrious profession
of arms. This is the domain where he will acquire honor and the desired
favor of his most beautiful lady, by making himself noticed, by presenting
himself first in line, and by accomplishing such feats of valor that he causes
stories to be told about himself above all others. When he is at Mass, he
should be the most devout; at table, the best mannered; in the company of
knights and ladies, the most courteous. His ears should be unsullied by vulgar
language; his eyes should never issue a false glance; his mouth should never
utter an uncouth word; his hands should not make a false pledge or an ill-
placed gesture; his feet should not stray into any forbidden place. What more
shall I say? He will be more favorably endowed with good qualities than
everyone else, and in feats of arms he will fight to the best of his abilities. He
should be equipped with the very latest and best in armor; he should have
the best mount and be the best dressed.

"For the love of his lady, he will fight on horseback and on foot, despite
the fact that it could be said that his chivalric exploits arise from the vanity
forbidden by the Church, just as it is written in the Decretals,[29] which, I have
heard, talk about such things. First, in relation to the verse where it is said:
Et alibi non temptabis Dominum Deum tuum.[30] The question is to know if
God will bring victory to those who fight in a judicial duel for the right
cause. See further: *Predestinaciones xxiii^e, questione quarta,* where it is said
that neither experience nor law endorses a combat of this sort. I hope hereby
also to prove that to indulge in a judicial duel is to test God, for the learned
say that to ask for something which might go against nature is to hope for a
miracle or to test God. To these authorities we might add, *'De Purgacione
Vulgary' per totum, in capitulo 'Consuluisti' secunda, questione quinta. Item:
capitulo 'Predestinaciones' vicesima tertia, questione quarta, et notabiliter in capitulo 'Gloriosus de veneracione sanctorum,' libro sexto. Item: codice 'Ut nemo in
propria causa sua jus sibi dicat,' per totum;* [31] *Codice 'De Gladiatoribus tollen-
dis,' lege una, libra xi.* I could cite innumerable other decrees forbidding any
judicial combat and other feats of arms that I am talking about here.

"But emperors, kings, and other princes of the high nobility acting
according to their right and to seigniorial custom, have ordered such battles
and insisted upon them when the matter required. This question was the
subject of a great debate between the Holy Father, Pope Urban V, and Good
King John of France about an engagement for combat between two knights,
one French and one English, at Villeneuve-lès-Avignon.[31] So strongly did the

Pope wish to uphold the law of the Decretals that he ordered and had posted on all the church doors a notice threatening to excommunicate anyone who went to watch the fight. Nonetheless our most Christian king, to assert his royal prerogative, refused to back down and insisted on applying the laws vested in his temporal powers, which decree: *Leges de pa., et eius pairapho 'Si quis homines'; eadem lege 'Et une re.,' parapho 'Si quis alium.' Lege lombarda que incipit ' Si quis,' parapho ult°. Lege lombarda ' De const.,' et lege 'Similiter,' parapho ult°. In lombarda 'De omicidio,' lege 'Si quem.' In lombarda 'De pariti.,' lege ultima. In lombarda 'De omicidio,' lege 'Liber homo.' In lombarda 'De fur.,' lege 'Si quis alium.' In lombarda 'De adulterio,' lege tercia.*[32]

"There are many other authorities concerning judicial battles of this kind; the so-called Lombard laws permit duels of this sort freely, and in several particular modes. [32]

"Even so, today individual combats of this sort are to a large extent forbidden by order of the most Christian king Good King Philip, in a law to which we subscribe at present: this permits duels in only four instances, and in none other.[33] The first situation relates to cases of proven, indisputable, and evident wrongdoing, and is covered by the clause specifying incontrovertible homicide, treason, or other similar crime where the evidence is very strong. The second situation relates to crimes that would merit the execution of the criminal. This would not apply to the crime of theft, which cannot be adjudicated by duel, because the death penalty would not be imposed.

"The third circumstance obtains when punishment of the offender cannot be exacted other than through judicial combat, as in cases of murder or covered treason, where the person who has committed the crime has no defense other than through bodily combat. The final reason is if the accusation is made on the basis of solid evidence or facts that are presumed to be true: this last exception is the case of evidence.

"Therefore even though such combats are forbidden, or limited to those circumstances dictated by the Church or in the Decretals, to avoid falling into the sin of seeming to test God or into the sin of vanity, to return to my point, the true lover will not engage in combat for one of these two sinful reasons, that is, vanity or testing God. He will engage in combat only to increase his honor and without quarrel or animus against his opponent. I stress that the honorable combatant should never seek to harm or to dishonor his opponent, any more than he would seek his own harm or dishonor. To ensure this, he should seek God for assistance and as his witness, for himself and so that God may hear him better. [33] He should be confessed and shriven because of the perils that may arise from their sworn oaths. I shall pass over the ceremonies governing the oaths of the combatants to make my story shorter.

"When the true lover leaves his pavilion* fully armed, as appropriate, bearing his shield and all the requisite armor, then he should make the sign of the cross and kiss his pennon; his lance or his rapier[34]—used for attack and for defending himself as best as he can—will be placed in his right hand. He will wait seated on his bench, or remain standing, until the call or word comes from the judge or the field marshal. Then this true, loyal lover will advance bravely and proudly, ready to devour his opponent and defend himself as best he can, protecting himself well; he will undertake his first blows cautiously and with prudence, as Valerius Maximus says in his sixth book, where he remarks that it's a great shame for a commander or a combatant to conclude, 'I didn't foresee that it would turn out this way.' For when it comes to steel on steel, and to battles that are the most dangerous form of fighting, no one can change the outcome by waging the same fight a second time. It is the same with feats of war; they too should be conducted according to wise, prudent counsel and thus brought to a good conclusion; this is confirmed by Vegetius in the first book of his *Art of Chivalry*,[35] where he says of those who wander through life without reason that 'they can rectify everything except errors made in wars and battles fought without forethought, and these no one can remedy—because once the harmful deed is done, punishment follows immediately.'

"For this reason, my friend, the wise, true, and loyal lover should be prudent and moderate in all his words and deeds. [34] Even if those who behave this way are not the strongest or the most numerous in battle, they are often victorious, triumphing in the most ferocious wars. They follow the dictum of the Wise Man who says, as was cited earlier: *Malo mori fame quam nomen perdere fame.*[36] Which means, my friend: 'I would rather die of hunger than lose my good reputation.' Furthermore, this perfect lover will show all due gratitude to all those who have done, or will do, him a favor, whether it is through their advice, their instruction, or their gifts; thus he will live always according to the principles of Aristotle, who says, *Diis parentibus et doctoribus non possumus reddere equivalens.* Which means, my friend, that we shall never be able to repay the same benefits that they have given us to the gods, to our teachers and to our relatives (that is, to God, to our fathers, mothers, and other blood relations)."

THE LADY AGAIN: "Now, my friend, I've shown and told you many things. I pray God that you've retained all or at least most of what you've heard. What do you think? Do you feel in your heart that you have the strength and courage to do all this? Pray tell me what you are thinking."

THE AUTHOR: When Madame had finished her speech, Saintré, like the child he was, felt overwhelmed by so many beautiful instructions; he could not utter a word.

Then she said, "What do you say, young sir? Do you have the courage and the strength to undertake these things?"

Then poor Saintré, hard pressed to reply, raised his eyes to her face and in a low voice said, "Yes, my lady, very willingly."

"You would do this, my friend?"

"Yes, my lady, with all my heart. But which lady of the quality you describe would want my service? Who would love someone like me?" [35]

"Why wouldn't there be someone to love you?" replied Madame. "Aren't you of noble blood? Aren't you a handsome young man? Don't you have eyes to see, ears to hear, a mouth and tongue to speak, arms and hands to serve, legs and feet to run, a heart and body to engage yourself to the loyal service that the lady would demand of you?"

"I do, my lady."

"Well then," she said, "why don't you take a chance? You don't imagine, do you, that however worthy you may be, there is a lady who thinks so little of her honor that she would beg you to serve her? Although it must be said that there are some ladies so driven by love that they can't help tenderly revealing their affections, thereby giving the lover license to proceed. So why don't you act boldly? For the more honorable your lady may be, the more she will esteem you for it, and think all the more highly of you."

SAINTRÉ: "My lady, I would rather die than offer myself and be refused, and then be mocked and made fun of, as I've heard has happened to others. That's why I would rather simply remain as I am."

When Madame heard him say this, and with good cause, and when she realized that he was failing to grasp what she was driving at, she could not refrain from revealing her feelings, and said to him:

THE LADY: "Well now, good Christian noble man that you are, will you swear to me by God, on your faith as a Christian and on your honor—there's no one here but you and me, and no one can hear us—that you will tell not a soul, living or dead, what I'm about to say to you, under any circumstances?

[36] Do you promise not to reveal or even hint at anything that I'm going to tell you, now or at any other time? Will you will promise me this by taking my hand with yours?"

"Yes, my lady," he said, "I promise."

THE LADY: Then Madame said to him, "Well then, Saintré, suppose that I were the lady I've been describing to you? Suppose I would promise to do you every favor. in return for your service and that I would lead you to great honor—would you be willing to obey me?"

THE AUTHOR: Little Saintré, who had never dreamt of love service to any lady, did not know what to say or do, except to kneel down and say, "My lady, I would do everything that you might command."

"And so, with your hand in mine, do you pledge me your faith?"

"Yes, by my faith. And upon my loyalty, my lady, I will carry out all that I promise, and I will do everything that you would wish to command."

"Then please rise and listen carefully to what I say and remember it."

THE LADY: "First of all, I desire and command that above all else you love God with all your heart according to the commandments of Holy Church, and to the very best of your abilities. Furthermore, I wish and command that, after God and as best you can, you love and serve the Blessed Virgin Mary above all else. Beyond this, I want and command that you love and commend yourself to the very blessed True Cross upon which Our Lord suffered and died to save us; the Cross is our true sign and our only defense against all our enemies[37] and evil spirits. [37]

"Further, I want and command that every day you say a *Pater Noster* or another prayer to your guardian angel to whom God has entrusted your body and soul, that he may guide you, protect you, and defend you if he should not be with you, and that he be there throughout your life and at the moment of your death.

"Further, I wish and command that you keep always in your heart Saint Michael, Saint Gabriel, or some other angel, in order that they be your advocates, sponsors, and ambassadors to Our Lord and Our Lady, just as those who cannot be present or speak on their own behalf often have advocates at a royal court to speak for them.

"Furthermore, I wish and bid that you respect and honor the Ten Commandments[38] with all the faith in your power, just as I recite them:

First, you shall not worship any idol or false god.
You shall never take the name of the Lord in vain.

You shall keep the Lord's day and the holy days.

You shall honor your father and your mother.

You shall not murder.

You shall not commit adultery.

You shall not steal.

You shall not bear false witness.

You shall not covet your neighbor's wife.

You shall not be envious of your neighbor.

THE LADY: "And then I wish and command that you believe completely in the Twelve Articles of Faith,[39] that is the theological virtues that foster good thinking, as Cassiodorus says in his commentary on *The Creed,* that faith is the light of the soul, the gate of heaven, the window of life, and the foundation of enduring salvation, [38] for without faith no one can please God. Saint Paul the Apostle says this on the subject, *Sine fide est impossibile placere Deo (xi^e cap^o.).*[40] That is to say, my friend, that without faith it is impossible to please God.

"Six of these articles concern the divinity of God the Father and the other six are about the humanity of Jesus Christ; those pertaining to the divinity of God are as follows:

To believe in God the Father omnipotent, creator of heaven and earth.

To believe in his true son made incarnate, Jesus Christ, our true savior.

To believe in God the Holy Spirit, true Love of God the Father for God the son, and of God the son for God the Father.

To believe in Holy Church and her commandments.

To believe in the communion of the saints and the remission of sins.

To believe in the general resurrection of the dead and in eternal life.

"And the six articles concerning the humanity of Jesus Christ are these:

To believe that the second person of the Trinity—that is, Jesus the son of God the father—was conceived by the Holy Spirit and born of the Virgin Mary.

To believe that he was crucified, suffered death and was buried by the order of Pontius Pilate.

To believe that after his death he descended into hell to free the holy
   prophets and the just.
To believe that on the third day he rose by his own power from
   death to life.
To believe that forty days after the Resurrection he ascended bodily
   to heaven in glory and that he was seated at the right hand of
   God the father.
To believe that on the fearful day of judgment he will come again
   to judge the living and the dead.
Beyond this, I wish and command that you believe and obey the
   Seven Gifts of the Holy Spirit,[41] [39] which are the gift of fear, the
   gift of piety, the gift of knowledge, the gift of strength, the gift of
   good counsel, the gift of understanding, and the gift of wisdom.
And I wish and command that you be willing to believe and follow
   the Eight Beatitudes,[42] first poverty of spirit, then graciousness of
   heart, tears for your sins and for those of others, desire to enact
   true justice, mercy and pity of heart, purity of spirit, peace toward
   all, and patience.

THE LADY: "And I also wish and command that the Seven Principal
Virtues be with you, of which three are divine and four are moral.[43] The three
Divine Virtues are Faith, Hope, and Charity, and the four Moral Virtues are
Prudence, Temperance, Fortitude, and Justice. I also wish and command that
you delight in the four gifts of the body, which are Clarity, Subtlety, Agility,
and Resilience in the face of suffering.[44] And I wish and command that the
Seven Spiritual Works of Mercy always be with you, which are to instruct
the ignorant, to correct those failing in their duties, to set in the right path
those who have strayed, to remain silent about the vices of others, to endure
insults, to comfort the afflicted, and to pray for all sinners. And I also wish
and command you to accomplish the Seven Corporal Works of Mercy:[45] first
that you feed the hungry, then that you offer drink to those who are thirsty,
give shelter to the poor, clothe the naked, visit the sick, visit those in prison,
and bury the dead. Saint Gregory has this to say on the subject in his letter
A Nepontiam: 'I do not recall having read or heard about anyone dying a
miserable death if he or she has willingly performed the acts of mercy, [40]
for mercy creates so many intercessors that it is impossible that their numerous prayers not be answered.' About this Our Savior says in the Gospel,

Beati misericordes quoniam ipsi misericordiam consequentur. (Mathei, vᵉ capᵒ).[46]
Which is to say, my friend: 'Blessed are the merciful, for they will find mercy.'

"Furthermore, I wish and command that you firmly believe in the seven
sacraments of the Church, which are Holy Baptism, Holy Confirmation,
True Penitence, the Holy Sacrament of the Altar,[47] Holy Orders, the Holy
Order of Matrimony, and Holy Unction.[48] And I wish and command that
with all your strength you refrain from falling into the seven deadly sins: the
first Pride, followed by Envy, Avarice, Sloth, Gluttony, Anger, and Lust."[49]

THE LADY: "I also wish and command that you keep from slipping or
falling, no matter what may happen, into the seven sins against the Holy
Spirit, which are Despair, Presumption, Deceit,[50] Persistence in Sin,[51] Envy
of one's neighbor, Lack of Charity, and Impenitence at the end of life. And
I also wish and command that at the beginning or middle of Lent, Easter,
and Pentecost, on the five holidays of Our Lady, on All Souls' Day, and on
Christmas Day, you make confession and that you seek a good doctor for the
soul, just as you seek a good doctor for the body. [41]

"And I wish and command that in whatever company of king, queen,
lords, and ladies you may be, wherever you may be, in fields, cities, or manor
houses, that when you see the image of Our Lord and Our Lady, in whatever
guise they may be—whether on a cross, as angels, as male or female saints—
that you adore them and that for shame of what people may say or think, you
not neglect to remove your hood, hat, or bonnet from your head if you are
wearing a head covering; otherwise, salute these images with your whole heart.
And it should be the same with the poor who may request alms from you: if
you are able to help them, you should, and if not, you should at least commis-
erate with them, with God as your witness. To refrain from doing this out of
shame before others is a mortal sin, driven by vainglory and worldly vanity."

THE LADY AGAIN: "I also wish and command that when you are grown
up and engage in the very noble profession of arms—as worthy men do who
fight battles at sea, on land, in one-to-one combat, or in battalions, whether
it is in skirmishes, by mines, in sieges, in sallies, whether on siege ladders or
at gates or in any other way—that you not forget the very holy blessing of
Our Lord, who told Moses to tell his son Aaron, who was a high priest of
the Law, to bless the sons of Israel, as the Bible says in the Book of Numbers,
in the xiiiith chapter: *Benedicat tibi Dominus et custodiat te. Ostendat faciem
suam tibi Dominus et misereatur tui. Convertat Dominus vultum suum ad te et
det tibi pacem.*[52] [42] For this blessing, uttered from the true mouth of Our
Lord, seems to me more commendable and more profitable than any other

that I know. I therefore bid you to repeat it every day at your bedside, each time that you rise and each time that you go to sleep.

"But since it seems that when you pray in this manner, you bless others rather than yourself, I think that as you make the sign of the cross you should pray as follows: *Benedicat michi Dominus et custodiat me. Ostendat faciem suam michi Dominus et misereatur mei. Convertat Dominus vultum suum ad me et det michi pacem.*[53] Then go about your duties joyfully, for no harm will ever come to you. This blessing was pronounced by Saint Francis to his companion, Brother Leon, when he was tempted by some devilish temptation that never came to pass."

THE LADY: "Furthermore, I wish and command that when you are grown and perform feats of arms and participate in battles and when you have overcome your enemies and might be tempted to engage in vengeance or an act of cruelty, that you remember the words of God in the first book of the Bible, in Deuteronomy: *Quicunque fuderit sanguinem humanum fundetur et sanguis illius.*[54] And HE also said during the Passion, *Qui gladio percutit gladio peribit.*[55] And HE said to David: *Non edifcabis michi domum quia vir sanguinium es.*[56] And again HE said to David: *Virum sanguinium et dolosum non dimidiabunt dies suos.*[57] Which means, my friend, that men who thirst for blood will never know the fullness of their time. And HE says, my friend, right here that he who kills with a knife will be killed by the knife. And HE says again, *Virum sanguinium et dolosum abhominabitur Dominus.*[58] [43] Which means, my friend, that the violent man of blood is an abomination to Our Lord. And he also says through the mouth of David: *Si occideris, Deux, peccatores, viri sanguinum declinate a me.* Which means, my friend, 'If you kill God's sinners, the blood of men will come to me.'[59]

"The Scriptures are full of many other invocations to pity and mercy that God himself has shown us; it would take far too long for even the most learned clerk to recount them in their entirety. Therefore, my friend, I wish and command that with all your strength you refrain from offending God, Our Lady, and the court of Paradise by committing this very inhuman sin as well as all the others, and that you take as a watchword the beautiful words of the pagan Seneca, who said: *Si scirem deos ygnoscituros et homines ygnoraturos, nom tamen dignarer peccare propter vilitatem ipsius peccati.*[60] That is to say, my friend, even if I knew that the gods had no knowledge and that all men were ignorant, I would still not deign to sin because of the great evil that is sin. So take counsel, good friend, from Seneca, who so abhorred vices and sins, even as a pagan; it follows that we who are baptized in the most

holy faith of Jesus Christ should abhor these sins even more. All these things
I wish and command you to accomplish with all your might."

THE LADY AGAIN. "And as for the rest, those matters concerning your
personal habits, I wish and command that every morning when you rise and
every evening when you retire, you bless yourself, [44] making the sign of the
cross meticulously, not crosswise or twisted in the manner of the devil's sign;
you must commend yourself to God and to Our Lady and to the True Cross
and to your good angel and to all the male and female saints who are your
advocates. You should rise early each morning, dressing yourself as honorably
and as agreeably as you can, without making too much noise. And when you
are laced in your doublet* and you have clean, well-fitting hose and your
shoes are clean, then comb your hair, wash your face and hands, clean your
nails if you need to, and cut them if need be, and then put on your belt and
fasten it around your gown.*

"When you are fully dressed, make the sign of the cross as you leave
your room, and commend yourself to Our Lord and Our Lady, to your good
angel and to all the male and female saints, and do as Saint Augustine says:
*Primo querite regnum dei.*⁶¹ That is, before any task, whatever it might be,
you should go first to church and take holy water, then attend Mass if you
are able to find one, and if not, kneel before a statue or image of Our Lord
and also of Our Lady, and, with your hands clasped together and your eyes
firmly set, not casting about, say your prayers and blessings with all your
heart, not to the images themselves but for the love of the One who is in
heaven.

"And then you may go to the presence chamber* and wait with the other
knights and squires while my lord the King and my lady the Queen, or either
one of them, attend Mass. You should accompany them and, if you have not
already heard Mass, you should kneel down, [45] not letting your eyes stray
other than to make sure that you are not in front of some lord, lady, knight,
or squire whose rank means they should be placed before you; do not, however, sit with the knaves, for of all the ranks the middle rank is the best, just
as the Philosopher says in the *Ethics*, where he says: *Virtus consistit in medio.*⁶²
Which means, my friend, that 'Virtue lies in the middle ground.' Or as the
poet says: *Medium tenuere beati.* That is to say, dear friend, 'Blessed are those
who do not strive to climb too high and who are reasonably satisfied.' Then
you should properly and wholeheartedly say the hour of the Mass, and then
fittingly accompany my lord and my lady back from Mass. If you are hungry
or thirsty, go discreetly to break your fast with a light meal before dinner.

Make sure that you don't indulge excessively in food or drink but rather that you eat lightly as I've said, following the precept of the Philosopher, who maintains that one should eat and drink to live, not live to eat and drink.[63] For it's true, as the saying goes, that the mouth kills more people than knives do.

"And I also forbid you to be obnoxious or deceitful or to repeat unpleasant gossip that can only cause harm. Cassiodorus says in his book *In Praise of Saint Paul* that the condition of falsehood is such that even if no one denounces it, it will lead to public disgrace, but that the condition of truth is the opposite, for it is so stable and firm that it grows all the greater in the presence of detractors. The Gospel has this to say on the subject: *Super omnia veritas (Secundum Esdre, iii^e capitulo).*[64] [46] That is to say that truth reigns over all things. Which is why, my friend, you should always be steady and truthful and why you should flee the company of liars and trouble-makers, for such people are truly dangerous.

"Therefore, be steadfast in your speech and with your hands, and serve everyone as best you can without disrespect and without reproach. Keep company with good people, listening to their words and retaining what they say. Be humble and courteous wherever you may be, without bragging or talking too much, nor being mute either—for the proverb says that by speaking either too much or too little you can be taken for a fool. Be careful that no lady or maiden, whoever she may be, is ever brought into disrepute on your behalf. Should you find yourself in company where the conversation is dishonorable, make it clear by your own graciousness that you disapprove, and then leave."

THE LADY AGAIN: "And I also desire and bid you to show compassion for the poor and never to denigrate the poverty of others. I command that you share what you have with the poor as much as you are able to, remembering the advice of Albertus, who said: *Non tua claudatur ad vocem pauperibus auris.* Which means, my friend, 'Let your ears be not closed to the voice of the poor.'

"And I further wish and command that if God has raised you to high estate with the gifts of good fortune, you take care not to forget the most glorious and enduring riches of heaven for those of this shadowy and transitory life. We have also told you what the Psalmist had to say about this: *Quando dives moritur, in tres partes dividitur: caro datur vermibus, percuniam parentibus, animam demonibus nisi Deus miseretur.*[65] [47] Which means, my friend: 'When the rich man dies, he and his possessions will be divided into three parts: and first of all his flesh will be given to the worms; his gold, his silver, his rings and all his other worldly possessions will be given to his relatives; and his soul will go to the devil unless God in his grace takes mercy on him.' On this subject, my friend, you should remember the beautiful words of Aristotle, who said:

Vir bone que curas res villes et res perituras,
Nil proffituras dampno quandoque futuras
Nemo diu manssit in crimine, sed cito transsit
Et brevis atque levis in mundo gloria que vis.

Which means, my friend, what Aristotle in his General Doctrine says: 'You, man who have striven with perilous effort to climb to the highest ranks of glory and wealth, take care that you are not brought down by that same effort. For no hard-won position is without great danger, and when all is said and done, the worst is that one must die.'"

THE LADY: "I also wish and command you to remember that in your great prosperity you should recall the word of Seneca in his last book *On Benefits*, chapter XXI, where he says that those who are raised to high estate have no greater need than to be told the truth. And following this is his judgment of the jealousies and great disputes that occur in the courts of powerful lords, where everyone seeks to outdo each other in pleasing their superiors and in subtle flattery.

"Here's what the *Politics*,[66] book three, chapter nine, has to say on the subject: the flatterer is the greatest enemy of truth; when a man flatters and his lord listens to him, it is as if he drives a nail into his lord's eye, for it blinds great lords [48] and causes them to lose God's love, as well as honor and true self-knowledge, so that they don't know which things to pursue and which to abandon, and they think that they are being praised for things which in fact are very much condemned, and that they are condemned for things for which in fact they are praised.

"This all comes about because no one tells them the truth. Therefore, my friend, above all else that I've said and will say, beware of, avoid, and flee the very perilous company of flatterers—if you have any social standing and wealth at all, you will find them aplenty. I've told you this so that you can be a true friend of God and a man of renown in this kingdom—indeed, in the whole world—from this day forward. If you follow these precepts in the service of your lady and of Love, you won't fail to be truly saved, not only in your body, but in your soul and your person. That's enough for now. When I see that you're conducting yourself appropriately—or at least that you're trying to uphold these rules as best as you can—then I'll love you and bestow benefits on you, and make you truly my friend.

"What do you say to all this? Do you have the courage to obey me?"

SAINTRÉ: Then little Saintré fell to his knees and said, "My lady, I thank you for all this counsel; God willing, I shall follow it all very well."

THE LADY: "You shall?" asked Madame. "Then I'll see how well you do it. Now put on a good face, whatever may happen, and don't be dismayed by what I may say to you. But don't laugh about it either—I don't want my ladies-in-waiting to suspect anything about our plans. [49] Instead, pretend to be just as tongue-tied before them as you were before me. Now wait for me here, for I'll soon return."

THE AUTHOR: Then Madame stood up and said out loud to her ladies-in-waiting:

"What do you think about this deceitful young man? Haven't I made him confess at great length? Yet I still wasn't able to find out who his lady is!"

Then as if angry with Saintré, she said, "Now get out of here, young man, for you'll never amount to anything."

And as she reached the door of her dressing room, she turned around as if she were angry and said abruptly, "Just a moment, young man, wait right there. For I still want to settle something with you."

Then, acting with assurance, he pretended to be surprised (behaving as she had instructed) and stopped in his tracks. Madame returned directly to the room, calling out loudly so that everyone could hear: "Well now, young man, might I able to find out who your lady is? And if I guess her name correctly, will you swear to confirm it? Is it such and such, or that lady, or this other one?"

"No, my lady."

"Or this one, or that one?"

"No, my lady."

"Gracious!" said Isabel. "My lady, now we're off the hook, for we were given his guarantee that by this time he would have chosen a lady. Yet you can see that it's no one you've mentioned; so he must have someone else in mind. Since that's the case, draw him aside. If he's the kind of man he should be, then he'll tell you, and he will have kept his word."

Then Madame, laughing heartily as if playing in a farce, drew the young Saintré aside, saying softly to him:

THE LADY: "My friend, I'm giving you this little purse, with twelve *écus**
inside. [50] From now on, I want the colors and the letters entwined on it to
be the device* that you wear for my sake. As for the twelve *écus*, I want you
to purchase a crimson doublet in damask or silk, and two pairs of fine hose—
one of fine scarlet cloth and the other of *brunet** from Saint-Lô, all embroidered with the same colors and device as the purse. You should also purchase
four pairs of linen underwear and four fine kerchiefs, as well as well-made
shoes and pattens;* I want to see you very handsomely fitted out by next
Sunday. If you're able to manage this very efficiently and graciously, then
God willing, I shall do even more for you."

Little Saintré, innocent and shamefaced like the child that he was, tried
to refuse the purse, saying, "My lady, I thank you; if you please, I'll take
nothing from you, for I haven't deserved it."

THE LADY: "Deserved it?" answered the lady. "I know very well that you
have not served me, but you will in the future, God willing. So I wish and
command that you take the purse."

As she said this, she secretly and discreetly slipped it into his sleeve,
carefully wrapped in fine cloth, and then said, "Now go away, and try to do
well, so that I'll have good news of you; God keep you. Don't come back to
the gallery until you're suitably dressed. I'll say nothing more for the
moment, except that I pray to God that all or at least most of the things I've
taught you will remain with you."

Then Madame, in a loud voice, pretending to be angry, exclaimed, "Get
out of here, right now! Go away! You're a coward and a dimwit [51]—be off
with you! You've not paid your debt yet; we'll settle accounts with you
another time."

THE AUTHOR: When Jean had left the room and had taken his pathetic
leave of her, she said laughing to her ladies, "I think that we'll be wasting
our time. He doesn't have any sense of what it means to find a lady nor has
he any intention of doing so; I don't think he's ever given any thought to
being in love. But at least we've been able to have a good laugh—and we'll
laugh again."

Then Madame was helped out of her gown, and she prepared for bed,
as did all the other ladies. Several of them were quite annoyed by Madame's
long discussion, since they had wanted to go to sleep. Now I shall be silent
for a while about Madame and her ladies, to come back to little Saintré.

THE AUTHOR AGAIN: Once he was far from the lady's room, little Saintré
stepped aside and glanced about to make sure that no one could see him.

Then, he drew the purse out of his sleeve and unwrapped it. When he saw how beautiful it was, with its twelve *écus* inside, no need to ask if he was delighted. His heart was so overcome with joy that he felt as rich as the King. He made many happy little plans about how he would do what Madame had commanded and was full of joyful little thoughts about how elegant he would look the following Sunday.

Then he went to see Perrin de Sole, the King's tailor, and said, "Perrin, my friend, how much would it cost for me to have by next Sunday a doublet made for me, out of fine crimson damask?"

Perrin looked him over, took out his measuring instrument, and then said, "Do you have any money?"

"Yes, Perrin, provided that it doesn't cost too much." [52]

And then Perrin, since he was so gracious to everyone, said "My son Saintré, by my faith, I can't do anything for less than six *écus*, but it will be of the very finest quality." Then Saintré, young and eager, put his hand into the purse and gave him the six *écus*.

After he had paid for his doublet, he went off to Jean de Busse, the King's hosier, and got him to sew two pairs of hose at two *écus* for both pairs, which he paid on the spot. Then he visited François de Nantes, the King's embroiderer, and showed him the purse so that he could embroider Madame's emblem on the hose, for which he paid two *écus*. After all this, only two *écus* were left.

Then Jean took himself off to a goodwife* of Paris, who had been recommended several times by his father, the Seigneur de Saintré, and said to her: "Marie de Lille, good mother, might I have two pairs of fine linen underwear for an *écu*?"

"Certainly," said Marie.

"Good mother, here is the *écu*; see to it that I'll be able to wear one of them on Sunday."

Then he drew the purse from the breast pocket where he kept it and showed her the two *écus*.

"Very well, my son," she said. "And who might have given these to you?"

"My lady mother, of course, sent me twelve *écus*. So I beg you use to use one of them for the linens, and the other one I'll keep along with the little purse."

When Marie saw the beautiful purse, she was delighted for the young man and said, "May God bless my lady your mother for taking such good care of her son." And then she said, "And where are the other ten *écus*?"

"Mother, they've already been spent."

"Alas, son, I'm afraid that you've lost [53] or wasted them."

"I've not done that, Mother, truly not, as you'll see on Sunday."

And so the whole week went by until Sunday morning, when the afore-mentioned Perrin de Solle, the tailor, Jean de Busse, the hosier, François de Nantes, the embroiderer, and Guillaume Soldam, the shoemaker, all purvey-ors to the King, proceeded to the chamber of Jacques Martel, first groom* of all the King's squires, where young Jean and the King's other pages were sleeping, all bearing the clothing they had made—one man carrying the dou-blet, the others the embroidered hose, the shoes, and the pattens. When Jacques Martel learned that they were assembled at the door, he had it opened for them. Once they had entered the room and he saw everything they were carrying, he asked whom all these things were for. "For our master," they said. "It's for our master, little Saintré. We're all at his service."

Then Jacques turned toward Saintré laughing and said, "Saintré, I see that you've relied on your creditors."

"Master," replied Saintré, "Madame my mother is the one who has relied on them, for she has sent me money to enjoy myself and to pay for my necessities. And it seems that I have no great need for money, other than to dress myself like a gentleman."

"Well really, I liked you well enough before, but after hearing this, I'm even more fond of you."

Then he turned to the other noble pages and said, "Ah, you wicked boys, you would never do such a thing. Instead, you'd go spending your money on gambling in bars and taverns and other disreputable places. Yet I've given you good beatings to correct you." [54]

Then he turned toward the master craftsmen and said, "Now be quick! Dress him for me at once and make him look handsome."

When he was completely outfitted and decked out, little Saintré, who had already paid in advance for everything, gave half an *écu* to the journey-men* and the other half to the squire's servants, who were already fonder of him than of any of the other page boys, since he gave away his old clothes so generously. When the squire and all the others were dressed, they followed him to Mass and then went to wait for the King in his presence chamber, not without a good deal of discussion about Saintré, of whom they were all greatly envious.

When the King emerged from his chamber and saw little Saintré so dressed up, he began to laugh and asked the squire how it happened that Saintré had become so elegant.

"Sire," explained the squire, "I was amazed this morning when Perrin de Solle, Jean de Busse, François de Nantes, Guillaume Soldam and their attendants all came to my room bearing these clothes; I thought they were playing a trick on me."

Then the King and all the lords in his retinue began to sing Saintré's praises, and the King said, "I wish he were three or four years older; he would be my *varlet-tranchant*."*

With these words, the King went into the chapel, followed by the Queen.

As they walked back after Mass, Madame saw little Saintré in the distance, dressed so very elegantly. Coming up to the Queen, she said, "Ah, Ma'am,[67] look at how pretty the little Saintré boy is!"

"Indeed, fair cousin." said the Queen, "What you say is true, he really is nice to look at." [55]

Then they went into the hall for dinner. Madame could not take her eyes off him; in order to observe him more secretly and to be able to speak with him, she called the other ladies and said to them, "Don't we want to see whose device young Saintré is wearing on his hose? God help us when such people want to wear emblems and pretend to behave like lovers."

"Ah, Madame, he has the best of intentions."

Then one said, "Oh, for goodness sake, let us see what it's all about," and the other said, "Madame, let's go talk to him now."

Drawing aside with her ladies into one of the windows, Madame called Jean over and spoke as if she knew nothing at all about the matter. "So, master Jean, very well! We want to know and to see whose device you're wearing on your hose."

Then little Jean, on his knees, held back as if to be coaxed.

"We'll certainly find out," said the ladies, "but let's do so quickly, since the King would like to dine."

So one of the ladies grabbed his arm, while another took him by the shoulder, and the others held onto his body, until they made him stand up on his feet. Then Madame and all her ladies, and several who had no particular business there, were able to see the devices, for which he was much praised. Madame was delighted, body and soul, by the pleasure of seeing her emblems.

After the tables were removed and grace said, to make a long story short, the minstrels began to play, and the joyous company began to dance and then to sing, until the King, who was ready to retire, called for the spices and the parting cup. And while they were all dancing, Madame's gaze was fixed

FIG. 2. Brussels, Bibliothèque Royale, MS 9457, f. 36r: Madame,
her ladies, and Jean de Saintré.

Reproduced by permission of the Bibliothèque Royale.

on Saintré, [56] so well did he sing and dance. Then she thought that she
would like to look more closely at his device and speak to him at greater
leisure. For the more she observed him, the more he pleased her—since there
was no man or woman at court who did not think him a worthy gentleman.

So as he passed with the parting cup, Madame said as he went by, "Do
as you did the other day, little Saintré," and he understood exactly what she
meant.

Madame then went off to her chambers and found little Saintré in the
galleries, just as she had instructed. Acting if she were somewhat amazed, she
exclaimed, "Oh! You handsome lad, is that you? Walk ahead; you've made
yourself scarce for five or six days; we have a bone to pick with you."

Then she turned to her ladies and said, "We'll have to inspect this boy's
devices and try to find out if we can who has given them to him and what
they mean. I can't believe that he has enough maturity or common sense to
be in love."

As she spoke, she arrived at her chamber, where she dismissed all the
men except Jean and had the door closed. And then, surrounded by her

ladies, she examined the devices and said, "So now, young man, you say that you've no ladylove, and yet you're looking so handsomely dressed!"

"My lady," he replied, "it's my mother who has dressed me so handsomely, with God's help."

"How can it be," Madame inquired, "that she has made you so handsome when she lives in Touraine and, I believe, has never even set foot here?"

"My lady," he replied, "it's the twelve *écus* that she sent me in a lovely golden silk purse that have made me so elegant."

"Is that so?" said Madame. "We'll have to see that little purse and know all about where those twelve *écus* went. [57] If they haven't been put to good use, I'll write to tell her not to send any more."

Then little Saintré withdrew from his breast the purse, which was wrapped in a fine little kerchief. And Madame, who knew very well that none of her ladies would recognize it, took the little purse and examined it in front of everyone, as if she had never seen it before. She looked at the emblem embroidered on the hose and saw that it was the same.

Then she said to Jean, "Well now, my lad, first of all, how much did the doublet cost you?"

"My lady, for the doublet made just so, I gave Perrin de Solle six *écus*."

"And the hose?" she asked him. "Who made them, and how much did they cost?"

"My lady, I bought these scarlet hose and another pair made of fine *brunet* from Saint-Lô for two *écus* from Jean de Busse, and I paid François de Nantes another two *écus* to embroider them."

"All right, sir, that makes ten *écus*; what did you do with the remaining two?"

"Lady, as for one of them, with three *sous** I got two pairs of fine linen underwear, and with twenty *sous* I had two pairs of shoes and three pairs of pattens, and the rest I spent in wine for the master craftsmen's journeymen and for the serving men of the squire who is our master."

Madame, who was very satisfied with this arrangement and who saw that his courtesies toward the master craftsmen had been useful to him, and that her largesse had been well spent, said in laughing to her ladies-in-waiting, "He has stolen half the money!"

"My faith, my lady," Jean replied, "I beg your pardon, but I didn't have a farthing left."

"Well in that case," said Madame, "I would like to know who your lady is. [58] So come over here to talk to me."

"Ah, my lady,' her attendants protested, "for goodness sake, you're making him suffer too much by trying to find out so much from him."

"Don't concern yourself with this," said Madame. "Stand back, since I intend to find out more about this."

And when everyone had drawn away, Madame said to him, "Well now, my friend, I'm very pleased with you up to now; try to do this well in all that you do, for you'll be all the more worthy. Above all else I order that no one, no matter how good a friend he may be, find out about our affair."

"He certainly will not, my lady; upon my word, I would rather die than divulge the secret."

"So now, my friend, I would like you to have two other gowns, one of which shall be made of fine Saint-Lô *brunet*, trimmed with sable, and the other will be a fine gray from Montivilliers, lined with fine lambswool; you should wear these every day except when you ride along with Monseigneur the King. I would also like you to have two hoods, one scarlet and the other black, as well as a blue satin doublet and two other fine pairs of hose, and kerchiefs, shifts, shoes, pattens, and other necessary things. And I want you to play tennis from time to time, too, and archery—both are very respectable games that will keep you in good shape. To buy all this and to keep yourself well maintained, I'm giving you sixty *écus*; I'll be observing how you conduct yourself."

"Since you don't yet have your own servant, I want you to retain Gilet de Corps, who's a solid, dependable squire's servant, at a wage of eight *sous* for him to take good care of your clothing, hose, and armor. If you conduct yourself well, [59] you'll receive a necklace, a chain, and a Bohemian belt as well as a damask gown, and many other fine things—provided you remain faithful, discreet, and a man of honor."

"My lady, I'll do as you say, God willing."

"Now listen to me, dear friend. Whatever threats or harsh words I might say to you in front of my ladies or anywhere else, don't be offended."

"As you like, my lady, I won't. Please don't worry about a thing."

Then pretending to be very annoyed with him, Madame scolded Jean in front of her ladies-in-waiting. Next, she went to her dressing room, opened her jewel box, placed sixty *écus* into a silk purse, and returned to him.

"Well now, young man! Have you thought it over and finally decided to confide in me? If you won't tell me, tell Lady Jeanne or Lady Katherine or Isabel, or whomever you please."

"But what should I tell you, my lady, when I have no ladylove?"

"Yet you're wearing devices and intertwined letters, and you give every sign of being a lover, you sniveling young man."

"Lady, upon my word, I've told you whom I love more than anyone in the world and who has made me wear these devices."

"Ah! Young man, young man, you're really abusing us if you expect us to think it's your mother. I'm sure that you love your mother and that she's paying for all this, but she's certainly not the one whose devices you're wearing. Come here, now! I've thought of someone else I haven't named."

Then drawing him aside, she said, "Take this little purse and make sure not to lose it. There are sixty *écus* here; I'll see how you manage. [60] You mustn't come to the galleries any more whenever I pass by. And don't come too close to me elsewhere, either. But when you see me pick my teeth with a pin, this will be my signal that I want to speak with you. Then you'll rub your right eye, and I'll understand that you've gotten my message, and that's when you'll come to see me. Do you understand what I've said?"

"Yes, my lady, very well."

"Well then, off you go. Do as I've said, and I'll love you all the more for it. When I see that you're conducting yourself properly, I'll retain you as my lover and I'll set you up very handsomely indeed."

"My lady, I'll do just as you say, God willing."

"Be off, then; I want to go to bed. Remember not to be upset when I scold you in public."

THE AUTHOR AGAIN: Then, pretending to be angry, Madame said to Jean, "Get out of here, boy, go away! You'll never amount to anything!"

"Goodness, my lady, let this not be the last time we see him!" said the ladies. "You see, Saintré, it would really be better if you told Madame the truth."

As instructed by Madame, Saintré pretended to be upset; he bowed and left without a word.

Then all the ladies all burst out laughing at the way that Madame had assailed him, saying, "Alas! Now we've surely lost him; we won't be able to have fun at his expense anymore."

Of course, they knew nothing about the sweet arrangements he had made with Madame.

"Now, be quiet." said Madame. "He hasn't paid his debt to me yet; the best part of the game is just beginning."

"Dear me," replied Isabel. "We're torturing that poor child."

Now I shall stop talking for a bit about the jokes and games that Madame and her ladies enjoyed at Saintré's expense, and I'll tell how he spent his sixty *écus*. [61]

THE AUTHOR: After young Saintré left Madame, he went straight off to count his treasure. He was so thrilled at the sight of the heap of coins in his hand, he did not know what to think or do. He spent the whole day pondering where to keep the money. He dared not entrust it to a squire or to anyone else, since Madame had expressly forbidden anyone knowing anything about it. He decided to hide the *écus* in his pockets until the following day before spending the money, and so he did. That night was longer than any he had ever known. The next day, as soon as he had risen and heard Mass, he went off to see Perrin de Solle, the King's tailor, and had him make the three gowns as Madame had instructed (these were lined with fur, and he wore one the following Sunday) and the blue damask doublet. He had enough money to pay for all this and still have a great deal left.

THE AUTHOR: When Madame saw young Saintré dressed in his sable-lined black gown and his blue damask doublet, she was far more delighted than she let on. Then she winked at him and signaled with her pin, and he responded in kind. When Madame returned to her room, she found him in the gallery. The moment she saw Jean in the distance, she said to her ladies, "Here comes our entertainment; we'll have to deal with him."

But as soon as he saw her, he pretended to turn away and take another route. So Madame called to him and said, "Well now, young man, is it proper behavior to run away from ladies? [62] You're a real good-for-nothing; come right over here."

Once Madame was in her room, she dismissed all her attendants except for Jean de Soussy, the Queen's squire, and her own squire, Thibaut de Roussy, the two men whose tongues were most likely to wag about things that couldn't be hidden, and she told them: "I've kept you here so that you can have a good laugh with us."

Then Madame began to speak to Saintré, "Well, now, young man, well, well! How many times have we all begged you to tell us who your ladylove might be. Neither our prayers nor our requests, neither our threats nor our insults have helped us learn a single thing. Since you haven't wanted to confide in any of us, perhaps at least you can tell Jean de Soussy and Thibaut de Roussy, or either one of them, since they're your good friends."

"But Madame," objected Jean de Soussy, "why would he want to tell us any more than he was willing to tell you?"

Young Saintré, who understood exactly what was happening and what Madame meant, pretended to be frightened and said nothing. Seeing that he remained silent, Madame said to Jean and Thibaut, "The young man you see before you is handsomely dressed in a sable-lined gown, a silken doublet and fine embroidered hose, yet he wants us to believe that he doesn't have a ladylove and—what's worse—that he isn't even in love. My goodness, when I consider it, any woman who claimed you as a lover would be extremely well served."

With these words, she became very stern with him and said, "Now, sir, however good your family may be, you're still a page: where did you get such a gown and doublet?"

"My lady," he said, "since my mother wants me to dress this way and ordered me to do so, I have to obey her wishes." [63]

"And how much has she sent you for this?" "Sixty *écus,* my lady." "Sixty *écus*? Sixty *écus*? You've squandered half of it!" she exclaimed.

"No, I truly have not, my lady."

"You mean to say that your gown, your hat, that doublet and those hose cost sixty *écus*? Tell me the truth."

"No, my lady, but besides all that you see here, I've another gown of fine blue, lined with the finest lambskin from Romania;[68] and another gown of fine Montivilliers gray, lined with fine white wool; two more hats; and two pairs of fine hose, one pair dyed carmine. And there are four *écus* left."

"And who helped you to plan for so many things?" "Truly, my lady, no one except Perrin de Solle and myself." "Perrin de Solle," said Madame, "I know that he's a worthy man, which your affairs have proved, since your money has been well spent, it seems to me. But didn't you tell me that your mother had already sent you twelve *écus*, so you could be finely attired?"

"Yes, my lady." "Then may God bless such a good mother and make you a fine son for her. Now everybody please leave, for we all must get some sleep."

At these words, everyone left, and as they departed Jean de Soussy and Thibaut de Roussy complimented young Saintré and urged him not to be offended by Madame's harsh words. Beyond that, they complained that Madame had pressed him too hard to find out about things that were none of her business. [64]

"Indeed," Jean said. "Who would be happy to hear such offensive things, just because I won't tell her who my lady is, especially when she repeats these things to her ladies? Why won't she simply believe that I don't have and don't want a ladylove? If I did have a lover, for heaven's sake, they've all pestered me so much that I would never tell them who it is."

And then they all began to laugh, and they left each other with these words. Jean and Thibaut then told Madame and all her ladies what had transpired, and the ladies all had a good laugh.

It wasn't long before Jean and Thibaut repeated the conversation between Madame and her ladies with young Saintré in several places, just as Madame suspected would happen (and as she realized another story would have been spread if they had known it); the gossip made for a good laugh. Just so did this good, loyal love remain a secret, until Fortune, in her inconstancy, chose to turn her back on them, as we shall see in what follows.

THE AUTHOR: Their loyal love remained a secret for sixteen years, during which time Madame devised a new way to speak to Saintré as secretly as possible, as she explained:

"My friend, it's not so hard to start the dance; but it's another matter to get out of it honorably. I've asked you to meet me here in the gallery so often that even though you've said that it's your mother who has dressed you so well and made you so handsome, some people might have other ideas about this nonetheless. It only takes one person to guess what's going on and publicize it everywhere. Which is why I've decided that I no longer want to meet you in the galleries; rather, when I want to talk to you, or you want to see me, we'll each make our signal, as we've said. Then you'll come and open my garden door when you see that I've retired for the night and returned to my room; here's the key. This way, we'll be able to speak to each other and talk at our pleasure."

THE AUTHOR AGAIN [65]: In the third year of their affair, when Jean was sixteen, Madame thought that he was old enough to advance beyond the rank of page boy. Since he was skillful at carving, she thought he would be well qualified to become a *varlet-tranchant* to either the King or the Queen, as appropriate. As she thought about how she might best accomplish this, she said to herself: If you ask the squire who supervises Jean, and he remembers the twelve *écus* and other things, he might think that you were the cause of his recent change in fortune. And if you tell one or the other of the lords, he might guess the cause. Nonetheless, he needs someone's support so that he won't have to remain a page any longer. So she concluded that she herself would make his case to the Queen, who would take the request forward to the King. So she signaled with her pin, and young Jean replied.

THE AUTHOR: When they were together in the garden, as she very lovingly embraced him, she said, "My best beloved, now that you're sixteen years old, you're too old to remain a page boy. I've thought about how to promote you and have decided to ask my lady the Queen to act on your behalf to ask my lord the King to move you up in the ranks, so that you'll become head carver for one of them. From the very first time the King saw you so handsomely dressed, he said laughingly that he wished you were four or five years older so that he could order you to carve at his table. So I'm warning you that if Madame speaks to you on the subject at any point, you should thank her very humbly, so that I don't get accused of being a liar."

THE AUTHOR AGAIN: Young Saintré was overjoyed at these words, and he humbly thanked Madame [66], who gave him leave after she spoke, kissing him tenderly. Then Saintré departed, and Madame closed the door quietly after him and then went to sleep.

THE AUTHOR: Madame, who worked day and night for the advancement of her very devoted servant, the next day, at the Queen's *levée,** said laughingly to the Queen, "Madame, I must take care of a matter that I've been meaning to attend to for several days. I would like to make a request on behalf of a very shy young squire, who is so timid that he dare not ask you himself."

"And who might this be?" asked the Queen.

"My lady, it's little Saintré."

"And what does he want?"

"My lady, he says that he's ashamed to remain a page any longer, because he's now sixteen or seventeen years old; he would like you to request that my lord the King make him his *varlet-tranchant*; he'll write to his father and mother for help in procuring the horses and anything else that's needed for the position."

"To tell the truth," said the Queen, "this seems to me like a proper and reasonable request, so we'll undertake it very willingly. For I know that my lord likes him and that he's a very gracious young man. I have every hope, my lady, that he will become at some point a distinguished gentleman."

It wasn't long before the Queen made this request to the King, who was happy to appoint Saintré, on account of his courtesy and their good relations. Not to delay things any longer, the next time that the Queen saw the chamberlain in the King's presence, she reminded him of his promise. So the King commanded that Saintré serve as his carver, beginning with their next meal, and he ordered that three horses and two servants be provided for his service. Aware of the King's good wishes [67] and of the Queen's smiling favor, the chamberlain observed young Saintré with the other young noblemen, and called him over to him. He asked, "Young Saintré, my friend, what is your first name?"

"My lord chamberlain," he replied, "my name is Jean."

"Jean, from now on you'll no longer be a page. The King has ordered you to be his *varlet-tranchant*, and he has sent you three horses and two servants. Therefore, my son, if you have ever worked hard in service, work even harder now, for it is because of your gracious service, and on behalf of all, that the King so loves you. And don't rest on your laurels, for I hope that he'll do even more for you. Keep your hands and your nails clean, and look after the rest of your body as best as you can; as with all the assignments for table service, your position requires it."

Everyone in the room who heard these words and learned about little Saintré's promotion was delighted. And for this reason, it is a very fine, profitable thing for all young squires to serve most agreeably to all, and to be polite, humble, and patient, in order to earn favor from God and from everyone at court, just as the well-known proverb says: "Whoever cannot endure the bad along with the good, will never achieve honor."

THE AUTHOR: Then, as befits a humble, polite, gracious young man, Jean de Saintré immediately knelt before the King and thanked him for the great honor he had bestowed on him. And the King, as befits a wise, benevolent, and courtly lord, said, "Saintré, devote yourself only to serving well, and we shall reward you for it."

Then Jean de Saintré, in all due humility, warmth and grace, turned to the chamberlain and there, in front of the King and everyone else, he thanked them for the good instructions he had received. He felt no embarrassment—as many would have been done—in thanking him publicly. [68]

At that, Jean departed and went to the Queen, who was in her chamber; then publicly, without giving any sign to Madame des Belles Cousines, he bowed before all the courtiers and ladies assembled in the room and very humbly thanked the Queen. And the Queen said, "Saintré, the services and the courtesies that you have shown to everyone, but especially to the ladies, have promoted you well beyond your years to make you advance from page to a squire serving my lord the King and myself. Therefore, my friend, devote yourself to serving well and to pleasing everyone, for there will always be one person who compensates for all the others."

Then the tables were set up, and the chamberlain appeared to invite the Queen to dine. Madame des Belles Cousines made a show of knowing nothing about all these things; she was with the other ladies and maidens who were all singing Saintré's praises. But Madame said nothing more than: "It's true that he has been and is still a fine young page."

THE AUTHOR: After the King and the Queen sat down, with Madame seated at the foot of the table, the chamberlain took a table napkin from the bread basket and placed the napkin over Jean de Saintré's shoulder. Jean then began to perform his service as *varlet-tranchant* and did this so graciously that the King, the Queen, and everyone else were greatly pleased. Madame des Belles Cousines glanced at him quite frequently from her seat at the foot of the table. She thought that it would be good for him to have the three horses and two servants that had been ordered for him. So she drew the pin from her bodice and, pretending to clean her teeth, she signaled to Saintré until he finally noticed. He replied with his own sign as prudently as he could.

THE AUTHOR: When night fell, Jean opened the garden gate and waited for Madame, who appeared not long afterward. [69] They greeted each other in a way that a man or woman who has never known love could not imagine. Madame said to him, "My one love and sweetest thought, since you can't remain here very long, give me a truly loving kiss. And take this little purse containing one hundred sixty *écus*. I want you to buy a fine, spirited, lively horse to ride with the King, a horse that will be sprightly and strong; spend whatever it costs up to eighty *écus*, and then buy another sturdy horse to ride every day, for up to twenty *écus*, and for thirty *écus* find another strong two-year-old horse to carry your trunk, and find a servant: this makes a total of one hundred thirty. With the remaining thirty *écus*, you should have beautiful caparisons* made, and your servants should be attired in matching liveries* when you ride together. Do as you like with the rest of the money, as long as it lasts. When you're out of funds, just make our signal, with no other fuss."

At these words, she said, "Farewell, my friend, farewell, my only hope, farewell my most precious possession and treasure, farewell."

"Farewell, my dear lady who can give me no command too great and whom I must and intend to obey."

With these words, they took leave of each other.

THE AUTHOR: That night, Jean de Saintré went off to sleep in the chamber of the squire who supervised the pages, who said, "My dear son Saintré, I'm very sorry that you're leaving us, but I'm delighted by your good fortune."

Then the squire turned to the other pages next to Saintré and said, "Now my children, mind what I say. Isn't it a wonderful thing to do good deeds and be humble, sweet, amiable, calm, and gracious to everyone? Just see how your companion's behavior has earned him the favors of the King and Queen and everyone else. [70] But you, you quarrel and gamble and play dice, all of you, and you keep company with ruffians in taverns and bars, in spite of my harsh beatings and punishments; so no matter how good your families may be, if you won't mend your ways as you grow up, you'll be all the more wicked and mean." After these words, everyone was undressed and went to bed.

THE AUTHOR: Little Saintré, who dared not reveal where he had hidden his one hundred sixty *écus*, tucked them into his pocket that night for fear they might be stolen. God knows that the night was long as he waited to buy the horses, but when day broke and as soon as he was ready and dressed, he went at once to the goodwife Marie de Lisle and said, "Marie, my good mother, I have news for you."

"What's that, my son?"

"The King in his grace has promoted me beyond page: he had me carve for him yesterday, and he has ordered me to have three horses and two servants. He also arranged very secretly, through one of his attendants, for me to get one hundred sixty *écus* to buy mounts and livery for me and my servants, so that I can be properly outfitted. He forbade me to tell anyone about this, lest they be envious. So I beg you, my very good mother, don't let a soul find out about it; please keep this a secret for me! "

"Oh, my dear son, praise the Lord!" said Marie. "Now make sure you don't tell anyone else, for it won't ever be revealed by me. But how will you manage? You need a man who really knows something about horses and who can help you find good servants."

"My dear friend and mother, I've thought of writing to my father and asking him to recommend a few people; [71] with respect to the horses, our squire will be very happy to help with this, and with other things as well when I ask him. But I don't want to rush into this, so as not to arouse suspicion."

What more can I say? Before the month was over, he had acquired servants and fine mounts, and he and his servants were appropriately dressed. Then the King loved him more than ever and esteemed him greatly, as did the Queen, which caused much talk. And when Madame observed the fine reception that the King gave him, she took her pin and made the signal so often that Saintré finally noticed it and then responded in kind.

When they were together in the garden that evening, Madame said, "My beloved and my dear heart, I see that my lord the King and my lady the Queen hold you in their good graces, thank heavens. We must think about how you might maintain that favor, which is a very hard thing to do at court, because of the lies and slander of envious people, unless you cultivate friends among those closest to the King, attracting some by your gifts and others by promises. Since you can't give everyone all that they want immediately, you can make assurances about what gifts you'll give and when you'll bestow them: promising a horse or a hackney* to one person, a gown to another. For by making gifts and promises—as long as they are promptly fulfilled—or by bestowing honors on people or giving them a warm reception, as may be appropriate, you'll never fail to delight them, binding and capturing their hearts so that they're all committed to you. You should offer gowns matching their livery to court officials, so that they'll be beholden to you. For Madame the Queen, you should offer on one occasion a fine hackney for riding and another time a fine horse for her litter or her carriage. Give the other ladies gifts according to their position: offer some ladies beautiful headdresses and others nicely gilded silver belts. [72] Present some ladies only with a fine length of cloth and others with beautiful clasps; offer some ladies lovely diamonds and rubies, and let others have delicately enameled gold rings. To the lesser ladies, give purses, gloves, laces, and pins, all according to their station. And in this way, out of regard for your largesse, the honor, grace, and love of all will be yours.

"And if you ask me where you'll be able to procure so many things, I'll answer: as long as you serve me loyally, I'll provide you with everything. As you grow physically stronger, I want you to undertake noble feats of arms, and then you will carry the *emprise** that I will give you. And by these means, you'll reach even greater heights in the love and grace of my lord and my lady, and everyone else. To begin the process, you'll find three hundred *écus* in this purse, of which one hundred will be for a fine hackney or other good horse that you will first give to my lady the Queen, thanking her for the honor that my lord the King bestowed upon you at her request. The other hundred *écus* you will spend on livery gowns for their grooms of the chamber,* everything made of the same cloth and in the same color, with our devices. And to stress how close you are to them all, you should wear a gown of this same livery and color at the upcoming feast of All Saints.[69]

"And by the time of the Christmas feast, you will have furnished each of the other officers with his own gown decorated with our same device but fashioned from another color of cloth. And the remaining hundred *écus* will be to buy New Year's gifts, as I enumerated, for the ladies, damsels, and others, as well as gowns that you will give to the kings of arms* and to the heralds,* trumpeters, and minstrels. [73] And with this, since we can no longer be together, my heart, my dearest, and my very loyal servant, kiss me and be with God."

THE AUTHOR: As Jean de Saintré observed all this and realized the great good and all the honors that Madame lavished upon him and sought to obtain for him even though he was so young, he very humbly thanked her on his knees, saying, "Ah, my most esteemed lady, the most perfect of the good and honorable beings that exist in the world. . . . Alas! How will I ever be able to repay you in service for even a thousandth part of what I owe you? But, my very true lady, I'll do what I can, and God who knows my true thoughts and my desires will enable me do the rest."

Then Madame made him rise, and said as she kissed him, "God bless you."

THE AUTHOR: The next day after Mass, Jean de Saintré worked tirelessly until he had gathered the King's and Queen's grooms and stablemen; he called them to his rooms and had a fine breakfast served to them, and then announced, "I would like to spend eighty or a hundred *écus* for a fine hackney, the best you can find." Then they sent off for the most experienced horse merchants and ascertained which were the best hackney horses available in Paris, which they went to see; they bought one for Jean to present himself as a gift to the Queen.

Jean drew the Queen aside and said, "My sovereign lady, as fully and humbly as I know and am able, I thank you for the benefits and honors that the King has bestowed upon me at your request and also that you have given me. In recognition of this, if you would kindly step over to the window, [74] my lady, you'll see a little hackney that I offer you; I beg you to accept it, with the understanding that a simple man has simple means."

The Queen at first gently demurred, but finally went over to the window to see the horse, which was a fine, well-bred hackney, adorned with a silk saddlecloth in the colors and device of the queen, which made her very happy. After Jean left, the Queen began to praise him to the skies; Madame reacted rather coldly on the surface, however much her heart rejoiced at the fine things all the ladies said about him.

When it was time for the Christmas feast, all the menservants, and then the officers, kings of arms, heralds, trumpeters, and minstrels, as described, were all provided with livery, and the ladies all received their New Year's gifts; Madame chose hers, which was the least grand of all the rubies. Then news of Jean's generosity traveled throughout the court, although this was not without provoking a good bit of envy, as usually happens in every court. Those who were worthy courtiers praised him so much, however, that the King and the Queen held him in even higher favor than he had been. Jean de Saintré comported himself so well in this fashion that the King grew more fond of him every day. In this way, he obtained the King's favor and acquired many good friends. But however highly the King might esteem him and no matter what favors Jean might receive, he was never overcome with pride. On the contrary, he strove to be agreeable to those who were his hidden enemies, and he maintained this mode of life for three or four years.

Madame, who observed and understood all these things, very soon wished to speak with him. So she signaled with her pin, to which he replied, and when they met together in her garden, [75] she said to him, "My only love, thank the Lord, there is no king, queen, duke, lord, lady, or maiden, down to the very least of them, who does not go out of his way to say good things about you, because you have been and remain still so humble and gracious. Because of your generosity, your reputation now flourishes; so I entreat you and order you to make no foolish or extravagant expenditures, since these would redound far more to your shame than to your honor, more to your harm than to your profit. May well-spent Largesse be your guide, for such Largesse bears in itself all manner of virtue: and above all, wise Largesse crowns the soul with everlasting glory, it remains beloved by each person who has benefited from it and so acquires new friends; it blooms into a good reputation, it extinguishes ire from angry hearts, and it provides every protection, for it makes enemies become friends. For all these reasons, my friend, I recommend such Largesse to you.

"And if it should please God that you be blessed with good fortune, use your time wisely, either in armed conquest, or in serving lords, or in being served by them, so that you desire nothing greater than the love of God and many friends. And do not entrust yourself to love of Fortune, if she has already shared her transitory earthly goods with you. Do not forget the words of Alain de Lille, who says in the *Anticlaudianus, Tempora felici, multi numerentur amici; cum Fortuna perit, nullus amicus erit.* That is to say, my friend, that when Fortune is a man's friend and she has raised him to a respectable position, then he will find innumerable false friends; but when Fortune turns her back on him, he won't find a single one. That's why there is no greater folly than to trust in Fortune."

THE LADY: "And beyond this I want and entreat you frequently to enjoy reading beautiful stories, [76] especially about the worthy and marvelous deeds written by the Romans.[70] About world politics and government, read Livy and Orosius. If you want to know about the twelve Caesars, or Caesarians, read Suetonius. And if you want to know about the Catiline conspiracy, read Sallust. If you want to know about the great war between Julius Caesar and Pompey, and also about the sovereign battle waged between their powers in Thessaly, where Pompey was defeated, read Lucan. And if you want to know about the Egyptian kings, read Matastrius. If you want to find out about the Trojans, read Dares Phrygius. If you want to know about Ptolemy, read Polybius. To find out about the diversity of world languages, read Arnobius. To learn about Jewish history and the destruction of Jerusalem, read Josephus. And if you want to know the history of Africa, read Victor. But Pompeius Trogus, according to Valerius, is the one who has written the most about the time before him, for he writes about the origins of all the regions on earth and about the disposition of their lands."

THE LADY: "Now I've come to the end of ancient histories, which I beg and order you to enjoy listening to and reading, for you could spend your time no better than in improving your mind with these noble and celebrated works. It's just as the poet says,

Ut ver dat florem, flos fructum, fructus odorem,
sicut studium mores, mos sensum, sensus honorem.

That is to say, my friend, just as the springtime brings the flower, the flower brings the fruit, and the fruit gives off balm, so does study teach good conduct, and good conduct lead to prudence, and prudence bring worldly honors. [77] Thus by listening to and retaining these noble histories, exempla, and teachings, you'll be able to acquire the lasting joy of paradise, honor in arms, honor in wisdom, and honor in wealth, and you'll be able to live happily and honorably.

"And when your lord or any other asks earnestly for your advice, follow the counsel of the poet Claudian when he urged honor for the emperor in his second book, where he says, *Te patrem civemque geras, tu consule cunctis; non tibi nec tua removeant sed publica vota.* Which is to say, 'Behave like a father and friend, comfort them with good counsel; do not attend only to yourself, love God and the public good.' For the good Romans lived this way, which enabled them to rule absolutely over the entire world, providing laws that we still use. On this, Saint Augustine in the twelfth chapter of the fourth book of *The City of God* recites one of Sallust's authoritative statements, where he records the words of Cato, who said that what made our Roman ancestors so powerful were sense, industry, taking honest counsel in our own hearts and in deliberative assemblies, and for this reason, my friend, I recommend these things to you, so that the counsel of your lord and of all others who have faith in you be loyally protected and kept secret. For your honor depends largely on these principles, as does the honor of those who behave otherwise. Now, my friend, I've said enough for today; I pray that God will grant you to accomplish all this, or at least the greatest part of it."

THE AUTHOR: When Madame had finished speaking, Jean de Saintré fell to his knees, and humbly thanked her, saying, "My most esteemed lady, the one whose commands compel me more strongly than anyone else's, as humbly as I can, I thank you." [78]

Then, as it was growing late, she kissed him and said, "Go along now, I know very well what you mean, let me do the rest."

THE AUTHOR: The following day, as soon as it was light, Saintré rose, and once he had been to hear Mass, he set out as soon as he could and was first in the presence chamber. Very soon the other knights and squires joined him. Then the King went to hear Mass, and when he saw Saintré so nicely and elegantly dressed, he said to the Seigneur d'Ivry: "Unless I am much mistaken, I predict that Saintré will one day be an excellent young man. But how does it happen that he is so well dressed?" "Sire," said the Seigneur d'Ivry, "I have heard it said that it is his lady mother who equips him, and no doubt it is his father's wish that he be so well turned out."

THE AUTHOR: The King said no more on that occasion, but said to himself that he would like to offer support to the young man, and when he went back into his chamber, he called for his treasurer and ordered that Saintré be given five hundred *écus*. And when the Queen heard of this, she ordered him given three hundred *écus* and a length of damask, and Saintré found himself higher in favor with the King and with the Queen than any of the other squires; all this stemmed from the good advice and the funds given him by Madame, who had loved him for seven years. And by the time he reached the age of twenty or twenty-one, the King had done him many favors—and so I shall say no more about the many times that Madame instructed him, for it would take too long.

THE AUTHOR AGAIN: When Saintré reached [79] that age, Madame, whose only wish was to make him worthy and renowned, realized that he now had the courage and the strength to acquire a reputation in arms. When they were together, and after they had exchanged loving words, Madame said with a smile:

"My true friend, my heart, my every joyous thought, since by God's good grace you are now so high in the esteem of my lord the King and of my lady the Queen, and indeed of the whole court, I consider that you are man enough to succeed in some particular deed of arms that will build your reputation in this kingdom and abroad, and to this end, on the first of May next,[71] I want you for my sake to wear a gold bracelet enameled with our devices and set with six good diamonds, six good rubies, and six good large pearls, each of four or five carats; I have wrapped them up in a little purse in this satchel, where I have also put two thousand gold *écus* for you to fit yourself out. And you are not to concern yourself with your expenses for your journey there and back, nor for your lodging, for I shall ensure that my lord the King, my lady the Queen, and my uncles the lords of Anjou, Berry, and Burgundy,[72] and other noble lords of our family, will each offer you financial assistance, and if they do not do so, my only love, you need not fear, until you have spent the thousand *écus*."

THE AUTHOR: When Saintré heard this token of the generosity, the honor, and the profound love that Madame felt for him, he was so overcome with joy that he could not speak. However, he knelt and thanked her as ardently as he could. Madame, who understood what he meant, said to him:

"My love, [80] I singled you out from all the rest to serve me, and I beg you to have no other thought than to be merry and joyful, and to be good company everywhere, for I shall always furnish you with gold and silver and precious rings to ensure you are well turned out. And when your bracelet is finished, on the night of the first of May, you will bring it to me and I shall fasten it for the first time around your arm. Then, as from the following day, you will swear an oath not to remove it, unless within a whole year you find a knight or a squire of impeccable lineage and blameless reputation in arms who will help you to achieve the *emprise** you will promise to accomplish: that is, that he will challenge you for it in combat, on horseback or on foot, the agreement being that he will return it to you unless, in combat on foot, he shall have the better of you, in which case it will be his. The articles* of the joust will be as follows: first, a joust with both combatants fully armed and on war saddles,* until one of you has broken three lances cleanly at a point no less than six inches from the lance head and a foot from the vamplate*; the first to achieve this, in the presence of the judge, will receive from his opponent, mounted on his horse, a diamond set in gold worth at least three hundred *écus*, to present to his fair lady. The following day, assuming, please God, that neither of you is wounded—otherwise, on the eighth day thereafter—at the time appointed by the judge, you will engage in foot combat together, armed with two poleaxes,* until of you is thrown to the ground or has dropped his poleaxe. And if after those courses of arms* your opponent has the better of you, I bid and direct you to give him the bracelet at once; and if God gives you [81] the victory, your opponent shall at once surrender his poleaxe to you, and also his armor, for the remainder of that day."

THE LADY: "And, my love, you need not fear any opponent, because although you are young and not one of the tallest or the strongest, it has often been the case that the weaker overcomes the stronger, and in battle the larger army is often defeated by a smaller one fighting in a godly cause. After all, in such an instance, man may fight, but God gives the victory to whom he pleases, and it is for this reason that with all your heart you must pray for God's guidance, for his might and his aid, and if you do so you cannot come to harm. And if Fortune were by any chance against you—and I pray God that that may not be the case—then you need not fear, for my devotion to you will be unchanged; indeed, I shall love you all the more, for according to the code of honor and chivalry you will be even more esteemed; and for that reason, whatever happens, you cannot do other than succeed, provided that God guards you from injury, which he will do if you commend yourself wholeheartedly to him.

"And I would much prefer that you have as an opponent a man who has already achieved a reputation in arms rather than one who is of your own age, and for that reason, before you make yourself known to your opponents, I direct and command you that a month before you leave you send a king of arms or a herald to the courts first of the King of Aragon, then of the King of Navarre—those being the greatest of the kingdoms of Spain—and then of the King of Castile and of the King of Portugal, all four of them Christian kings, and the herald should present a letter of challenge;* if the challenge is not accepted in the first of these courts by a knight or [82] squire ready to undertake to free you from your oath, the herald should proceed to the next, and once he has an acceptance he should return to you with a letter from the challenger sealed with his seal. And if God, as I hope, is for you in whole or in part, then, my dear heart, you will achieve a high reputation as a squire, and in that case God knows that my lord the King and my lady the Queen will love and cherish you; that thought alone should give you the strength to defeat a giant. Therefore, my love, apply yourself to be valiant and pray for God's guidance and help; if you do so you cannot fall short. And on this we must part; I shall say no more for the present."

THE AUTHOR: Then Saintré fell to his knees and said:

"My most revered lady, my goddess, my dearest one, I thank you as humbly as I know how, and from the bottom of my heart. And as concerns the deed of arms you ask me to undertake, God knows, as do Our Lady and the Archangel Michael, that beyond your love and your favor there is nothing I desire more. For by God's will, you will hear such news of me that you and my lords will all be content." Then he took his leave of her, with a loving kiss, and ten, or fifteen, or twenty returned, and many a "God bless you . . ."

THE AUTHOR AGAIN: Saintré spent the whole night mulling over this new enterprise, and when day broke and he had heard Mass, he called for Gillebert Lorin, the King's goldsmith, who was a renowned expert, and took him aside and said:

"Gillebert my friend, I want a gold bracelet enameled with my arms and my device, and studded with six diamonds, six rubies and six pearls—and here they are."

Then he showed the jewels to Gillebert, who was very pleased and impressed, and, to cut the story short, in only a few days the bracelet was ready. [83] And when Saintré was in Madame's presence, he rubbed his right eye, the signal that they had agreed upon, and she responded with her pin. That evening, when they were in the garden together, Saintré showed her the bracelet, although in the moonlight she could not see it clearly. Madame said:

"I'll examine the bracelet by torchlight, and also in daylight tomorrow, and I'll return it to you tomorrow evening when we meet here again, and then we can speak as long as we like."

THE AUTHOR: The following morning, when Madame saw the exquisite, costly bracelet, she was delighted and gave her signal to Saintré; he responded immediately, and when they were alone together, Madame said to him:

"My love, here is your bracelet, which seems to me so magnificent that it is difficult to imagine anything better. When I sat down to dine today, I determined that tomorrow, the eve of May Day, you should host a fine supper for a number of lords, knights, ladies, and damsels of the court, and others; you'll invite me, but I shan't accept. And then, in order to have your *emprise* proclaimed with all possible honor by the King of Arms or by a herald, you'll announce that the lady or the damsel, the knight or the squire, who sings most tunefully during the dances after supper will receive a fine diamond if a lady or a damsel, a fine ruby if a knight or a squire, and that you'll give the same gifts to whoever, of the knights and squires, ladies and damsels, is the best dancer.

"And after the dances and the songs have taken place, as we have arranged, you will have ready a copious, elegant rere-banquet* which will have *entremets** and exotic dishes in plenty, [84] and you will have a dressed peacock brought in so that the lords, the ladies and damsels, the knights and squires can swear their oaths on it,[73] and when they have done so, then you will swear, before the ladies and on the peacock, that on May Day, which is the following day, you will fasten to your left arm a bracelet that will remain there a whole year unless, during that time, you find a knight or a squire of good birth and with a blameless reputation at arms—and so on and so forth, just as we have said—assuming, of course, that the oath meets with the agreement of the King. And when once you've done that, and when you've duly escorted the ladies to their quarters, you'll keep the bracelet hidden next to your heart so that I can fasten it to your arm for the first time."

"My lady," said Saintré, "may the true God who rewards all virtue reward you for your kindness and make me worthy of your favor, for my heart and my every thought have no other wish."

And at those words, Madame, as always, gave him leave to go.

THE AUTHOR: The following day, the last day of April, as soon as day broke, Saintré busied himself with organizing cooks and dishes of all sorts, and—to make a long story short—he arranged a supper and a rere-banquet just as Madame had said, and then invited lords, ladies and damsels, knights and squires, burghers and their wives from Paris, and plenty of other guests. And when the supper, the rere-banquet, the dances, and the ceremony of the oaths had been duly concluded, and the ladies of the court had been escorted to their lodgings, and the King and the Queen had been offered a parting cup, and everyone had left, Saintré went, as Madame had arranged, to the garden; very soon afterward Madame came to join him, and then for the first [85] time she kissed the bracelet and fastened it to his left arm, although it was now so late that they could be together only for a short time. As she fastened it to his arm, she said:

"My love, my only desire, I pray God and Our Lady that this very hour when I give you this bracelet will be so propitious that you will return laden with honors, and in order to bring that about, I swear that on Fridays and Saturdays, as long as you are away, I shall wear no underlinens against my bare skin." "Ah, my lady," he said, "how have I deserved—how can I ever deserve—that a lady like you should swear such an oath for my sake?" "Yes, my love," she said, "now that you are equipped as I wish, I believe that as soon as possible you should obtain the consent and goodwill of our lord the King, send your letter of challenge, by a herald or pursuivant,* to the four royal courts that we listed, and solicit replies via the herald."

And having said this Madame gave him leave to go, and thus, with aching hearts and tears in their eyes, they parted.

THE AUTHOR AGAIN: The following day, May Day, Saintré dressed in his new clothes, made sure that the members of his household were dressed in their best, and put on his bracelet; then he went to hear Mass—he had the priest say the Mass of the Holy Spirit*—and gathered his friends together, just as Madame had instructed him. Then all of them accompanied him to the audience with the King—and indeed, many of them volunteered to attend him for the duration of the whole enterprise. And when the King appeared from his chamber, attended by my lords his brothers and a number of others of his family, Saintré and his companions fell to their knees [86], and Saintré began a joyful speech:

"Your Majesty, it is the custom for all men of birth to seek to enhance their reputations by the noble exercise of arms and by other means, and since my greatest desire is to gain a reputation for arms, I hope for your gracious consent and indispensable permission in a new enterprise. Yesterday, at my little banquet, I swore an oath before all these my esteemed lords and ladies, damsels, knights and squires here present"—and here he gave their names— "that this morning I would wear on my left arm this very gold bracelet, and you will find inscribed in this letter, if you will deign to read it, the articles of my oath."

Then the King took the letter of challenge and had it read publicly in front of him; he spent some time considering how he should respond, given how serious the weapons were and how young Saintré was—for he was very attached to the young man. When Saintré saw how the King was hesitating, he was very much afraid of a refusal, and said: "Ah, Sire, this is the very first petition of arms* that I have addressed to you; I beg you to give your consent."

Then my lords the King's brothers and all those present, impressed by Saintré's courage and daring, added their voices to his, and they all pleaded with the King so fervently that he agreed.

Then the King proceeded to Mass, and Saintré, having thanked him most humbly, went to the Queen, who had followed her husband into the room; he and all his companions fell to their knees, and Saintré said:

"My sovereign Queen, it has pleased the king to give me permission to pursue my *emprise*, with the help of God and Our Lady and the Archangel Michael, [87] according to the articles set out in this letter of challenge; here is the bracelet I spoke of, and I hope, Ma'am, that my plans will also be pleasing to you." "Oh, young man," said the Queen, "do you intend to undertake an *emprise* when you are so young? Who has advised you?" "Ma'am," he said, "God and honor have been my only advisers." "Well then, since they are your advisers, I pray that they will ensure a happy result." "Oh, Your Majesty," said a number of those present, "please have the articles read so that we can see what the conditions are." "We shan't do that until we have heard Mass."

At these words, Madame, who, like all those present, was looking on Saintré very warmly, came forward to hear what he would say. Then the Queen said:

"Saintré, since my lord the King has consented, I must consent too. And now that we have consented, I pray God, Our Lady, and the blessed Saint Julian[74] that they will give you every happiness and every success in your *emprise*."

Then the Queen went to hear Mass. When she returned, she asked that the letter of challenge be read to her, then said:

"Alas! This is a young man who is scarcely more than a boy! How has he had the audacity to undertake a challenge like this? It can only be the result of sterling character. And if by God's grace he returns unharmed, he will surely never need to undertake another deed of arms, since he is launching himself so young into a chivalric career."

Fig. 3. © The British Library Board: MS Cotton Nero D IX, f. 32v:
Saintré in the lists.

And with these words, the Queen went to table to dine.

THE AUTHOR: When the tables had been removed, the King, the Queen, her ladies, and all those present went to the stands to watch the jousts that were about to start. Then Saintré came into the lists* on a destrier* caparisoned in white damask embroidered with forget-me-nots, and the *mêlée** was joined between the defenders within and their opponents outside—but in order not to prolong the story, I shall say nothing about any combatant except Saintré himself, who broke lances, threw one opponent out of his saddle to the ground, overturned two others, horse and man; he wore his helmet for so long that he was made the champion, being the last to leave the lists. Needless to say, Madame was delighted, and so were the King, the Queen, and all the rest of the court; they were astonished to see the excellence of his jousting. And for the first time he was presented with a prize by his opponents: a very fine diamond that he presented to Madame.

THE AUTHOR: The following day he returned to the jousts, his horse caparisoned this time in green satin embroidered with pansies, and he in the same colors. [88] What more can I say? Once again he performed so well that all those present were amazed. But the King, afraid that the young man might suffer some hindrance to his *emprise*, made him withdraw from the lists, and for that day he jousted no more.

THE AUTHOR AGAIN: And when these first celebrations were over, Saintré diligently sought out the best-bred destriers, and gathered knights, squires, relatives, friends, kings of arms, heralds, trumpeters, minstrels, and two drummers; he also had made gowns, jewelry, armor, accoutrements,* helmet plumes, and other things essential to his forthcoming journey and to the success of his deed of arms. And when everything was ready, he made their signal to Madame, and that evening, when he came to the garden, he explained in detail all that he'd done: how he'd engaged three knights—he gave their names—with fourteen horses, [89] nine squires with twenty-three mounts, a chaplain with two horses, Anjou King of Arms with two horses, Touraine Herald and Lusignan Herald with four horses, four trumpeters with six horses, two drummers with two horses, and four excellent and powerful destriers that were to be ridden south by four handsome little pageboys, and led by two grooms who were to take charge of the horses and organize their fodder, two cooks with three horses, a forager,* a blacksmith, an armorer with four horses, and eight pack-horses, "four for myself and four for my retinue, and twelve further mounted men to act as my personal servants, and another one with three horses to act as my Steward: a total of eighty-nine horses, all to be dressed, Madame, in your colors and with your device."

He listed all these people and horses rather hesitantly, as if he felt his retinue might seem too large and too self-indulgent.

THE AUTHOR: But when Madame, who had listened to him with great pleasure, realized that he was hesitating because he was afraid that he could not afford such expenditure, she said to him:

"My love, I believe you have done better than anyone else possibly could, and as far as your expenses are concerned, I do not wish you to be anxious: I hope that my lord the King, my lady the Queen, and particularly my fine lords my uncles will offer you help on that score. And if they are not willing to do so, your honor and reputation need not suffer, since you have enough to finance you for a year. And now, my love, what of the trappers* for your own horses?"

"My lady, I have three sets, all very sumptuous. One is of crimson damask heavily embroidered with silver thread and trimmed with sable; another is of blue satin covered in gold-edged lozenges [90] and beaded with our initials, and that one is trimmed with ermine; the third is of black damask with the pattern picked out in silver thread; it's tufted with ostrich feathers in your colors—green, violet, and gray—with a fringe of white ostrich feathers, and strewn with swags* of black and ermine. This third one is the one I want to have made up as a trapper for my jousts, if you agree. And everyone tells me that these trappers and caparisons are very handsome and a delight to see.

"And I've had a fourth set made, with a matching coat of arms* for myself: that's the one I'll wear to enter the lists for my duels on foot. It's made of crimson satin all sewn with gold spangles enameled bright red, and across the crimson is a bend in white satin scattered with silver spangles, and on the bend *a label of three points Or* scattered with fine gold spangles: that is what I shall use for my device."

"But, my love, what is to be the blazon*?" "My lady, my arms are *gules, on a bend argent a label of four points Or*." "Good heavens, that all sounds superb. I should love to see all your accoutrements, but I am afraid of causing gossip. But I shall find a way to see it all without arousing suspicion: I shall prompt the Queen to ask."

"Well, now, my lady," said Saintré, "henceforth I am at your service when you give the word, for I think that the sooner I set things in train the better. I think that Lusignan Herald is here. If so, I shall try to meet him on his arrival."

Then they fixed on the following month, July 15, as the due date for his departure. And with those words they parted, with many a deep sigh and many a loving kiss. [91]

THE AUTHOR: The following morning, in the Queen's robing room,* Madame, who had not forgotten her desire to view Saintré's magnificent accoutrements, said pleasantly to the Queen:

"Your Majesty, I have heard tell that young Saintré has had several superb sets of trappings made for him; I find that difficult to believe! But on the other hand, Ma'am, although he is keeping them under wraps, if you were to ask him to show you them, in private, to us ladies of the court, then I believe he'd readily agree." "Are they really so superb, fair cousin?" "Ma'am, according to rumor, they are even more magnificent than I can describe." "Very well, then," said the Queen, "if we are not refused, we shall inspect them." "Ma'am," she said, "because he clearly wants to keep his outfits concealed, tell him to bring his four destriers into the small courtyard, with the trappers packed away; we'll get him to array his horses behind closed doors, and set a guard." "Ah yes, indeed," said the Queen, "you're quite right; remind me when you see him."

With these words, the Queen went to hear Mass, and saw Saintré in the presence chamber. Then Madame stepped forward and said discreetly:

"Ma'am, there's Saintré."

Then the Queen called for Guillaume de Lurs, her gentleman usher,* and had him summon Saintré.

"Saintré," said the Queen, "may God grant all your wishes! We beg you to show us the trappers you have had made for your destriers; everyone says they're magnificent."

"Oh, Your Majesty," said he, "with all due respect to those who have told you so, the trappers are very ordinary. I'd be ashamed to show you something so lowly." [92]

"Ah, fair sir, we beg you to let us see them for ourselves after dinner in the small courtyard; we'll lock the gates and set a guard. And if you want to keep them truly secret, have your men bring the caparisons in under cover, and then bring in your destriers; when the trappers have been fitted, have us called in private."

"My lady," said Saintré, "since this is what you wish, your wish is my command."

THE AUTHOR: When the King and Queen had dined and the tables had been removed, Saintré sent for his trappers and his destriers. The gates were closed, as had been directed, and the trappers were fitted to the horses. Then Saintré went to the Queen as she had asked. The Queen, urged by Madame and very eager to see the outfits herself, could not resist telling the King about them.

"Really?" said the King, "Are they truly so magnificent?" "My lord, if you wished you could come and see them." "Very well," said the King, "let them serve the parting cup." "Ah, my lord," said the Queen, "let there be very few present."

After the parting cup had been served, the King and the Queen left the room and went to the galleries above the courtyard, from which they saw the destriers fully caparisoned: a splendid and elegant sight. Then all the ladies and damsels began to sing Saintré's praises, and to pray God in his mercy to bring him back laden with honors. And when the King was ready to withdraw, he called Saintré to him and chatted to him about one thing and another, then withdrew into his robing room and [93] sent Saintré by his manservant Jean de Suffle three thousand *écus* to spend on his chivalric enterprise.

And when the Queen heard that the King had given Saintré three thousand *écus*, she was delighted. Then she called Madame and said: "Fair cousin, I am delighted that my lord the King has given Saintré three thousand *écus* to defray his expenses. Truly, I must give him at least a thousand, and I entreat you to give him two or three hundred." "Well, my lady," replied Madame, "you make very free with someone else's purse."

And she pretended to be reluctant. And when the Dukes of Anjou, Berry, and Burgundy heard what the King and Queen had given Saintré, each of them gave him a grant of a thousand. That made up some seven thousand, to which should be added other gifts given him by other lords; indeed, he never had to ask or to solicit a penny, and for this he was admired; people said of him:

"Surely we ought to help out a young knight like him, who is scarcely more than a boy but who is proposing such a valiant project out of the goodness of his heart? Truly, he deserves our love and admiration."

THE AUTHOR: And when the date of his departure drew near, eight or ten days prior to his leaving, Saintré, with his three knights, his nine squires, his King of Arms, his heralds, and all the rest of his retinue—all of them dressed in gowns decorated with his device—as well as a number of his other friends, lords, knights, and squires, all came to kneel before the King, in the presence of the King's brothers the Dukes of Anjou, Berry, and Burgundy. And Saintré said very humbly:

"My lord King, [94] Your Majesty gave your consent to my wearing this bracelet as a spur to deeds of arms on horse and on foot; you have seen the letter of challenge. Now I come before you to beg you most humbly, on my own behalf and that of my lords my brothers and my friends who have been courteous enough to agree to attend me, to give leave for my party to set out, under the protection of God, Our Lady, and the Archangel Michael, on July 15, so that I can begin my journey."[75]

THE AUTHOR: The King—who had already given leave, as we have shown—said: "Good heavens, Saintré, are you ready so soon?" "Sire," he said, "yes."

Then the King said:

"Saintré, you are of good birth; in your family there have been many men of valor. May God grant that you match them; I am hopeful of it, since you are beginning so young. And you need not be uneasy: whatever happens to you—for you are as inexperienced in arms as a schoolboy—I believe that in time God will make you a master of chivalry. But remember one thing: in whatever deed of arms you undertake, whether you win or lose, you should do so gladly and fairly."

And then the King gave him leave to depart, for which Saintré thanked him humbly and joyfully. And then the King withdrew, and Saintré made sure to thank all the lords for the generous gifts they had given him.

THE AUTHOR AGAIN: And as July 10, 12, and 14 came, Madame was filled with feelings of great regret and anguish on Saintré's behalf, and every day she gave him the signal with her pin, and he responded. And when they were in the garden together, they sighed and wept at the thought of his coming departure. [95] Then Madame said:

"My only dearest, who means more than I can say, my lord the King has given you three thousand *écus*, my lady the Queen one thousand, my fine lords my uncles each one thousand: that is seven thousand, not counting gifts from other lords. But since it is impossible to know how things will develop for you, I shall give you another three thousand, which will make up a round ten thousand. As long as you are not too extravagant, that will allow you to live comfortably for some time. But one thing I beg of you: that while you are still on your knees at the end of your daily Mass, you ask your priest, after the prayer of blessing, to say over you the blessing that God gave Moses, according to the Bible, out of His own mouth—the one, let me remind you, that I have often told you about: *Benedicat tibi Deus et custodiat te. Ostendat faciam suam tibi et misereatur tui. Convertat Deus vultum suum ad te et det tibi pacem.*[76]

"And when you are about to take up arms, on foot or on horseback, I entreat you to make the sign of the cross and to ask the same blessing with a true heart: *Benedicat michi Deus et custodiat me. Ostendat michi faciem suam Deus et misereatur mei. Convertat Deus vultum suum ad me et det michi pacem.*

"After that you can leave with confidence and perform your duty virtuously. Provided you do so, everything, win or lose, will be to your honor; whatever happens, [96] I shall never fail you."

And at these words, tears from her heart poured out so profusely that she could no longer speak.

THE AUTHOR: And at this Saintré, who was painfully conscious of Madame's great benevolence and favor toward him—something for which he felt himself to be the most fortunate lover in the world, especially so as every day she multiplied the benefits and honors, and princely and chivalric teachings, that she provided—was overcome by distress and said:

"Ah, my most sovereign and noble goddess beyond compare, you to whom I look to comfort me for the deep despair I feel at parting from you as I take my leave from you who are my sole desire, my sole delight, and my greatest prize, now that I see your grief my own is doubled and assails and vanquishes my heart, so that it is wounded to death—and thus I leave you, to die elsewhere, and, my lady, I bid you farewell."

And at these words he turned his back and made to leave.

THE AUTHOR: Madame, her torrent of tears almost exhausted, and hearing Saintré's words, spoke to him with many a wonderful and heartfelt sigh.

"Ah, my love, do not turn away so soon . . . ! You know that we women have tender hearts, full of pity for those we love. Do not go in sadness, for I take comfort in the hope that God will bring you back in triumph. Now my most faithful of lovers, now my dearest, now my every thought, now the love of my life and of my death, smile and go with a glad heart, and for your sake I shall be [97] happy and gay. But on your life, do not write to me; send full details to my lady the Queen, and that way I shall know everything about your doings without any risk of discovery—and now, my love, we must kiss and part."

And then there were kisses given and taken, kisses countless and untold, kisses blended with the deepest sighs, and in that state of painful pleasure and sorrowful bliss, to their dismay, they heard midnight strike. And that moment brought the dread parting, and as they said farewell, Madame kissed him and slid onto his finger a fine and precious diamond: "And God be with you. . . ."

THE AUTHOR: The following morning, July 15, was the day of departure. After Mass, and when the priest had given Saintré his blessing, Saintré and his retinue, all dressed in his livery, came to bid farewell to the King, who said:

"Saintré, God's blessings on your journey and your deeds, and may you return with great honor. I have asked only one thing of you, and I ask it again: ensure that you win or lose honorably and fairly." "Sire," he said, "please God you will never hear of my behaving in any other way."

Then the King touched his hand. And then Saintré went to the Queen, who said:

"Ah, Saintré, since you must go, I and all my ladies will pray that you will have success in arms and joy in love."

"Ma'am," he said, "as for success in arms, please do pray for that, but my desire is only to serve the King and you." And with these words he took leave of her, then, briefly, of Madame—[98] although she whispered with a sigh: "I have already taken my leave of you."

Then he went to the other ladies and damsels, and gave each of them a little gold ring enameled with forget-me-not flowers, and at that none of them could refrain from bursting into tears, they were so fond of him. And when the Queen heard the conversations about the rings, she called Saintré over and said to him, laughing:

"Now then, young master Saintré, aren't Belle Cousine and I ladies like the others? Why aren't we part of your following, as well?"

"Oh, Ma'am," said Saintré, "forgive me! I didn't dare think that ladies like yourselves would deign to accept such small gifts from me."

"Of course we shall," said the Queen, "although we would not do so from just anyone."

At that, Saintré gave them the choice of all the rings he had—although in fact they were all identical—and they said: "Saintré, heartiest thanks."

And at these words Saintré took his leave again, and as he left Madame could not stem her tears. Then, to excuse herself, she said to the Queen: "However sorrowful I feel, however full of regrets, I never weep except when I see others weeping." "And indeed, Ma'am," said the other ladies, "what woman could be so heartless as to refrain from weeping at the sight of a mere boy riding off to his peril? And when we've nurtured him in our service, and when he has always paid us such delicate and pleasing attentions?"

THE AUTHOR ON SAINTRÉ'S DEPARTURE: When Saintré had taken his leave of the ladies of the court, [99] he went to take leave of the lords, and all of them were very gracious to him; then he went with all his retinue to his own quarters to dine. And as they were dining, the Queen sent him a length of fine cloth of silver,* the Duke of Anjou sent him a handsome, well-trained courser, the Duke of Berry sent him a great cloak and five hundred sable pelts, and the Duke of Burgundy sent fifteen marks'* weight of silver plate. And everyone who gave Saintré gifts gave him at least a hundred écus in love and honor of the Queen and the said lords. And when they had all dined and the horses were saddled and bridled, all the knights and squires of the King's court and the Queen's, and all the lords we have mentioned, and many others, in all at least a thousand horse, came to escort him.

Then Saintré had his retinue set off in the following order: first, his two foragers, his cooks, and his chaplain, then the four trumpeters bearing his banner, then his three heralds, and then, two by two, his three knights and his nine squires, then all their serving men wearing his livery, then his five packhorses with saddle blankets with his blazon, led by two grooms, then his drummers, then his four destriers caparisoned with fine Florence taffeta* in grey, green, and violet, with his device lettered large in silver, each of them having a magnificent steel shaffron* with elegant crests of embroidered ostrich plumes covered in silver spangles. The destriers were ridden by four pretty pages wearing his device, their sleeves embroidered with silver spangles, each of them wearing a handsome feathered hat in Saintré's colors. [100] And after the destriers came the two grooms and the blacksmith.

After them came several more drummers, and then the minstrels who were accompanying him. And after the minstrels came the pursuivants, and then the heralds of the various lords, and then those of the King, and then the royal kings of arms. And after them came all the trumpets and clarions,* first those of the lords, then those of the King. And after the trumpeters came Saintré, wearing his own device like his pages, his sleeves heavily embroidered with gold and silver spangles, and wearing a feathered cap like those of his pages, and mounted on the fine courser given him by the Duke of Anjou as a parting gift; Saintré rode in the middle of four lords, two in front, two behind, and then behind them came all the lords, knights, squires, in what-ever order they pleased—and all these escorted him out of the court and out of Paris, for a good league*. . . . And on his departure, he invited all the kings of arms, heralds, pursuivants, trumpets, minstrels, drummers, and other sworn companions to supper with him in Bourg-la-Reine, where he spent that first night; he gave them excellent hospitality, and the following morning he gave each of them fifty *écus*. And now I shall say no more about his departure, and turn to his journey and to the arrival of Lusignan Pursuivant.

THE AUTHOR: When Saintré arrived in Avignon, and when news of his arrival spread across the town, Anjou King of Arms, who was carrying a sealed letter with a response to Saintré's challenge, came to meet Saintré as he came out of church after Mass and gave him the letter. And when Saintré had read the letter and taken note of it, he went straight back into the church and publicly offered thanks to God; [101] then he turned to the King of Arms and in front of everyone asked how his challenge had been accepted, and who the champion was who had taken it up. Then Lusignan King of Arms said:

"I arrived in Barcelona on June 3, quite late in the evening, and spent the night there. The following morning, after I had heard Mass, I returned

to my lodging and dressed in a coat of arms with your blazon—as was right—
and slipped the little pouch where I carried your letter of challenge into my
doublet; then I had a groom from the inn conduct me to the King's palace.
And God be thanked, at the gate I met a very well-built, handsome knight,
with a considerable retinue, named Enguerrand de Cervillon, and as he
passed, I offered him humble greetings. When he saw that I was wearing
your coat of arms, he suddenly called out to me and said: 'Herald—for such
you seem to me given the coat of arms that you're wearing—what is your
name?' 'My lord,' I said, 'my official status is King of Arms of Anjou, Touraine, and Maine.'

"Then he replied: 'King of Arms, you are most welcome; I believe you
have come to this court bearing a challenge, and if that is so, I beg you to tell
me what it is.' 'My lord,' I said, 'it is indeed the case that I am here on behalf
of a noble and renowned squire of the kingdom of France, named Jean de
Saintré; on the last May Day, in the presence of many ladies and damsels,
lords, knights, and squires, he undertook an *emprise* according to which he
vowed to wear on his left arm, for a whole year, a magnificent gold bracelet
studded with precious stones, [102] unless within that time he found a knight
or squire of good birth and *sans reproche** who would deliver him from his
vow by combat on horse or on foot, as spelled out in the terms of this letter;
in pursuit of his vow he comes first here to this kingdom and to the court of
this noble King, and he will remain here a full month, hoping to be released
from his vow by a knight or squire of the rank I have described. If no challenger presents himself, he will proceed to the court of the King of Navarre,
then to the court of the King of Castile, and then to the court of the King of
Portugal; in each of these courts he will stay for a full month if he doesn't
immediately find what he's looking for.'

" 'Now, King of Arms, I beg you to let me see the letter, and I promise,
on my honor as a knight, if the challenge is an honorable one, that if it is
God's will, and the will of Saint George and of my lord the King, I shall be
ready to help your master to fulfill his vow.' And when I heard him speak
with such dignity, when I saw him so stalwart and so well escorted, and when
I heard the terms of his promise, I thought that I had found what I was
seeking. So I drew the letter from my doublet and gave it him, and when he
had read it at his leisure, he said to me: 'King of Arms, come with me.'

"Then he went and spoke to a number of knights and squires of the
court; he showed them your letter of challenge, and then said again: 'King of
Arms, come with me.' Then he took me by the hand and led me to the King,

who was just leaving Mass. Then hand in hand we knelt together, as did the rest of those present, and then he said, in his own language: 'Sire, as I left this your palace, by great good fortune I found Anjou King of Arms, here present, [103] and I realized, from the fact that he was wearing his tabard,* that he must have come on some errand of arms, especially so since he had come to the court of so high a prince as you. I called out to him and asked him whence he came and why he was wearing his tabard at your court, given that you are at peace with all other Christian princes. And he replied in terms that I shall repeat to you if you wish to hear them.'"

THE KING OF ARMS: "As he was speaking, the King, who had been staring at me, touched my hand and bade me very welcome, then told me to tell him what I had said to Messire Enguerrand de Cervillon. So—to be brief—I repeated word for word what I had said. 'And where is the letter?' said the King. 'Sire,' said Messire Enguerrand, 'here it is.' Then the king had it read, and when it had been read Messire Enguerrand said: "Sire, the most noble privilege of true worldly honor demands of noble hearts that in order to match the most noble pursuit of arms, they should make every attempt, as best they can, to acquire the noble gift of the highest honor, whether in *emprises* or in duly declared war, or in any other fashion that honor may permit. And since good fortune has meant that this adventure was presented to me first, and although many others here present at your court are nobler, more mighty, and worthier than I am, nevertheless, Sire, in recognition of the chance that made me first, I beg and beseech you, as humbly as I know how, as I should and as I can, if you are inclined to allow this challenge to be accepted by one of your court, that that one might be me.'" [104]

THE KING OF ARMS: "And when the King heard this petition, and before he gave an answer, he withdrew a little, with a number of lords and other knights and squires, all of them experienced; when he had consulted them rapidly, he called Messire Enguerrand to him and said publicly: 'Sir Enguerrand, we have heard your humble and honorable request, and for love of you and in your honor, as for that of the noble squire who has carried this challenge, we accord our permission and appoint for your encounter a day fifteen days after his arrival; may God bless you and keep you. And in this way you will give great pleasure to the ladies.' Messire Enguerrand and his friends thanked the King most humbly for his gracious response, and I did likewise on your behalf.

"Then the King went to dine, and Messire Enguerrand led me to his house and sent to get my horses and stable them with his own, then had me dine with him. After dinner he bade me take off your blazoned tabard and gave me an elegant, costly gown of blue velvet richly brocaded in gold and lined with sable—I have it here in my traveling trunk—and then had me stay with him all that day and the next; indeed had I wished I could have stayed longer. And while he was devising his response to you, the King's heralds came to take me around the town and to celebrate my visit.

"And when Messire Enguerrand's response was drawn up, he took me to take my leave of the King, who received me very cordially for love of our own lord the King, and for love of you, and had me given a tabard of black brocaded velvet lined with sable, and a hundred Aragonese florins,* [105] and as I took my leave he said to me, most graciously, that I should greet you on his behalf."

THE AUTHOR: And when Saintré and all his companions heard Anjou's report, with the excellent news that his challenge was soon to be taken up, they were all delighted, and the news soon spread everywhere and was carried to the King and Queen so that Madame heard it, as did all the court and the rest of the kingdom. At that the ladies and damsels started to fast, to offer pledges, pilgrimages, and prayers for love of Saintré. Saintré himself, however, good Christian that he was and knowing how his honors and his advancement at court were God's gift to him, returned to the church and knelt, bare-headed and hands folded, to give thanks devoutly to God and to Our Lady in his prayers. And then all the company retired to dine.

THE AUTHOR ON THE ENTRY INTO BARCELONA: While these things were happening and Messire Enguerrand was making his preparations, it was not long before Saintré arrived in the town of Perpignan. The King was notified of Saintré's arrival, and of the great display and splendid retinue with which he was traveling. [106] The King naturally assumed that he was a man of substance, as did his court, and immediately sent orders that worthy lodgings be prepared in the city of Barcelona; these arrangements were completed by the King's commissaries* two days before the young man's arrival.

And as Saintré made his entry into the city, Messire Enguerrand, with a fine retinue of lords and knights and squires, was awaiting him a league outside the walls. And all were astonished, just as spectators had been when Saintré left Paris, first, by Saintré's remarkable youth, and second, by the lavishness of the young man's own retinue. And when Messire Enguerrand saw how very young his adversary was, he was dismayed to find himself committed to combat on such terms against someone who could have been his own son; he could not stop staring at him, amazed that so young a man would undertake such an *emprise*.

And when they reached the lodging prepared for Saintré, Messire Enguerrand, embarrassed at the thought of the combat in which he was to engage, took Saintré aside and said:

"Jean de Saintré, my brother, you are a noble young squire, and I am a noble old knight; if you were willing to release me from the vow that I have made in response to your challenge, I would be happy to offer you a different opponent, my nephew, who is your age and already, just as I am myself, a knight. I would beg you to accept this offer."

Saintré, wise and courteous, responded thoughtfully on his own account:

"My lord Messire Enguerrand, it has pleased God and been my good fortune that my challenge came first to your hand, something for which I am profoundly and humbly grateful—and you of your goodness, as a most chivalrous knight, [107] have given your sworn word to accept the challenge. And although my lord your nephew is a most admirable knight, and worthy to stand against the bravest knight in France, nevertheless since a favorable chance has brought me to you, I would wish, with all due apology, to maintain our agreement. And if by some chance, which I cannot foresee, you were unable to take up my gage,* I would legitimately consider myself released from my vow."

THE AUTHOR: And when Messire Enguerrand heard such an honorable and elegant response from so young a man, he was astonished; he understood just what Saintré, without expressing it in so many words, had meant, as to how he would take Enguerrand's demission* as freeing him from the terms of his vow. So he determined to complete the deed of arms promised, and said:

"Saintré, my brother, I have heard your excellent response: by God's grace, and that of Our Lady and of Saint George, I shall fulfill my oath on the day and at the hour that my lord the King has assigned. And in order that all shall be done as quickly as possible, and in all due form, I propose that I come to fetch you as soon as the King leaves vespers. You will be all prepared, and will come to pay your respects to the King and to the Queen, who will be delighted to see you. And there, in the presence of my lord the King, I will unfasten your bracelet. I will return it to you tomorrow, as your letter dictates; I have every hope that, with the help of Saint George, I shall do honor to Madame."

And on that Enguerrand bade Saintré farewell; he did not at first wish to stay to dine, but Saintré, eager to see more of his behavior and his temperament, persuaded him to stay a while.

THE AUTHOR AGAIN: Then Messire Enguerrand [108] went to the King and told him of Saintré's remarkable generosity and his gracious way of speaking, and the King, who had already heard something of this, felt a great deal of respect for the young man. He was very eager to see him, as were the Queen and all the ladies of the court, and had him summoned after vespers; he had him very well escorted, with Messire Enguerrand holding him by the arm; the latter knelt and presented Saintré, both of them kneeling, to the King, in the presence of the Queen. And when the King saw them, he stepped forward two or three paces, and said: "Welcome to a squire of such remarkable promise!"

Then he had them rise, and Messire Enguerrand presented him to the Queen, who said: "Jean, you are very welcome," and took him by the hand and had him get to his feet.

Then Enguerrand and Saintré came back to the King, and both of them knelt. Messire Enguerrand said to the King:

"Sire, you have read my brother Saintré's letter of challenge laying out the feat of arms he proposes, and by your grace you have given me leave to assign a time and a place for me to take up his challenge. So, with your kind permission, please give me leave to complete the terms of his vow: that is, in the first place, to unfasten the bracelet that he is wearing on his left arm."

Then the King, in his wisdom, insisted on hearing in person that this was Saintré's wish. He had the letter publicly read aloud, and had Saintré acknowledge its terms, then said:

"Jean de Saintré, are you indeed wearing this bracelet as a challenge, in the way that your letter lays out?" "Sire, yes," said Saintré. "In that case," said the King to Messire Enguerrand, "I give you leave to release him." [109]

Then Messire Enguerrand took off the bracelet, and once he had done so he threaded it onto a gold and silk ribbon and wore it round his neck for the rest of the day, and returned it to him the following morning. And once this was done, he and Saintré went to the Queen and the other ladies, who paid them great honor and made them very welcome; then they all retired to the presence chamber and there they played a variety of games until it was time for supper. Then Saintré took his leave, and Messire Enguerrand and a number of knights and squires invited him to supper—and for many days thereafter, Enguerrand never tired of talking of Saintré's good looks and his gracious manner, and those also of his household.

And on the fourth day, the King had the Queen issue an invitation to summon Saintré, and all the noblemen who had accompanied him, to dine. And after dinner there were dances and songs, in which Saintré, who like some of his companions had a very fine singing voice, gave great pleasure to the King, the Queen, and all the court. And thus they were made welcome every day at court—and now I shall cut a long story short, and turn to the feat of chivalry for which Saintré had come.

THE AUTHOR ON SAINTRÉ'S ENTRY INTO THE LISTS: Fifteen days after Saintré's arrival in Barcelona, on the day that had been ordained for his combat with Messire Enguerrand, the two champions were armed and equipped by ten in the morning. At that hour, the King, with the wisdom and dignity required, sent a cavalcade to honor the visitor and escort Saintré with all due ceremony into the lists: four of the noblest lords and knights of his court, the Count of Cardona, Don Federich de Luna, Messire Arnaut de Pereillos, and Messire François de Moncade, all splendidly equipped and with a fine retinue. And when that had been arranged, the King set off himself and made his way to the stands that had been set up to the side of the lists [110] and furbished with magnificent hangings; with him were the princes and lords, knights and squires of his household, all escorting many princesses, ladies, and damsels from his own court and from the wider region, all present to see the feats of arms promised for the day. And when the King and Queen were all installed in their stand, at the King's order the heralds and kings of arms attended the combatants to order them to fulfill the pledges they had given. At that, Saintré, already armed, mounted his horse along with his retinue, and as instigator and deviser of the *emprise* entered the lists with his retinue, in the following order:

First to emerge from his pavilion were his drummers, on horseback, with all those who were to escort him to the fight. After the drummers came three packhorses carrying trunks with his armor, all duly covered with trappers embroidered with his coat of arms, and each led by a groom on foot. After them there came on foot the two armorers. After the armorers came, two by two, the pursuivants wearing their tabards. And after the pursuivants came Saintré's minstrels. And after Saintré's minstrels came the minstrels and trumpeters of the King of Aragon. And after the trumpeters of Aragon came the heralds of Aragon. After these came the heralds of the kingdom of France. After the heralds of France came the two Kings of Arms of Aragon and Anjou, each bearing the coats of arms of their lords, and then the French Kings of Arms bearing Saintré's own arms, richly embroidered. [111]

After the Kings of Arms came Saintré's four trumpeters and buglers, and after them knights and squires carrying across their thighs twelve great lances, six of them with the lance heads attached and draped in cloth of silver in his colors trimmed with marten* fur, and the remaining six richly decorated in the same manner.

After the twelve lances, on a magnificent courser, came Don Bernard de Cardona, carrying at his saddlebow* a lance with a banner in the richest crimson velvet, lined with ermine and trimmed with a fringe of finest gold. And on the four quarters of the banner were richly embroidered the four blazons of Saintré's four principal bloodlines.[77]

After the banner came Don Federich de Luna on a most powerful courser. He bore at his saddlebow a lance decorated like the six previous lances, on which was carried Saintré's tilting helmet,* crowned with a helmet crest* consisting of a great thistle flower set on four gold leaves; from the base of the flower hung a long mantling* of gaudy Plaisance linen,* richly trimmed with big pearls and thread of gold, and spangled all over with gold initials.

And after the helmet came Saintré himself on a magnificent, spirited destrier; on its head it had a steel shaffron decorated with three ostrich plumes, richly embroidered in Saintré's three colors; he and his destrier were dressed and caparisoned in crimson silk sewn with ermine tails, with a border checkered also in his three colors and fringed with silver. On his head he had a fine, jaunty feathered hat; [112] he was wearing only his pauldron,* his chausses,* and his sabatons*; in his right hand he carried his banner, which showed the Madonna and Child, and as he rode along he made the sign of the cross.

After Saintré came Messire François de Moncade and Messire Arnaut de Pereillos, side by side, each on his fine courser, and after them a great number of knights and squires who had been ordered by the King to escort him. So accompanied, in such fine style, he came to one of the great pavilions, carefully pitched, which the King had had erected at each entry to the lists. And there he dismounted, accompanied by the four lords who were his seconds,[78] and by those of his household that he had chosen.

And following Saintré and preceding the four lords, there came his four pages, each on a fine courser, the horses caparisoned and the pages dressed as they had been when they left Paris, as we described earlier.

THE AUTHOR ON SIR ENGUERRAND'S ENTRY INTO THE LISTS: When Saintré had dismounted, the Kings of Arms, the heralds, the pursuivants, the trumpeters, and the minstrels went to find Messire Enguerrand to offer him an honorable escort, and they found him on the point of mounting his horse. Then they formed a procession, with the drummers first, then the minstrels; after the minstrels came many lords, knights, and squires who had come to escort him.

After the knights and squires came his four destriers, [113] all saddled up and with the saddles covered in the same cloth of gold as their trappers. The first destrier was caparisoned in a costly figured blue satin embroidered with gold thread and with a wide border of a subtle gray cloth.

The second destrier was caparisoned also in figured blue satin embroidered with gold thread, but this time trimmed with sable. The third destrier was caparisoned in rich purple figured satin embroidered with gold thread, and this was another of Enguerrand's colors; it was trimmed with ermine, and the horse was led forward by three grooms on foot.[79] After the three destriers came twelve knights also on fine coursers, six of them riding two by two with twelve lances covered in the same cloth of gold, with the same trimmings, as the trappers. After the twelve lances came the King's trumpeters, and after them Aragon King of Arms, wearing a sumptuous tabard; at his neck he bore a shining lightweight steel targe,* surrounded by thirds with three draperies of gold, and in each of the four quarters of the targe was a coat of one of the four lineages from which he, the King of Aragon, was descended, and in the center, his own coat of arms.

After the King of Arms came the Count of Orgel, riding on a powerful, fine-bred courser. On the tip of his lance he carried Messire Enguerrand's bascinet,* which had a helmet crest consisting of a *demi-deer Or naissant*,[81] *collared*, the collar having three jewels, a fine ruby, a fine diamond, and a fine Balas ruby,* each set between two very large pearls.

After the bascinet came Messire Enguerrand himself, fully armed except for his head, on which he wore a beautiful chaplet made of a variety [114] of flowers and leaves; he was mounted on a magnificent, powerful destrier caparisoned in costly crimson figured velvet embroidered all over in gold thread, and having a deep border of ermine; in his right hand he held the lance grip on which his arm rested.

After Messire Enguerrand came the Count of Prades and the Count of Cardona, who were his seconds, and then the many other lords, knights, and squires who had come to escort him. And he too came and dismounted at his pavilion, and there he put on his bascinet and was provided with everything that he needed.

THE AUTHOR ON THE COMBATANTS' ARMS: When both combatants had presented themselves, the King had their lances measured: they were to be, from tip to lance rest,* exactly thirteen feet long. And when each lance had been measured and returned to the combatants, the King ordered that Saintré be first to enter the lists, and so it was done. But once he was mounted on his destrier, he called for his banner and used it to make a sign of the cross, while reciting the blessing that Madame had taught him, as we described. Still making the sign of the cross he rode slowly into the lists, to his appointed place, and with him came the four lords who were his seconds; they were escorted by the agreed number of attendants, on horseback and on foot. He circled the lists around the tilt barrier,* which was made of fine scarlet canvas.

And as he went out and back, when he was in front of the stands where the King and the Queen were seated, he bowed as low as he could as a mark of respect; the King was impressed and said to his courtiers: "Truly, in everything he does and says, this young squire shows his quality, [115] and demonstrates how much the French court where he has been trained is a true school of honor." The Queen and all her other ladies were just as loud in his praises: they competed to speak well of him, and most of them prayed for him. Then he rode slowly to his appointed place, rested his lance on his thigh, and rode his horse prancing up and down the lists.

The King now summoned Messire Enguerrand, and, to cut the story short, had him do just as Saintré had done. And when each combatant was stationed at his own end of the list, the King ordered them to do their duty.

THE AUTHOR ON THE FIRST DAY: Then Saintré, holding his banner, again made the sign of the cross and recited his blessing three times. Then he and Enguerrand fitted their lances into the lance rests, couched* their lances, and galloped toward each other at full tilt. At this first course of arms, however, there was no result.

At the second course, Messire Enguerrand lodged his lance head just under Saintré's visor;* Saintré meanwhile lodged his lance against the bottom of Enguerrand's pauldron; the lance broke, and Enguerrand swayed a little in his saddle. At this, the trumpeters sounded a loud clarion.

At the third course, Messire Enguerrand angled his lance too low, and it broke against Saintré's saddletree;* Saintré meanwhile struck off Enguerrand's stag's-head helmet crest. Then the trumpets began to sound, but because the lance had not been cleanly broken, the King commanded them to be silent. [116]

At the fourth course, Messire Enguerrand caught Saintré squarely on his breastplate and broke his lance cleanly. Saintré struck Enguerrand on his bascinet; the lance slipped off the breastplate and slid between Enguerrand's hand and his gauntlet. The gauntlet was torn off, and although his hand was not wounded, it was so bruised and swollen that the remainder of the jousts had to be postponed for four days. Saintré's lance broke just below the lance head, but the blow was disallowed.

Thereafter the King had a herald read the articles of agreement governing the jousts, whereby appellant* and defendant engaged that in case of injury one should await the recovery of the other for eight days; in keeping with this agreement, the King ordered both contestants to return to their lodging. Each of them rode back fully armed except for his helmet, but in order to do honor to Saintré, who had, he thought, had the better of the day, the King had Enguerrand leave the lists first.

THE AUTHOR: After they had both disarmed and rested a little and Messire Enguerrand had had his hand treated, the King sent for them to have supper with him, and he had Saintré, as the visitor, sit on his right hand, and Messire Enguerrand, as the King's subject and one of his household, on his left, with his hand in a sling. And when the tables had been removed, the King had the Queen and all her ladies join them, and at that point the dancing started, and the Queen took Saintré as a partner, and the other ladies and damsels took the other knights and squires who had come with Saintré. There Saintré was much praised by the knights and ladies; Messire Enguerrand also made every effort to do honor to Saintré and to make him welcome—and Saintré was indeed honored and made welcome at court until the time when Messire Enguerrand was healed. [117]

On the fourth day, in order to complete their *emprise*, the King ordered that they be in the lists fully armed, and they appeared accoutred* just as they had been previously (apart from their helmets), with themselves and their destriers decked out with new accoutrements.

And when both of them were fully ready in the lists, the King commanded them to do their duty; and at that point they spurred their horses against each other, with their lances in rest.*

In this fifth course, Messire Enguerrand was struck on the edge of the double gardbrace,* and Saintré just below the bascinet, and both their lances broke cleanly so that the shards flew into the air, and their destriers staggered and nearly fell. And at that the trumpets sounded, and those present shouted so loudly that they could scarcely be silenced, and it was agreed that both contestants had broken their lances very honorably.

In the sixth course, Messire Enguerrand struck Saintré on the pauldron, and Saintré him at the bottom of the beaver,* and both contestants broke their lances cleanly; thus each of them had broken his three lances.

In the seventh course, just as the lances were about to cross, Messire Enguerrand's horse spooked leftward, and thus the course was null.

At the eighth course, when Messire Enguerrand's horse saw Saintré galloping up, it bucked and swung round, so that if Saintré had not reacted quickly and raised his lance, he would have struck Messire Enguerrand in the back; his quick thinking was highly praised by the King, the Queen, the lords and ladies, and all the spectators. And then Messire Enguerrand left the lists [118] and went to his pavilion to change horses, and when he came out again they lowered their lances and spurred against each other so hard that the horses were not close enough for them to strike each other.

In the ninth course, Messire Enguerrand was carried away by his fresh horse; he raised his lance a little too far, and Saintré's lance struck him just on the besagew* and glanced off the breastplate,[82] and the blow unriveted the besagew and tore off the lance rest, and as it ripped away Messire Enguerrand swayed heavily in his saddle, and thus Saintré achieved his four lances broken, and Messire Enguerrand had to withdraw to change his breastplate. And when Enguerrand had returned to the lists and when each of them had his lance rested on his thigh, they spurred toward each other at full speed but the lances did not make contact.

At this tenth course, as luck would have it, the two lances crossed, but the destriers were moving at such speed that the tilt barrier, made of red canvas hanging from rods, could not prevent Messire Enguerrand's destrier falling, and Saintré's had its shoulder dislocated. Then Saintré dismounted and took a rouncey* and went to his station* to change destriers; he refused to take off his helmet no matter how much he was urged to do so. And when Messire Enguerrand had got to his feet and returned to his side of the lists, he waited for Saintré—who reappeared very soon.

At the eleventh course, Messire Enguerrand angled his lance somewhat too low and caught Saintré on the lowest of his lames,* and Saintré struck his opponent on the vamplate and distorted it badly. Then Messire Enguerrand, because he had struck Saintré so low down, fell forward over his saddlebow, and both contestants broke their lances cleanly [119] so that the shards flew out everywhere across the lists: Messire Enguerrand had by now broken four lances, and Saintré his full tally.[83] Then the trumpets sounded, and the spectators cried out so long and so loud that they took some time to fall silent. And at this point, when Saintré's five lances had been broken as specified in the articles of the *emprise*, Messire Enguerrand, aware that Saintré had duly broken his five lances and that he was therefore the victor, challenged him to a final joust in honor of the ladies,[84] and Saintré agreed. And when the King heard that the two champions were proposing this final joust, he sent to have it forbidden, in order not to compromise the combat on foot. And then he commanded that both of them should be brought before him immediately, and when both were present, he commanded them to dishelm;* then he had the following words read by his own King of Arms, whom he had requested to come up into his stand.

ADJUDICATION OF ARMS: "To the two lords here present (he had no need to name them): our lord the King has witnessed your jousts performed valiantly and completely, so much so that no man could do better, as described as follows in writing. . . ." Then in the presence of all, he read the results as he had noted them, course by course and point by point, and then said: "And until your last course, you were equal, but then, noble squire Jean de Saintré, you broke your fifth lance cleanly and thus completed the terms of your challenge on horseback; our lord the King therefore awards you the prize."

And at that point Messire Enguerrand came up to Saintré to present him with the promised ruby. [120] But when Saintré saw him approaching, he spurred his destrier and went forward to meet him; then he bowed low and touched his hand and saluted him as ceremoniously as he could, saying:

"My lord and brother, I thank you from the bottom of my heart for the great honor you have done me."

And then Messire Enguerrand answered as a wise and gracious knight should:

"What are you saying, brother? It is I who should thank you for your victory over me, and I pray God and Saint George that he will grant you to perform better and better. And may your fair lady, to whom I commend myself most humbly, give you your reward. In token of which, and in her honor, I present you with this ruby that she has inspired you to win, and beg her duly to accept it."

Then Saintré bowed low and took the fine ruby and thanked his opponent most humbly, then said:

"Now, my lord brother, it is by your leave that I have won this ruby, for you have pretended to lose; so that your most cherished lady may not be the loser, I beg you to offer her, with my most humble respects, this small diamond."

And when Messire Enguerrand saw the huge, magnificent diamond, and Saintré's nobility, generosity, and outstanding courtesy, he turned to the knights who were standing around them and said, in his native Castilian:

"Truly, this is the flower of noble young men!" Then he said to Saintré:

"Truly, brother, I thank you on behalf of my señora and myself, and we are as grateful to you as if I had accepted your gift or as if she had received it; but I must refuse you on this occasion, [121] for I cannot accept the diamond; you must give it to her who has deserved and won it."

Saintré continued to press him, and Messire Enguerrand continued to demur and to refuse, until the King asked what was afoot; and when he and the Queen were told, Saintré was highly praised, needless to say, by the King himself, the Queen, the lords, the ladies, the knights, the damsels, the squires, and all the ordinary spectators. But the King, at Saintré's ardent entreaties, told Messire Enguerrand he must accept the diamond: Saintré's courtesy was such that his opponent could not refuse. Then Messire Enguerrand took it, and as he did so, the trumpeters and the minstrels began to clamor, and the King told the combatants to go and disarm.

Sir Enguerrand and Saintré, elaborately courteous as ever,[85] each wished to escort the other; there were entreaties on both sides, but in the end Messire Enguerrand prevailed, and to show his courtesy even more fully, he begged Saintré to ride on his right; they went forward side by side. And when they reached Saintré's lodging, Saintré made strenuous and dutiful efforts to be allowed to escort the other back again, and he would indeed have done just that if the lords of the court, on both sides, had not held him back by main force. Saintré begged all the lords, his own supporters,* and others, to have supper with him that night, but however much he entreated them, none of them wished to remain, and all of them left him to rest for that night; and it was the same thing for Messire Enguerrand, since they both knew that they were to engage in combat on foot the following day. But that night the King, wise, benign, and gracious sovereign and prince that he was, took note of the pain and the effort that each had endured the previous day, [122] and postponed their combat so that they could rest.

THE AUTHOR: Two days later, on the day agreed for them to take up arms again, Saintré went very first thing to hear the Mass of the Holy Spirit and had himself given his blessing. Then he had two heralds and a page carry Messire Enguerrand the two poleaxes, covered,[86] so that, as the articles of his challenge had specified, he could take his choice of weapon; once Messire Enguerrand had made his choice, the heralds came back to find Aragon King of Arms announcing in the first instance to Saintré and on behalf of the King the time—two o'clock that afternoon—when their combats on foot were to be fought. Then Saintré sent thanks to the King via the King of Arms, most humbly, and presented the latter with a fine cloak of crimson damask shot with silver and lined with sables, to thank him for the excellent and joyful news that he had brought—and the King of Arms reported their conversation to the King.

THE AUTHOR: When the first hour after noon had sounded, the King and Queen, as we have said, went up into their stand, and sent word to the participants that they were to present themselves. Then Saintré, as the *entrepreneur** and challenger in the jousts (although not the appellant),[87] made the sign of the cross with his pennon and said his blessing as before; and his retinue processed in the following order:

THE AUTHOR AGAIN: First came the drummers and then the packhorses with his armor under cover, as we have described, led by pages; after the packhorses came his two armorers on foot, and then his four minstrels, two by two. After them came [123] the pursuivants and then the heralds of the local lords, all heralds and pursuivants dressed fittingly in their tabards and livery. After the heralds came the French knights and squires of his own company, also all dressed in his colors; and after them came the Kings of Arms and the heralds of the King of Castile, side by side with those of the King of France and riding to their left. And after the heralds came Saintré's trumpets and clarions and then those of the King, and after the King's heralds came the Count of Prades carrying Saintré's poleaxe before him on a powerful courser, and one on each side of the Count came Don Bernard de Cardona and Don Federich de Luna.

And after them came Saintré himself, completely unarmed apart from his bracers,* his greaves,* and his sabatons, mounted on his magnificent, powerful destrier; he was wearing a handsome cap beautifully embroidered with three fine ostrich feathers, filigreed with small diamonds, Balas rubies, and other precious stones, pinned on with a fine, valuable brooch made up of a great diamond set between three large Balas rubies and three very heavy pearls. Saintré and his destrier were caparisoned in crimson satin, sewn with spangles of pure gold enameled in scarlet, with a great bend of white satin covered with silver spangles on which was enameled his own blazon, *argent a label of three points Or*. And in his right hand he carried his pennon, embroidered with a Madonna and Child, and with this, as he rode, he made the sign of the cross.

And after him came his pages mounted on fine destriers draped in rich trappers, [124] and after them, two by two, came the aforementioned Messire Arnaut de Pereillos and Messire François de Moncade, and after them, all the knights and squires whom the King had sent to escort him. And in such state he came and dismounted at his pavilion, which was close to the gate into the lists, at his own end; and there he had himself fully armed, apart from his helmet.

And when Messire Enguerrand had also arrived and dismounted at his pavilion, the King commanded his King of Arms to sound the call to arms. Then Saintré, escorted by his chosen supporters, lords, and others, came into the lists on foot, and there he found the King's Marshal, who asked him who he was and what he intended, to which, with a humble smile, he replied:

"My lord Marshal, I am Jean de Saintré, come here on the day and at the hour that the most excellent prince, the King here present, as our true and expert judge, has appointed for me and for my lord and brother Messire Enguerrand de Cervillon, so that we may proceed to our combat on foot as specified in my letter of challenge."

After these words were pronounced, the Marshal went to report to the King. The King commanded that the gate to the lists be opened to him so that Saintré might take up station in his pavilion, and when the gates were open and he made to go through, he made the sign of the cross with his pennon, then kissed it and went into his pavilion; and Messire Enguerrand, to be brief, did the same.

But when once both of them were in their pavilions, very soon thereafter the Marshal, [125] along with an escort of four men at arms, came first to Saintré and led him fully armed, with his appointed supporters, and presented him to the King, who was in his stand. And on the way Saintré passed in front of the stand where the Queen and her ladies were sitting, and there, bowing low, he knelt—and you would have seen all the ladies folding their hands and praying to God that he might be protected from harm. And then he proceeded to the presence of the King, and made the same obeisance,* and as he did so, Messire Enguerrand came up too; then Saintré bowed low before his opponent—something which was not customary—and said: "My lord and brother, without prejudice to either of us, I pray God that He give you merit and honor." "And likewise to you," said Messire Enguerrand; and then both of them knelt before the King.

Then, to make a long story short, the King commanded his Marshal to administer the appropriate oaths. Then the Marshal had them swear on the Gospels that, on their faith in God, on their lives and on their honor, they had nothing on them, nor intended to have anything, nor would have anything, such as spells, incantations, charms, simples,* invocations, or any other devilish or evil device, which might act as a weapon or a defense; that they bore no hatred, envy, or ill will toward each other; that they intended merely to pursue honor and renown and the much-longed-for favor of their ladies. These oaths duly sworn, both rose and went to their pavilions; but as Saintré got to his feet, he turned and repeated his obeisance to the King, and also to the Queen [126] and to her ladies, in just the same way as he had already done; and then retired to his pavilion, as did Messire Enguerrand, to have his helmet strapped on.

How the champions emerged from their
pavilions to perform their arms

When both of them were ready, and when, again to be brief, all the appropriate cries and challenges had been issued, the King commanded that they should sally out of their pavilions. As Saintré came out, his visor raised, he kissed his pennon, spoke the blessing that Madame had given him, made a great sign of the cross, then kissed the pennon again and handed it to one of his supporters. Having done this, he lowered his visor and, holding his poleaxe in his hand, he began to work his arms and his shoulders, and to fall first to one knee and then the other, with as much ease as if he had been wearing nothing more than a doublet.[88] And when both champions had emerged from their pavilions, and the pavilions had been withdrawn from the lists, then, at the King's command, the Marshal standing in the middle of the lists cried in a loud voice:

"Let the fight begin . . . !"

How Saintré and Messire Enguerrand set upon
each other and fought with great valor

And when the Marshal had pronounced these words, they charged toward each other as if they had been two lions unchained. And as Saintré charged, he cried:

"For my most honored lady whom I serve!"

And then they began to rain blows on one another. Messire Enguerrand, a most valiant knight, strong and powerful, and taller than Saintré, raised his poleaxe [127] and struck him such a blow on his charnel* that he staggered;

Fig. 4. © The British Library Board: MS Cotton Nero D IX, f. 46v:
Saintré and Messire Enguerrand.

and Saintré caught him with the haft* of his poleaxe such a blow on the
opening of his visor that he fell back a good pace.

Then Messire Enguerrand raised his poleaxe again and brought it down
with all his might, as he had previously, but Saintré, who was still affected
by the first blow, covered himself with his poleaxe so effectively that he was
untouched.

Then Messire Enguerrand raised his poleaxe again to strike Saintré, but
as his adversary stepped forward, the latter caught him with his axe blade on
the fingers of his right hand so hard that even the roundel* could not prevent
his fingers being bruised and numbed. In the heat of the moment, Messire
Enguerrand was unaware of the damage he had suffered and tried to raise his
poleaxe, but was unable to. When the pain hit him and he could no longer
hold his poleaxe in his right hand, like the bold and valiant knight he was he
took his poleaxe in his left hand and spread his arms to grapple with Saintré.

But when Saintré saw what he intended—although he hadn't realized the
damage he'd done to his adversary—he hammered on him with the hammerhead of his axe to prevent his getting any nearer. And then, when he realized
what had happened, he struck a sudden blow at Messire Enguerrand's left hand

that held the poleaxe, so that the weapon fell from his grasp; and when Messire Enguerrand found himself thus disarmed, in a last desperate effort he seized Saintré around the body, and Saintré did the same with one arm, since the other was still holding his poleaxe. [128]

And when the King saw Messire Enguerrand's poleaxe on the ground, and saw the two champions grappling with each other, he cast down his baton,* as prince and impartial judge, and said "Hold!" And then the guards separated the two combatants, and the King had the Marshal bring them before him, and had his officials say to them:

"You, Messire Enguerrand, and you, Jean de Saintré: the King commands me to say that you have both performed your arms, your duty, and your honor, with such valor and such nobility that no one could have done more. But your letter of challenge, Jean de Saintré, says that you must 'fight with poleaxes until one is knocked to the ground, or until his poleaxe has fallen from both his hands'—so in those terms my lord the King here present awards you the prize."

Then the King commanded both of the combatants, who were kneeling before him, to get up and have their helmets removed. And when Saintré heard the King's adjudication and his ruling, he thanked him as humbly as he knew how, saying:

"Ah, most excellent and omnipotent prince, I thank you with all humility for the honor that you have condescended to do me, and for your ruling in my favor. But as for the prize that you award me, I beg you as humbly as I can that you bear in mind the way in which my lord and brother here present has done me honor with his poleaxe. Any success that I have had, Sire—and please remember this—has come from sheer luck."

All those who were listening marveled in their hearts at these words of Saintré's, [129] and the tongues of all the lords and ladies were loosened to praise him; and no matter how much they had favored Messire Enguerrand, they could not refrain from saying that Saintré was the very summit and epitome of honor and modesty. The King himself and all those in his stand were astounded; the Queen, along with Madame Alienor de Cardona, Messire Enguerrand's wife, and all the other princesses, countesses, baronesses, and ladies who were in the main stand with the Queen, all began to sing his praises; and Messire Enguerrand himself could not refrain from saying:

"Just listen to how noble this young man is! Where would we find any other knight, living or dead, who would wish to divest himself of such honor in order to invest his opponent with it?"

The King, who had been so delighted to hear those present singing Saintré's praises that he had forgotten that the young man was still on his knees, commanded him to rise and said:

"Jean de Saintré, you have asked me to change my ruling; I declare that the ruling remains in place, and I wish you to retain the prize so that all may recognize the honor you have today, by God's grace, been granted."

Then the King ordered that Messire Enguerrand should courteously surrender his poleaxe, and that when he was disarmed he should do his duty.

Then Messire Enguerrand had his poleaxe returned to him, holding it as best he could in his wounded right hand supported by his left, and he surrendered it courteously, saying: "My brother, I render this poleaxe to you, [130] and will accomplish all the other things specified in your letter of challenge, with a prayer to God and to Saint George that they increase your renown yet further."

When Saintré heard the King's ruling, and Messire Enguerrand's gracious words, he had his bracelet handed to him by one of his men; then, taking the poleaxe, he bowed to Messire Enguerrand and said: "My lord brother, if this is the King's wish, I bow to his command. But to you, who have richly deserved it, I hold myself quit and give you my bracelet, begging you with all my heart to accept the gift."

Sir Enguerrand and all those present were even more amazed than before, and Messire Enguerrand responded: "Ah, brother Jean de Saintré, is there no end to your sense of honor? For your bracelet and for the honor you do me, I thank you from the bottom of my heart, but truly you must return the bracelet to your fair lady."

And the King demanded to know what entreaties the two men were exchanging. The Marshal said:

"Sire, Jean de Saintré is absolutely insisting on giving Messire Enguerrand his bracelet, as if he had won the prize."

"The bracelet?" said the King; then he turned to the princes and other lords that were with him and said: "What are we to say about the honor and the valor of such a young squire? Never have I seen anything like it."

"Indeed," said the other lords, "nor have we. And it is clear that his origins are noble, and that he has listened and learned in the noble court where he has been raised and trained; and those who accompany him show the same nobility." [131]

And at these words, the King immediately ordered that Saintré keep his bracelet. And when Saintré heard the ruling, he fell to his knees and said:

"Ah, Sire, in God's mercy, at least allow me to make use of it elsewhere."

"Elsewhere we agree to," said the King, "The bracelet is yours to do with as you wish. But we would not wish it to be said that we or our judgment played any part in your decision as to where to bestow it."

"Sire," said Saintré, "I thank you."

Then he called for Anjou King of Arms, Touraine Herald, and Lusignan Herald, who had accompanied him, and he handed the bracelet to the King of Arms, and sent all three of them to Madame Alienor de Cardona, Messire Enguerrand's wife, who was in the Queen's stand:

"And you are to say to her that I commend myself to her most humbly and consider her the one I believe most worthy to have the bracelet; I beg and pray her of her grace to accept it as if from the hands of my own most esteemed lady who gave it to me; I only regret that it is not a richer gift, and thus more worthy of her."

I cannot begin to describe how astonished were the Queen, Madame Alienor, and the other princesses and ladies there present, and the King himself in the stand to their right, and the other lords who attended him.

Then Madame Alienor replied to the King of Arms and the heralds:

"King of Arms and you other heralds, my friends, I thank the most gracious and valiant squire Jean de Saintré, but begging his indulgence, I have not deserved this bracelet; rather, it is due to her for whose sake today [132] he has achieved such grace and honor, so I beg you to take it back to him, with my excuses."

The Queen, wise and sagacious as she was, said when she heard this response: "In truth, fair cousin, you should not refuse such an honor from a young man so talented and so noble as this; I beg you to accept." Then Madame Alienor acceded to the Queen's request, and the Queen insisted in her turn on being the one to fasten the bracelet around the lady's left wrist.

Once the bracelet was on her arm, Madame Alienor took from her necklace a pendant made up of a fine large pearl of four or five carats, in a setting of three large diamonds and three fine rubies, and gave it to the King of Arms, saying:

"You, sir, and you also, heralds, you are to give this little jewel to that most gracious of squires Jean de Saintré, with my most heartfelt respects, and you will tell him that although his bracelet was due far more to his fair lady than to me, I have accepted his gift. And in order that his fair lady may share in the honor that he has this day acquired, I ask you to present him with this little pendant, begging him to bestow it on her with my greatest compliments."

When the King heard of the words that had been spoken, and of the exchange of the jewels, he was delighted; then he commanded that both men be disarmed. Then each mounted his horse again, and once Saintré was on his horse, he immediately went over to Messire Enguerrand, [133] whose injured hand was being dressed. When the latter saw Saintré he said: "Ah, brother, was it your lady who told you to serve such a meal to friends?" "Ah, my lord brother," said Saintré, "or was it your lady who told you to dish out such punishment to people who've joined your game?"

And when they were both mounted, there followed an exchange of civilities, each wanting the other to leave the lists first and more honorably.

The King, who intended that Saintré should be honored, sent immediately to say that they should leave side by side, but since Saintré had won the prize, he was to be on the right; then each should return to his lodging as he had come. But as they were to part, there was another lengthy exchange, since each wished to escort his companion. When the King saw how protracted this was, he again sent to say enough of the civilities, they should part and go their separate ways.

Then each took his leave of the other and went to his pavilion to disarm and rest for the remainder of the day, until time for supper, when the Queen sent for them. And then, to cut the story short, they were lavishly served, with good wines and good meats, subtleties,* and *entremets*, after which the occasion was joyously celebrated with songs and dances and *morisques** of all sorts. And now I shall say nothing more of the great honors, the dinners, and the suppers that were offered by the King, the Queen, and the other lords and ladies to Saintré, and by Saintré to his hosts, and I will come to his farewells, and to the gifts that they all presented to each other. [134]

How Saintré took his leave of the King, the Queen, and all those of the court, and of the gifts that were presented

After Saintré, as you have heard, had completed his *emprise*, he stayed two more days in Barcelona, feasting and reveling, and on the third day he took his leave of the King, the Queen, the lords, the ladies, and the damsels of the court, and of the other princes, princesses, and ladies of the region who had come as spectators to deeds of arms of a sort that was then held in much higher esteem than it is today.

And the King and Queen insisted that at their parting, both for Saintré and for his knights and squires, the normal civilities should be suspended: that each of them should be kissed by the ladies. The Queen gave the lead, by kissing first Saintré and then all the knights and squires of his company, and she was followed by all the rest of the ladies, something that the customs of the country had never allowed before, nor since, other than as an exception and for the closest of friends. But at this sad parting—alas!—Love had already lit painful flames in the tender hearts of some on each side, so that they could not prevent tears of sorrow running from their eyes and down their cheeks, whatever efforts they made to keep fixed smiles on their mouths.

And after the leave-taking and after the baggage train had left, Saintré presented the King with the finest and strongest of his four destriers, draped in the costliest of his caparisons, [135] ridden by a handsome, well-born page, his nephew, elegantly dressed; he presented the Queen with a hundred yards[89] of the finest lawn,* and with a further hundred yards of finest quality white linen of Reims,[90] the finest he had been able to procure in Paris; he also presented her with a very beautiful Book of Hours* adorned with pure gold and fine jewels, and he presented to the ladies and the damsels of the court a further two hundred yards of the same fabrics as he had given the Queen. He presented a hundred *écus* to be shared between the King's household and the Queen's, and the officers of the court; he presented another one hundred *écus* to the Kings of Arms and the heralds of Aragon and other foreign regions; he presented fifty *écus* to the trumpeters and the minstrels; he presented Madame Alienor with a fine hackney, a gray, saddled and bridled, with a saddle blanket of crimson cut velvet, thickly embroidered in pure gold, trimmed with gold and checkered in silks in her colors. To Messire Enguerrand he sent another of his best destriers saddled and caparisoned with one of his most costly trappers, along with a very fine sword with a hilt embossed with pure gold, and to each of the other four lords who had been his supporters, he sent a fine courser.

The King for his part sent Saintré a fine, thoroughbred Apulian courser[91] and two fine Andalusian jennets,* and a magnificent chalice and cover with a gold pitcher; he also sent twenty marks' weight of gold cups and fifty marks' worth of fine whiteware;* he presented each of Saintré's knights with a length of crimson velvet, his nine squires with three lengths of crimson damask, his heralds, trumpeters, and minstrels with two hundred Aragonese florins, and the remainder of the retinue with a hundred florins. [136]

The Queen sent him a length of the finest velvet cloth in crimson-purple brocaded with silver (as befits a squire),[92] two lengths of fine damask, one crimson and one black; she sent each of his three knights a length of blue figured satin, and to each of his nine squires a length of plain blue satin.

Madame Alienor sent him a superb gold chain of three marks' weight, Messire Enguerrand sent him a very fine Spanish courser and a fine Andalusian jennet, each ridden by a Moorish page dressed in Moorish style, and a length of crimson damask embroidered with silver.

The Count of Cardona sent him fifty marks' weight of silver tableware. Don Federich de Luna sent him twelve fine, heavy steel crossbows and twelve brigandines,* four of them covered with velvet embroidered with silver, four covered with blue velvet, four covered with damask in various colors, and all twelve trimmed with gilded silver.

Messire Arnaut de Perillos gave him a black Moor, richly dressed, mounted on a fine, strong jennet, man and horse dressed in Moorish fashion, and Messire François de Moncade sent him two magnificent suits of armor, one for war and one for the joust, both with costly adornments, and a beautiful sword with gold scrollwork, all enameled white. He also gave him a Turk, with his wife and their two children, who were expert workers in gold threads and silks; Saintré presented them later to the Queen, who was delighted.[93]
[137]

And there was not one of the ladies and damsels of the court who did not make him presents of undershirts in fine silks worked in fine gold stitches, of purses and gloves all embroidered in Spanish style, of musks* and Cyprus pomanders* and so many sorts of sweet-smelling perfumes that it would take me too long to list them, for the ladies' regard for him was limitless. What more can I say . . . ? Never have I read, or seen, or heard say, that any nobleman, or indeed his companions, was so much loved and so universally admired.

How Saintré, accompanied by all the lords, left Barcelona to return to France

And when Saintré was ready to mount his horse, he bade farewell to his host and to many others. Present to escort him were the Counts of Prades, Cardona, and Urgel, and the other lords I have mentioned, and many other knights and squires, somewhere between a thousand and twelve hundred horse; moreover, the King had their expenses defrayed as far as the frontier by a steward and by one of the clerks from his treasury. And here I shall say no more about the honors paid to Saintré, about the gifts given and the farewells made, and describe his return to the King's court, and the vows and the pilgrimages that Madame made for love of him.

How Saintré and his companions returned, and of the warm welcome that the King, the Queen, Madame, and others gave them

When Saintré reached his lodgings on the evening after he left Barcelona, he considered what would be the most honorable way to let [138] Madame know the outcome of his *emprise*, the date of his return, and what had become of him; he feared that if he sent one of his heralds to court, he might be thought to be seeking his own glory, and if so, certain people might secretly condemn him. For this reason he decided to confide his dilemma to Messire Pierre de Preuilly, whom he trusted; the latter agreed with him that it would be more proper to have the news given by a third party, and not by one of his heralds—although it was their role—nor should he write a letter to the King, the Queen, or anyone else.

"But if you so wish, it would be best for me to send Guillaume my cousin, as my representative, and I shall write to the King, to the Queen, and to the ladies to tell them about the honors you have received; Guillaume is a man of good understanding, and he will convey everything just as I shall explain it to him." And this was what they did.

And when the King, the Queen, Madame particularly, and all the rest of the court heard what had happened, there was such joy at court that for several days no one spoke of anything else, and everyone longed for Saintré's return. Madame, who since he left had spent most of her time, night and day, in prayer on his behalf, had fulfilled the vow that we mentioned, that until he returned she would never wear underlinens against her bare skin on Fridays and Saturdays; in addition, when she had heard the news that at the court of Aragon he was to be freed from his vow by a knight so authorized by the King himself, she had redoubled her vow so that she had spent every Wednesday hearing Mass and giving alms to the tune of ten *écus*, and on top of that, she had made pilgrimages incognito throughout the town.

She took great pains over these measures, especially around the time when she knew the combats were scheduled—[139] so it was while she was at prayer that Guillaume de Preuilly arrived, sent by his uncle Pierre, to bring the news as I have described it, and when Madame heard this much-longed-for news, which Isabel ran to bring her, she immediately felt her heart reassured, raised her eyes to heaven, thanked Our Lord, and then returned to her chamber and knelt with folded hands to thank Our Lord yet again. What can I say? On the one hand her joy was so great that she could scarcely keep her countenance; on the other, she so longed to see Saintré that she had no rest day or night, indeed so much so that she could scarcely enjoy the news of his success. And at this point I shall stop talking about her great joy— which her longing to see him again turned into great distress—and I shall describe Saintré's arrival before the King, and the great welcome and the great honor that he was afforded.

How after this journey Saintré made his way into the King's presence, the welcome and great honor that he was afforded, and how Madame's heart was healed

And when Saintré and his retinue had made such progress that they were two leagues away from Paris, they were met by many barons, knights, squires, townspeople, and others of the court and of the city of Paris, who had all come to meet him, to honor him, and escort him, so much did everyone love him and wish him well; there was such universal joy that it was a pleasure to see them all. And when he had paid his respects to the King and to the Queen—who welcomed him most warmly—he went over to Madame, who could scarcely contain herself for her delight, [140] although wise as she was she hid the extent of her joy; then he went over to the other ladies, who greeted him very warmly. Then when he had kissed them all, the Queen commanded that the court should dance, and as they danced, Madame, who was sitting beside the Queen, said: "Ha, my lady, as you've heard, Saintré has danced quite enough in Aragon, and he's tired. For God's sake, have him called over to sit with us, and ask him about the dress and the fashions of the ladies of Aragon." "Indeed, fair cousin," said the Queen, "you are quite right."

The Queen had Saintré summoned, along with another three ladies, and said to him: "Saintré, my friend, we wish you to have some rest." Then turning to the other three ladies, she said: "Please sit, all of you, and the most courteous among you shall let him sit on the train of her dress."

Madame, who was determined to be able to watch him closely face to face, did not wish to volunteer that courtesy, and pretended she hadn't heard. Then the Queen first asked Saintré about his arrival in Aragon, about the welcome that had been afforded him by the King, the Queen, the lords, and especially the ladies; then she asked about his feats of arms, on horseback and on foot, about the beauty, the manners, and the fashions of the ladies. Saintré, as was right, passed lightly over his own feats of arms, and what he did say did more to applaud Messire Enguerrand than himself, but for the rest, he extolled the ladies very highly and in every possible way, as he did the King and all the lords; he could not praise them enough. And here I shall speak no more of the praise and honor that accrued to him through his response to the Queen's and to her ladies' questions,[94] [141] and turn to the absolutely joyful welcome that Madame afforded him, and to the way in which from time to time, when she dared, she feasted her eyes on him.

THE AUTHOR: As she listened to them talking, Madame looked nonchalantly right and left, here and there, and finally allowed her loving gaze to linger on him, and as she did so she took out a pin from her headdress and started to pick her teeth with it in the usual signal. When Saintré saw her signal, he immediately responded by rubbing his right eye a little, and thus, their hearts torn between joy and distress, they passed that long and tedious day until night came and the time that they had arranged to meet in the garden, and then they started to delight in each other, with many kisses given and many received. Then they took their pleasure, then they shared their delight, then their hearts and their sorrows were healed, and there, in those delights, they spent the time from eleven o'clock until two o'clock in the morning, at which time they were obliged to part. And at this I shall say no more about their perfect happiness, and turn to Saintré's progress and to the friendship forged between him and Boucicaut, first of that name.[95]

Here I speak of how Saintré became chamberlain[96] to the King, and of his alliance with the squire Le Meingre, known as Boucicaut

The King, who as you have heard was already very attached to Saintré, became more and more fond of him until, not long afterward, he ordered that Saintré sleep in his chamber, and very soon made him his principal chamberlain. Saintré, whom Madame in his childhood had instructed in the ways of virtue and good breeding, [142] remembered the words of Albertus

Magnus: *Non tua claudatur ad vocem pauperibus auris*,[97] and also Aristotle's
fine verses:

> *Vir bone que curas res ville res perituras;*
> *Nil proffituras dampno quandoque futuras.*
> *Nemo diu mansit in crimine, sed cito transit.*
> *Est brevis atque levis in mundo gloria que vis.*[98]

And he bore in mind also a number of other teachings as to those raised to
high office—and remembering these, however high his estate or however
great the favor he enjoyed with the King, he never allowed his heart to
become proud or his manners arrogant; rather, as time passed, he showed
himself to be more pleasant and amiable and courteous.

At that time there was at the court a very courteous young squire from
the duchy of Touraine, who was called Le Meingre but who was known, in
jest, by the name Boucicaut.[99] He was the grandfather of the present-day
Boucicaut family: a sensible, accomplished, and most agreeable young man,
quite in favor with the King. This Boucicaut, seeing Saintré in such high
favor with the King, made every effort to seek his acquaintance. Saintré, still
young, seeing how admired Boucicaut was and knowing him to be from his
own region of the country, was delighted to make him a friend, and the two
of them spent as much time together, and were as good friends, as if they
had been brothers; their mutual affection was such that the King—who was
already very fond of Boucicaut—agreed, indeed ordered, that the pair of
them should sleep together on the trundle bed* in his bedchamber when he
was not sleeping with the Queen.

What more can I say? The two squires were devoted to each other, and
were such steadfast friends [143] that there was never any discord between
them, and when one of them needed to be absent on business, or for an
emprise or a deed of arms—something that was often the case—the other
kept his privileged place in the King's bedchamber and allowed no one else
to usurp it. And although Boucicaut became thereafter a most valiant knight,
more skilled and prudent than Saintré himself, nevertheless, in expertise with
arms Saintré was thought to be the better. And for this reason the Kings of
Arms and the heralds devised a common saying, which went:

> When it comes to assault,
> Saintré's better than Boucicaut;

When it's time for a treaty,
Boucicaut's better than Saintré.

Which is to say, one of them preferable for arms, the other for strategy—and
thus, as long as they both lived, their friendship and their alliance were unas-
sailable. And now I shall leave them aside and turn to a new feat of arms
that Saintré accomplished against the Seigneur de Loisselench, a baron from
Poland, who bore *argent, an ox rampant gules horned and hoofed sable*; this
feat of arms was performed in Paris in the presence of the King, the Queen,
Madame, and innumerable lords and ladies.

How Madame ordered Saintré to take up the challenge
issued by the Seigneur de Loisselench

A year after Saintré had completed his feat of arms against Sir Enguerrand, there arrived at the court the Seigneur de Loisselench, a baron from
Poland, a tall, strong, and most powerful knight who had come in pursuit of
honor and of the favor of his lady [144] with four other Polish barons: the
Seigneur d'Endach, who bore *gules, a saltire pierced vert*; the Seigneur de
Nulz, who bore *Or, an ox's head sable*; the Seigneur de Morg, who bore
argent, three heads sable; and the Seigneur de Terg, who bore *Or, a cross voided
gules*. The four of them intended, once the jousts were over, to proceed
together on the pilgrimage to Santiago de Compostella.

The Seigneur de Loisselench, as a pretext for arms on horseback and on
foot, was wearing a gold circlet just above his left elbow and another just
above his ankle, the two circlets being fastened together by quite a long gold
chain; he was to wear them for a full five years unless in the meantime he
was able to find a knight or a squire of good birth, *sans reproche*, who would
release him from his vow by the means we shall discuss here. And in order to
achieve his ambition more quickly and with greater honor, he had decided
to come to the most noble court of France, where men of birth and chivalry
were received warmly and with great honor; he was eager also to become
acquainted with such men and to acquire their friendship.

Then he had Brunswick Herald, who was in his train, read his letter of
challenge, translating from Polish into French; the letter said briefly: that the
challenger and he himself would run ten courses on horseback, in full battle
armor and with war saddles, with *lances d'armes*[100] of a length prescribed by

the prince:[101] the ten courses would be run in succession, without a break, unless the prince were able to declare that three lances had been well and properly broken. [145]

And provided that at the end of the ten courses, or after the due breaking of the three lances, the two of them by God's grace had avoided injury, then two days later they would each deliver ten thrusts in succession with their lances, on foot; they would then have a breathing space in order to exchange their lances for poleaxes, rigorously identical, with which they would deliver another ten strokes, according to preference with the spike, the hammerhead, or the blade. And after another breathing space, they would deliver ten further thrusts with their sword points, and then ten strokes with their roundel daggers.*[102] And as concerns the choice of weapons—combat with the lance on foot or on horseback, style of lances and poleaxes, as above—Loisselench would engage himself to offer that choice to his opponent in the lists. And should it happen that in the course of these deeds of arms one of them should lose an item of his armor, he would nevertheless be bound to continue without it, or be judged to have lost the prize for that particular bout.

And to he who, in the five modes of combat, was judged, with God's help, to have gained the prize, his opponent would make awards as follows: for the combat on horseback, and there and then, a diamond worth at least three hundred *écus*; for the combat with *lances d'armes*, a ruby of the same value. For the combat with poleaxes, a fine pearl of at least four carats. For the combat with swords, a Balas ruby of the same value. For the combat with daggers, a sapphire of the same value.

And if it happened—which God forbid!—that in accomplishing the jousts described, on horseback or on foot, one of them should be so injured that he could not complete that day's sequence, or if either of them should be unhorsed or knocked to the ground, or should have his head, body, or arm disarmed so seriously that because of his condition he might refuse to complete the sequence, then that particular bout, and the remainder, should be considered fought, [146] and the defaulter should be obliged to donate the prizes as if he had lost all of the remaining bouts. "And in order to ensure that the prizes would be available for awarding, each of us should be required, before the arms begin, to place the prizes in the hands of the prince, to be awarded at his discretion."

THE AUTHOR: When the terms of the *emprise* were announced, Madame did not hesitate for a moment: she had Saintré called and said to him, discreetly and as briefly as she could:

"My love, with the arrival of this Polish knight who has publicly announced his challenge, the day has dawned which was promised to you by God and Fortune, the day on which you will earn honor and status. And I beg you, as urgently as I can, that you be the first to go to the King and ask to be allowed to take up the challenge and free the knight from his gage; take no thought for the expense, for God, and I, will provide for everything. And although you are my only love, my greatest blessing, and all and more than I can say—which should mean that I more than anyone else should discourage you, or even forbid you, from putting yourself in such danger—nevertheless such is the love that I bear you that I would wish to see you recognized everywhere as the best and the most valiant, and I pray God that He will ensure you your due honor."

And when Saintré heard Madame speak so generously—although he had already made his own decision in his heart—nevertheless he knelt and thanked her most humbly, and said:

"My most honored lady, on the love and loyalty I owe you, I had been thinking that very same thing, and wondering how I might broach the subject with you."

"Make haste," she said, "so that you may be the first." [147]

Then he hurried off to the King and threw himself on his knees and made his appeal in the approved way. The King, who was very fond of him, smiled at him as if amazed that so young a man, and one so slightly built, had the audacity to undertake so arduous a feat of arms against a knight so tall and powerfully built as was the Polish knight. Then he said:

"Ah, Saintré, have you considered this carefully?"

"Considered, Sire?" he replied, "Yes indeed, since the moment I laid eyes on him, I have had no other wish."

And as they were speaking, the Viscount of Beaumont came up to make the same request, and as he was doing so, there arrived the Seigneur de Craon, and after the Seigneur de Craon, the Seigneur de Vergi, quickly followed by the Viscount of Quesnes, the Seigneur de Saucourt, the Seigneur d'Hangest, and many others, all making the same request to the King. And when the King heard the same request from so many of his lords, he said to them:

"My friends, in such cases, first come first served—and as you see, here is Saintré, still on his knees, who was the first to address me. And indeed, young as he is, Our Lord is the God of the strong and the weak, of the young and the old. And since God looks with as much favor on the weak as on the strong, on the young as on the old, it would seem wrong to us to deprive him of the favor he has requested."

At that everyone got to his feet, praising the King's wisdom and judgment, and better pleased about Saintré than they were for themselves. Then Saintré thanked the King with all the humility he could muster.

The King had the Seigneur de Loisselench invited to dine with him the following day, along with his four barons [148] and the knights and squires of his retinue; they were received with great honor, and after the dinner there were dances with the ladies in the presence of the Queen, who received them all most affably, and then, through those who could speak both languages, she asked them questions about the ladies and about fashions and customs in their own country, saying how disappointed she was not to be able to understand them.

And when the dances were over, before the spices and the parting cup were brought in, Montjoie King of Arms of France,[103] at the King's command, read aloud again the letter of challenge before the Queen, and before the many lords and ladies. After the letter had been read, Montjoie asked the knight concerned to confirm that it was indeed his coat of arms on the seal, and if he could confirm all that was contained in the letter. And when these demands were translated for the knight, he confirmed that the arms on the seal were indeed his, and that he validated all the terms.

Then Saintré knelt before the King and asked him to confirm the permission that he, Saintré, had been given. He then rose to his feet and said to the knight:

"My lord, you are most welcome. With the help of God, of Our Lady, and of our lord Saint Michael I shall free you from your vow, and from the circlets and chain that bind you."

And then he stepped forward to remove the circlets. But when the knight saw Saintré looking so slight and so young, he took a step backward, shamefaced, and said to his people in his native Polish:

"Is this really the one who is to free me from my vow? Is there no one here in this court who is as bold as he is?"

Then the bystanders explained who Saintré was, and how fond the King was of him, and how formerly he had fought before the King of Aragon on horse and on foot, and that he had triumphed in both exercises. Then the knight stared hard at him, and said [149]:

"I can scarcely refuse him; let it be as he wishes. And indeed I must admit that men like him are sometimes more to be feared than the strongest."

Then Saintré, who was about to question him further, was told:

"Saintré, carry on as you planned, for he thanks you from the bottom of his heart."

Then Saintré took off the circlets, and at this the King set the date for their deeds of arms on horseback for thirty days hence, and then retired into his chamber. And then Saintré, wearing the two gold circlets on their chain round his neck, one in front and one behind, escorted the knight to his lodging, along with a number of other members of the court. And at this I shall say no more about the great honors and the warm reception that were given to the visitors as long as they were there, and turn to the great heartache that Madame felt, and to the fine words that she addressed to Saintré.

How Madame grieved for Saintré, and of the fair words that she spoke to him

Madame, who had not set eyes on the Polish knight before the ceremony of the circlets, was dismayed when she saw how tall and well-built he was, and was so sorry for what she had said to Saintré that she could know no happiness. On the other hand, matters were so far advanced that she could not withdraw. Day and night she grieved and sighed, saying to herself:

"Ah, alas, how unhappy I am! What have you done, and what were you thinking of, when you advised the one whom you love most in all the world to expose himself to such danger, when you should have done everything in your power to dissuade him? Alas! He is to confront a man of such height and strength [150] that there is no one who shouldn't fear him! And if there should arise from this encounter some personal harm to Saintré or to his honor—which God forbid!—then alas, unhappy wretch that you are, you will never be happy again. Worse yet, perhaps he will never again love you—and rightly so—although all I wished was for him to win renown among the good and the brave . . . ! And I call on you to bear witness, Our true Lord, and also Our Lady of Liesse in the Laonnois,[104] to whom I shall dedicate an image of him done in wax, fully armed and mounted on a destrier caparisoned with his arms, weighing a full three thousand pounds, begging you, Holy Virgin, on my knees and with hands joined, to bring him back to me safe and sound. And otherwise, come what may!"

After Madame had spoken these words, she went to the Queen's chamber, and very soon thereafter she saw Saintré, took out her pin and made the signal. Saintré, who was for his part very eager to talk to her, responded immediately, and when the time was right, and when they were together, Madame, seeing him so joyful, had a change of heart, from despair to joy, and said:

"Now, my love, make sure you perform well and gallantly, and win or lose honorably, for whatever the outcome against so powerful an adversary, you can win nothing but honor. Have no fear in taking on such a giant of a man, so much taller and stronger than you are yourself, for God rules all and will help those who need him and who pray devoutly for his help, and for this reason: the stronger despise the weaker and fight with arrogance, whereas the weaker know how much they need the help of God who comforts and supports them, [151] so that in any contest man to man, strength to strength, only God can foresee the outcome. And even in those cases where the contest is equally balanced, and where everyone asks God's help with a full heart, let he who is in the wrong beware—for God who is a just arbiter gives everyone his due.

"And so, my love, let the outcome be as God wills; if Loisselench concedes you even a little of the honors, that little will do you more honor than any other deed, and if he defeats you, giant that he is in comparison to you, he can scarcely damage you so much that you will not be admired more than if you had not confronted him. For I have often heard those expert in arms say that a noble man who is defeated in a deed freely undertaken is nevertheless more admired than previously, for man may fight but God gives the victory to whom he pleases. And so, my love, think only to do your best, and as for your expenses and your dress and equipment, here is a pouch containing six thousand *écus*; spend them worthily—and now, God be with you."

THE AUTHOR: Saintré, seeing Madame's love for him grow and flourish further day by day, thanked her as humbly as he knew how, and then, to cut a long story short, he took his leave. He then spent the whole night filled with such elation at this new prospect that he could not sleep. And once day broke, he heard Mass and said his Hours and then busied himself all day so that, with God's help, and the King's, and Madame's, he was equipped with arms, destriers, and splendid accoutrements, so elegant and fitting that— quite frankly—they would have been appropriate for a baron of royal blood. And I shall now leave aside all these things, [152] as well as the talk that his feats of arms were inspiring everywhere, and all the prayers offered for so young and slightly built a young man faced with a Polish knight who looked as if he were certain to defeat his opponent at every blow, and turn to the deeds of arms that were done on the day duly appointed.

How the Seigneur de Loisselench and Saintré entered the lists on horseback, in the presence of the King, the Queen, and several princes, lords and ladies

On the thirtieth day after Saintré had taken up the challenge of the Seigneur de Loisselench, the day that had been ordained for them to begin their *emprise*, that very morning the Seigneur de Loisselench had twenty stout lances carried to a position below the King's grandstand; they were completely combat-ready in all respects, apart from the lance heads, without roundels* or vamplates, as is correct in such circumstances.

And when the King, the Queen, and the other royal lords and ladies had mounted into the stands or were placed at the windows of the rue Saint Antoine in Paris, the Seigneur de Loisselench sent a herald to take Saintré a leather casket full of the finest lance heads suitable for their joust, thus allowing him to choose the size and shape that suited him. And while the lances were being fitted with the points, the Seigneur de Loisselench came to the lists with a large and splendid cavalcade consisting of the lords, the knights, and the squires whom the King had assigned; with him also were the knights and squires of his own retinue, more than a hundred and fifty horse, all dressed and equipped anew, and before him came five particularly fine destriers, four of them in trappers of velvet of various different colors and embroidered in gold and silver in different patterns; [153] the fifth was caparisoned with figured velvet embroidered with his own blazon in gold thread: that is, *an ox rampant gules, horned and unguled sable*; on each of the horses was a pretty, well-born page very richly dressed.

And following this last destrier came the Count of Étampes bearing on the tip of his lance Loisselench's helmet, which bore a crest *on a torce argent and gules, an ox's head coupled between two wings argent.*

And after him came the Seigneur de Loisselench himself on his very powerful destrier, fully armed apart from his head on which he was wearing a stylish hood in different shades of purple; he and his destrier were both caparisoned in a rich crimson cut velvet,[105] embroidered with gold and lined with sable; to his right rode the Duke of Berry, who by order of the King escorted him to do him honor as a visitor. And when he reached the entrance to the lists, the King had him go in without ceremony and take his place under an arming pavilion with a tapestry roof, hung around with a curtain on rings; here he could dress and arm himself, and here also were refreshments: wines, fruits, and spices in plenty.[106]

And while Loisselench was still ensconced under his canopy,* Saintré came in also fully armed apart from his head, on which he wore a very fine hood of beaver fur trimmed with gold embroidery, and with a mantling made of Plaisance linen; at the front was a most valuable brooch made up of a very large diamond in a setting of three Balas rubies and three large pearls of four carats each (given to him by Madame) [154]; he and his destrier were caparisoned in trappers of fine ermine lined with sable—a magnificent sight. I shall say nothing of the accoutrements of his other six destriers and of his elegant pages; I leave that to the reader's imagination.

After the six destriers came the Count of Alençon, Saintré's close friend, who loved Saintré so much that he had deigned to carry his jousting helmet before him on his lance shaft, and after him came Saintré himself, and on his right the Duke of Anjou and Touraine, so eager was he to do Saintré honor. And after them came the innumerable lords, knights, and squires who wished to be in his retinue. And when he was about to enter the lists, as a good Christian, he made a great sign of the cross with his banner embroidered with the image of Our Lady, and pronounced the blessing that—as we saw—Madame had taught him.

And when Madame saw this, she thought him even more handsome than he had ever been, and both for the great love she bore him and for the great peril in which she feared she had put him, she was filled with such painful feelings of remorse that as she sat there in the Queen's own stand, her heart failed her. And the Queen and the other ladies, who did not realize what ailed her, saw her fall into a swoon so deep that she seemed dead: quietly, in order to avoid disturbing the King, they sprinkled her face and hands with vinegar and tried all the remedies they knew; by and by, they rubbed her temples so energetically that she revived. Then she opened her eyes and looked here and there and everywhere, then found her voice and said:

"Ah, Blessed Virgin, comfort me!"

Then [155] all the ladies present did their best to comfort her, but however much the Queen encouraged her, she could not bear to turn her head to watch the combat.

THE AUTHOR: Saintré meanwhile came smiling into the lists, looked up as he passed at the stand occupied by the King and the other by the ladies, and doffed his chaplet, bowing as low as he could—but he was rather surprised not to see Madame. He soon guessed what the problem was, however, and that Madame had not had the strength of mind to watch the contest, just as she had earlier said. Then, still mounted, he retired under his own canopy—as richly decorated as was the Seigneur de Loisselench's—along only with their lordships the Duke of Anjou and the Count of Alençon, and with those deputed to serve him.

THE AUTHOR AGAIN: Once both combatants had arrived in the manner I have described, the King, who had already had the lances measured and the lance heads attached, ordered that they should arm themselves completely, and that the Seigneur de Loisselench, as instigator of the jousts, should enter the lists first, and this was done. And next he ordered that Saintré should enter the lists, and that he should wear the beaver-fur chaplet he had worn on his head on top of his helmet. And when both combatants had presented themselves in the lists, the King sent out ten identical lances by ten of his knights, then summoned the Seigneur de Loisselench and instructed him to choose five for himself.

The Seigneur de Loisselench, wise and gracious as he was, thanked the King most humbly and then sent the ten lances to Saintré so that he might make the choice, just as his *emprise* had specified. Saintré—to cut [156] a long story short—thanked him and told him that he should retain the five sturdiest, and then the Duke of Anjou, wishing to be of service to him, selected one which he rested across his thigh until all was ready. And when the two chosen lances had been supplied, the King, in God's name, gave the word for them to lay on.

At these words the two knights spurred their horses forward as if they could not meet too quickly; at this course the Seigneur de Loisselench struck Saintré on the left couter* and ripped it away, and Saintré struck his opponent on the plastron,* but because the lance hit at a low angle, it bent and splintered. At that the trumpets sounded, and the cheers of the crowd rang out long and loud.

At the second course the Seigneur de Loisselench caught Saintré on the wrapper* so hard that he almost numbed him, and Saintré struck him on the brow of the helmet and caught his silver bull crest so hard that it spun the helmet round as their horses crossed with each other, and for that course Saintré had some respite.

At the third course the Seigneur de Loisselench returned the compliment: he speared Saintré's beaver-fur chaplet, all decorated as it was, and carried it away on his lance point, and Saintré struck him high on his gard-brace and buckled it and the couter, and tore away the arming-points,* and the gardbrace flew to the ground, and at that the cheers of the crowd and the braying of the trumpets redoubled, so that it became difficult to silence them.

And the Seigneur de Loisselench having been disarmed like this, the King asked to see the letter of challenge again [157] so that he could determine precisely what the terms were. In it he found three clauses: the first specified that if one of the two combatants, during a duel on horseback or on foot, was so badly wounded that he could no longer continue for that day, or if he lost his stirrups, or if his feet touched the ground, or if his head, his body, or one of his arms was disarmed so completely that he refused to continue the bouts in that state, then the remainder of the bouts should be considered done, and that combatant should be held liable for all the prizes, just as if he had been defeated in one bout after another.

And on that basis the King had the jousts stopped, and he had the terms of the letter shown and expounded to the Seigneur de Loisselench by the lords of Endach, Nulz, Morg, and Terg, the Polish barons who, as we saw, had come in his train and who, by order of the King, had had the terms of the letter read to Loisselench in their presence. He asked them to explain to Loisselench that he, the King, did not wish him to put his soul or his honor, even his very life, in danger.

The Seigneur de Loisselench, hearing the King's words, thanked him very humbly, but was visibly chagrined by his mishap; he maintained that, whatever might happen to him, he was truly determined to complete that day's bouts. He would not be deterred by the French lords whom the King had directed to serve him, but the Polish lords told him roundly that they were not prepared to be at his service in such conditions. Then the Seigneur de Loisselench said:

"You understand my honor and my shame better than I do; I leave them in your hands."

Then they said that they would take responsibility for the decision, [158] in view of the dangerous state in which they saw him. They consoled him by saying that he could make up the lost ground in the combat on foot; at that, doleful and heartsick, he accepted their advice.

When this news was given to the King, he had both of them withdraw and take off their helmets, and then present themselves to him on horseback, each carrying the prize that he was to offer. When the Queen and the other ladies saw that the Seigneur de Loisselench was disarmed, they ran over to

Madame, who was lying on the gold silk cushions and praying to Our Lady of Liesse, to whom she had dedicated prayers and orisons. The Queen said to her:

"Ah, fair cousin, get up and see the fine sight, and see how that nice young man Saintré has disarmed the Pole so that our husband the King has had them leave off combat and present themselves before him—I don't know why, unless it's to present the prize."

Madame was so joyfully consoled by this welcome news that her heart was beating wildly; she pretended that she was quite uninterested. Then the Queen said:

"Ah, fair cousin, we can see that you are not particularly pleased about the honor that this most valiant squire has won, whereas my lord the King and I share the general delight. And now, up! You must get to your feet!"

Then the Queen took Madame by one hand, and her ladies by the other, and pulled her to her feet until she could see the lists. Madame, who had taken great care to conceal her delight behind her conversation with the Queen, masked her recovery from her faint by saying to the Queen:

"Why, my lady, what's this? Do I see that the noble Polish knight has lost his gardbrace?"

[159] Then the Queen explained to her exactly how the combat had transpired, and how Saintré had broken his first lance, how he had impaled the silver bull crest that the Polish knight had worn, and how he had disarmed his opponent.

Listening to the Queen's account, Madame could not for sheer joy tear her eyes away from Saintré, and Saintré himself glanced here and there until his gaze fell on Madame; at that moment Madame made her signal, and he responded with all due grace. And when the two combatants were presented to the King, the latter had Montjoie King of Arms of France, say to them:

"Monseigneur de Loisselench, and you, Jean de Saintré, the King here present bids me say that both of you have carried out your combats today with such skill and with such honor that no other could have done better. But since you, Monseigneur, have lost your gardbrace to you, Jean de Saintré, the King, following the terms of the challenge, has deemed you, Saintré, the winner of today's prize; you therefore, Monseigneur de Loisselench, must comply with those terms—and here are the means with which you must do so."

Then Montjoie handed him the valuable prize diamond that had been given to the King for safekeeping.

At these words, Brunswick Herald, who had accompanied the Polish knight, came forward and had the latter repeat word for word after him the required phrases. Then the Seigneur de Loisselench bowed to the King and in his native Polish thanked him most humbly for the honor that he had done him. He conceded that Saintré had duly and completely won the prize, and with these words he took the diamond and advanced toward Saintré and, in his own tongue, thanked him most politely, and put the diamond into his hand. [160] Then the King ordered that each of them should go and disarm, and this was done. But as they parted, Saintré insisted that they should exit the lists side by side, with the Polish knight on his right. Then the trumpeters, the clarions, and the minstrels sounded a fanfare, provoking indescribable joy in the city. And at this point I shall say no more about the two champions—who went off to disarm themselves and to have supper with the King, who paid the Polish knight and his suite great honor; rather, I shall describe the way in which the Queen wished to retain Saintré at her side at the King's supper.

THE AUTHOR: When the supper was ready, the King sent an escort for the Seigneur de Loisselench, his four barons, and all the other Polish knights and squires. Saintré was in command, and he went very well attended; when the party came back into the royal presence, the King made them very welcome and did them much honor. Then the tables were set up and the supper laid out: the King had the Seigneur de Loisselench sit on his right, and on his left the four barons, and the remainder of the Polish contingent were seated at the second high table immediately beside the King's. They were served with wines and meats and all manner of dishes; I shall not describe them, since everyone will understand that the fare was of the best.

Once they were all seated and served, Saintré went to take supper in the Queen's apartments as she had said. No need to ask if he was warmly received by the Queen, by Madame, and by the other ladies and damsels: not one of them held back. Madame, who of all of the ladies had least need to do so, could not refrain from staring at the fine diamond which was Saintré's prize, and which he wore on a gold chain around his neck. [161]

Then the Queen also wanted to see it, as did many other ladies. Madame said to him:

"To be sure, Saintré, the lady who is given this as a gift is very lucky indeed."

The Queen heard her, and said:

"I pray God, Saintré, that you go on to win all the other prizes one after the other."

Then he knelt and said:

"Ah, ladies, I thank you all, but I have not deserved such success from God, and if I have already won a prize, it was because of your good prayers."

At these words the Queen's Steward came to offer her water to wash her hands, and when she was seated, she insisted, in spite of his protestations, on having Saintré at her right hand. What more can I say? The whole company was so joyful that I can hardly describe it. But when the tables were removed, the King on the one hand, the Queen on the other went into the Great Hall for dancing. There were all sorts of dances and *morisques*, but because of the hard work that the Seigneur de Loisselench, and indeed Saintré, had had that day, the King ordered that parting cup and spices be brought early, then retired to his chamber, and the guests all took their leave of each other. Saintré and the other French knights each took the arm of one of the Polish knights and squires, and thus gave them a fine escort to their lodgings. And here I shall cease to describe the honors, the wines, the dishes that the King provided for the Polish party every day, and postpone talking about the next day's combats on foot, to talk about Madame and Saintré, and the perfect pleasure that they had that night when they met in the garden.

THE AUTHOR: That night, as they intended, given Madame's signal, Madame and Saintré met in the garden. There they exchanged kisses most generously [162]—what can I add?—so much so that neither could imagine greater pleasure. And then Madame said to him:

"Alas, my heart! Alas, my love! Alas, my joy! Alas my sole and greatest desire! Today I was convinced that you could not survive, and when I saw you enter the lists, I was so afraid for you that my heart failed me, and I fell to the ground as if I were dead. Had I not been taken care of immediately, I should certainly have died. But when I heard the news of your glorious victory, my dying heart was revived, and Madame and her ladies came to raise me to my feet and take me to watch from the stand."

"Alas! My highest and only lady, what are you saying? Alas! Had I known all this, what would have become of my sorrowing heart? I would have preferred to die rather than to live . . . ! I would have abandoned arms, no matter what the dishonor. But thanks and praise be to God, I knew nothing of it. When I rode into the lists, I saw you beside the Queen, but then, as I came fully armed to take up my position, I looked up at the stands and saw the

Queen and all her ladies other than you, and I thought that perhaps you hadn't had the heart to watch the champions knocked to the ground in the joust—as you had said—and so I thought no more of it. But now, my most revered lady, I thank God and Our Lady for the honor that I have acquired this day through you, and I hope, my lady, that I shall do more and better in future. And I beg you to be of good cheer and to have no fear, for God, who has been our help so far in arms, will be so for the remainder."

And at these words they took most gracious leave of each other. [163] And I shall now leave aside the affairs of Saintré and his lady, and turn to the champions' feats of arms on foot, and how they were played out.

How the Seigneur de Loisselench and Saintré came to the lists and undertook arms on foot

On the day and at the hour at which the arms were to be staged, the King, the Queen, the lords, and the ladies took their places on the stands. The Seigneur de Loisselench sent the King, via the lords of Endach and of Morg, two matching thrusting lances,* metal-tipped and supplied with vamplates to protect the hand, and painted scarlet; he also sent two poleaxes, two swords, and two roundel daggers, all of them absolutely identical. Then, to cut a long story short, the King took four of the weapons and sent them to Saintré, and handed the other four back to the said lords of Endach and Morg to be returned to the Seigneur de Loisselench.

And thereupon the Seigneur de Loisselench, fully armed except for his helmet, rode out of his quarters in the same pomp as for the previous combats on horseback—more so indeed, since the Counts of Nevers, Boulogne, Tancarville, and Rethel rode in front of him carrying the four arms allotted to him, and since after them came the Duke of Berry, carrying Saintré's jousting helmet; next came Loisselench himself, fully armed, his horse caparisoned in fine velvet of the same color as his arms, and after him came numerous barons and other noblemen. In that array* he rode into the lists and dismounted at the new pavilion that the King had had erected for him, and so did those who had been delegated to accompany him.

And once Loisselench had dismounted, Saintré very soon came up with a fine large escort; [164] before him rode the Counts of Le Perche, of Clermont, of Saint Pol, and of La Marche carrying his four arms, followed by the Duke of Anjou, who carried Saintré's full jousting helmet. Saintré, escorted by this fine company, went to the other pavilion that the King had also had erected for him. To save time, I shall not detail the Kings of Arms, the heralds, the pursuivants, the trumpeters, the buglers, and the other musicians who led the combatants onto the field.

When both of them were ready, the King ordered them to come out, and at that point the dukes gave their respective champions their thrusting lances. As Saintré took his lance, he kissed his pennon and made the sign of the cross, then stepped briskly forward first and confronted the Seigneur de Loisselench just as the latter took his first steps. As Saintré struck his first blow he cried aloud:

"For Our Lady, and for my own dearest lady!"

At this encounter, the Seigneur de Loisselench had fully expected to knock his adversary to the ground in short order, and to have the better of him and force him back—and indeed, I believe that he might easily have done so because of his much greater strength and weight. But even though it is men who choose to engage in combat, God, at the appeal of Our Lady, is a source of strength for those who commend themselves to him wholeheartedly, and gives victory where he pleases.

Then the Seigneur de Loisselench gathered all his strength and struck Saintré just below his ribcage, but his lance glanced off the top of Saintré's plastron and skidded off a couple of yards.[107] And at this first bout, Saintré's lance also glanced off, [165] and as it did so it caught Loisselench between the lance itself and his hand, so that no fewer than three of his fingers were damaged, as was the gauntlet. And when they went to exchange the second set of blows, they found that Loisselench could not free his hand, nor Saintré his lance, so inextricably were they joined.

Then the Seigneur de Loisselench let his lance fall so that he could grapple with Saintré directly, but in vain, for Saintré used his lance to push his adversary away as hard as he could. And when the King saw Loisselench's lance on the ground, he ruled that Loisselench was no longer in possession of the lance and that therefore God had declared for the younger man. Then he had both of them escorted from the lists and taken to their pavilions to have their helmets removed and to deal with Loisselench's hand, and then he had both of them brought in front of him.

I cannot describe even the half of Loisselench's mortification, both because of his own misfortune and because so young a man had defeated him both on horseback and on foot; and in his then state, although his hand was bleeding so badly that, for very annoyance and in the heat of the moment, he was unable to stanch it, he wanted to move straight on to combat with the other weapons. But the blood spurted from his wound so much that he was obliged to desist.

And when his wound had been treated, his hand had been bandaged, and the gardbrace had been removed from his arm, he came out of his pavilion. As he did so Saintré came over to him to console him, and the Seigneur de Loisselench embraced him warmly and said, in his Polish language:

"Brother Saintré, if you continue to fight as well as you have begun, there will soon be no one who can withstand you."

When his compliment had been translated, Saintré smiled and said: [166]

"Ah, my lord brother, everything that you say is to your honor. And if I have indeed done well, it is not my work but rather that of my lady who directs my aim."

And at these words their lordships the dukes led the two combatants before the King. And here I shall leave off describing how the prizes were awarded, and turn to the delight felt by the Queen, by Madame, and by all the ladies and damsels, and to Madame's fervent devotions.

The Queen and Madame, along with the other ladies, were laughing and celebrating for love of Saintré and for delight in his victory; Madame's gaze was fixed on Saintré, and she determined, given God's grace to him at the intercession of Our Lady, that she would give her most heartfelt thanks. So she pretended to have a headache, and said to the Queen:

"Ma'am, forgive me, but I must go and lie down for a moment."

"Fair cousin," said the Queen, "do as you wish."

And when Madame was lying down in the withdrawing room* in the stand, she dismissed all her women, then got up and knelt on her bare knees, with her hands together and her eyes cast up to heaven, and gave thanks at length to God and Our Lady for the grace they had allowed Saintré. And when her devotions were complete, she came gaily back to the Queen as if completely cured. Saintré, who had glanced regularly and often at the ladies and had not seen Madame, was afraid that she was suffering as before; [167] when he saw Madame had come back, his heart was a hundred thousand times more joyful. And here I shall cease to talk about these things and describe the awarding of the prizes.

How the King ordered the prizes to be awarded

The King, who had in his keeping the eight superb jewels that were to be the prizes, four from Loisselench, four from Saintré, and who was to award them to whichever of the combatants was appropriate, ordered Montjoie King of Arms of France, who was on the stands, to convey the following words to those present. Then a herald was ordered to cry, "Silence, in the name of the King!" so loudly that everyone would hear. Then Montjoie said:

"My lords Loisselench, and you, Jean de Saintré, the King, our sovereign lord here present, commands and orders me to say that in these your most recent deeds of arms, you have both of you performed well and most valiantly. But since you, my lord Loisselench, are unable to complete the bouts as specified in your letters of challenge, the King, as your sole appointed judge, orders you to meet your obligations as to the four prizes, which following his command, his leave, and his license I return to you."

And when the Seigneur de Loisselench saw that Montjoie had finished speaking, he asked what had been said, and when Montjoie's words had been translated and Loisselench had absorbed the King's judgment—which he had foreseen—he fell to his knees and said that he thanked the King most humbly, that he greatly regretted that his own misfortune had made it impossible for him to prolong their deeds of arms on horse and on foot to the greater enjoyment of the ladies; since, however, Fortune so wished it, [168] he was ready to do his duty as the King had ordered, and as was correct.

And at these words, Montjoie dismounted and returned the four jewels to Loisselench to enable him to satisfy his conditions, and when Loisselench had the jewels, he advanced toward Saintré to present them to him. At this his heart was so full that he was unable to say a single word. The four other Polish barons saw how overcome he was with grief and outdid one another in begging forgiveness for him. Then Saintré was led forward by the Duke of Anjou, and bowed and took the jewels, and then said, smiling:

"My lord brother, I thank you as warmly as I know how for the honor that it has pleased you to afford me."

Then trumpets and clarions were sounded, so long and loud that it seemed they would never fall silent.

And after this, the King ordered that each should return to his own pavilion and remount to return to his lodgings and disarm. And when Saintré was mounted, the said Duke of Anjou said:

"Saintré, we wish you to behave with the greatest grace and honor."

Then Anjou led Saintré to the Seigneur de Loisselench, who was already mounted on his destrier. The two adversaries were set to ride side by side, and before them rode Anjou and the Duke of Berry, and thus Loisselench was escorted back to his lodging. I shall say nothing of the honors or entreaties the two champions exchanged, nor shall I say anything about what was done between then and supper; I shall concentrate on the delight shown by the Queen, by Madame, and by all the ladies and damsels, and indeed by the whole city, all that day and well into the night; no one could refrain from praising Saintré. [169]

How Loisselench took supper with the Queen

When the King and the Queen arrived at the Hôtel Saint-Pol, the King ordered that the Queen instruct her chamberlain to invite the Seigneur de Loisselench and his party to supper, and he wished Saintré also to be invited. And when the supper hour arrived, Saintré, with an elegant escort, went to seek out his adversary. And when they had arrived and were chatting with the ladies, the chamberlain came to lead them to supper. Then the Queen took Loisselench's right hand and had him sit beside her, and then said to Saintré:

"Saintré, since today is one of the days of your challenge, I wish to sit between you both."

And whatever his excuses, demurrals, and obeisances, Saintré was obliged to obey. Madame, delighted at the great honor paid to her lover, said to him as she sat down:

"Saintré, fair sir, may God give you all honor."

"My lady," he said, "you can see that if I take my seat here, it is because of the Queen's command and not because of my own worth. And if I have indeed achieved anything, it is because of one whom may God let me serve to the best of my ability."

And then the Queen summoned the Seigneur de Morg because he spoke French, and had him sit opposite her and Loisselench so that they could talk to each other. The other Polish barons, knights, and squires she had sit among her ladies and damsels, who honored and celebrated them. You need not ask about the wines and the different dishes—nor need I write about them. And—to cut the story short—when the tables were removed, the minstrels struck up for dancing. The King, with my lords his [170] brothers and other nobles of the blood royal, very soon came to join the ladies.

After many dances, and many songs sung, because Loisselench was weary and wounded the King called for wine and spices, and then all withdrew. Then Saintré, with a large and elegant retinue, came to escort Loisselench to his lodging. As they left the court, Saintré invited him and all his party to dinner the following day. What more need I say? At that dinner there were lords and ladies and damsels, knights and men of standing—so much so that it seemed a long time since such a dinner had been offered. And so—to be brief—once the tables were withdrawn, the minstrels struck up for dancing. Then there were *basses-danses*,* songs and other entertainments, and *morisques*, and no one could remember a feast more elegant and delightful and well ordered. But because the Seigneur de Loisselench was still suffering from his wounded hand, the feast had to be cut a little short, and then all the company took their leave.

THE AUTHOR: Five days later, the Seigneur de Loisselench was somewhat better, and he invited Saintré and some of the lords and ladies to dine with him in the Polish fashion the following evening. They were most abundantly served with wines and with Polish dishes. Then, when the tables were withdrawn, there were many dances and many songs. And then, after a copious rere-banquet served with the greatest good cheer and as they rose from table, the Seigneur de Loisselench came out with a great silver dish piled with diamonds and rubies set in gold, [171] and he went along the table asking each lady and damsel to choose one for herself. That done, all those present took their leave, and parted for the night.

How Loisselench took leave

The following day, the Seigneur de Loisselench and all those of his retinue went to take leave of the King and of my lords the King's brothers, and of all those of royal blood, especially the ladies, to be ready to leave the following day for their pilgrimage to Santiago de Compostella. And that evening the King sent money to defray their expenses to all those who had played host to the Polish party. And the following morning he sent the Seigneur de Loisselench a length of deep purple-crimson cut velvet embroidered with gold threads closely laid and couched;* he also sent gold tableware of twenty marks' weight, and gold-plated silver tableware worth two hundred marks, and a very fine Apulian courser. To each of the four barons in Loisselench's retinue the King sent a length of crimson figured velvet, and also a fine courser; and to each of his other knights a length of fine crimson velvet, and to each of his squires [172] a length of crimson satin; to Brunswick Herald, he sent one of his own fine robes, and one hundred *francs a cheval*.*

And the Queen gave the Seigneur de Loisselench another piece of blue cut velvet embroidered with gold, and a valuable brooch consisting of a table-cut* diamond set with three large pearls and three good rubies. And to each of the other four barons she gave a length of blue figured satin embroidered with gold. And to each of his knights she gave a length of blue figured satin; and to each of the squires, a length of plain blue satin. And Madame sent Loisselench a valuable diamond worth five hundred *francs*. And every single vassal of each of the King's brothers sent a gift: some a courser, some silk cloth embroidered with gold, others pieces of fine gilded or whiteware. And when the visitors saw the great honor that was paid to them, and the rich gifts sent by the Queen, by the King's brothers, and by Madame, even after they had officially taken their leave they insisted on returning to thank the donors most humbly.

And as the Polish party left its lodging, Saintré, who was escorting them everywhere, presented Loisselench with a very powerful destrier, saddled and with plumed shaffron and full barding* made of shining gold-plated silver, trimmed with figured cut velvet and fringed with gold and silk in his own colors—something wonderful to see. In return, the Seigneur de Loisselench gave Saintré his own destrier, caparisoned in cloth of gold trimmed with sable fur—the one on which he, Loisselench, had fought, and which was now groomed and fit for a gift. Then each of them mounted his destrier, and with his fine retinue Saintré escorted Loisselench for more than a league. But now I shall leave the subject of Loisselench and his party who were on their way to Santiago, singing the praises of the King, the Queen, the lords, Madame herself, and all the French court, amazed by the gifts and honors that they had been granted, and saying everywhere they went that the court of France was the flower of generosity and the very lodestar of all honor.

THE AUTHOR: After the departure of the Polish lords, Saintré was much commended by the King, [173] the Queen, the ladies, and all the court. I need not describe, and you need not ask about, the most sweet and loving welcome that Madame offered him, for everyone can use his or her own imagination. And things remained so for about a year, at which point Madame decided that it was time for him to undertake some other exploit that would create a stir—and since he was French, and in such favored service with the King, that it would be a good idea for him to undertake arms in some form against the English.

And when they were alone together, she said to him:

"My only desire, my only love, day and night I think of nothing but how to enhance your honor, and it strikes me that although you have done all sorts of deeds of arms, you have never matched yourself against the English. I beg you therefore, given that God and Our Lady and good fortune are on your side, that you seek the permission of his majesty the King and the trusted safe-conduct of the King of England to offer a *pas d'armes** for three days of each week in May, between Gravelines and Calais;[108] they are no more than three leagues apart, and the road is ideal to permit the challenge of a knight or a squire, whichever of them is the first, on one of the three days to present himself on horseback, fully armed and with a war saddle, ready to spur his horse against yours, and yours against his, for ten courses, with lances all of one measure, until one or other of you has broken three lances, or has been wounded.

"And the one to whom God has given victory will win a diamond or a ruby worth a hundred nobles* at least, provided of course that the would-be adventurer has letters patent from [174] his King or from a prince of the royal blood, with their seal, certifying that he is a man of name and noble blood and that he has pursued arms *sans reproche*. And to ensure that you have expert judges, and indeed to attract them to your *pas d'armes*, our King and the King of England should each nominate one of his Kings of Arms in his official capacity—thus one French and one English. And assuming that God has kept you from harm as I earnestly pray he will, if, when your *pas d'armes* is complete, some other nobleman, of the rank I have just mentioned, should happen to request that you undertake another combat on foot or on horseback, then, my love, I wish that with God's help, or Our Lady's, or Saint Michael's, you undertake such combat, before our lord the King, in Paris or elsewhere, so that your reputation may flourish better still."

And with these words, Madame ended her speech.

THE AUTHOR: These words, splendid and noble as they were, greatly pleased Saintré, and for that reason he fell to his knees and thanked Madame as humbly as he knew how. And when they had parted, he did not rest day or night until, in secret and with considerable difficulty, he had obtained the King's permission. Having granted permission, the King nominated as judge Anjou King of Arms (who was also King of Arms for Touraine and Maine). And thereafter Saintré did not rest, day or night, until he had sought out good destriers, and had arranged for arms and for twelve trappers for the twelve days of the *pas d'armes*, all costly, elegant, and eye-catching. And while he was preparing things like this, he sent word to Norroy King of Arms, herald to the King of England,[109] of his *pas d'armes*, begging him not to object to a suspension of hostilities for two months, that is from April 15 to June 15, in the French and English counties of Guines [175] and Boulogne, and at the frontiers around Calais,[110] so that both parties could present themselves at the *pas*. These agreements having been most willingly and joyfully drawn up, the news of the *pas* was spread abroad, drawing a considerable number of spectators.

THE AUTHOR AGAIN: And when April 15 arrived and the truce was in place, Saintré sent craftsmen and other workers from Paris to construct two identical houses[111] made of timber and wood, one for himself and one for the English lords and their retinues who would come to take part in the *pas*. In each of the houses were elegant reception rooms, bedchambers, private chambers, four-poster beds, dressers, stools, benches, tables, crackets,*[112] and other necessary furniture, and each of the houses was hung with tapestries. They were set up about half a bowshot apart, each surrounded by a palisade, and within the enclosure was stabling for three hundred horses. And on each side of the lists, at the point where the combatants would encounter, he had a fine stand constructed, nicely tapestried and carpeted, where the two judges and the heralds were to take their places.

And when the date of the *pas d'armes* drew close, Saintré said farewell to the King and the Queen and Madame, and to all the lords, and he arrived in Gravelines with a fine retinue of three hundred horse, and spent the night there. To be brief, I shall say nothing as to the gifts, the good advice, and the fine words that Madame gave him. And when he saw the two houses so nicely equipped and furnished, he was delighted. Then news reached Guines and Calais, and all the frontier areas, that Saintré had arrived, so the Duke[113] of Buckingham, already in Calais to prepare for the deeds of arms, was pleased to hear of Saintré's presence. [176] Then Buckingham sent Garter King of Arms,[114] who had been designated a judge for the English side, along with four heralds, to greet him and to attest, on behalf of the King of England, that all twelve candidates for his *pas d'armes* were of noble blood, barons who had been nominated by the King from among the many who had come forward—and Saintré greeted the King of Arms and his heralds most warmly. After dinner, he escorted them to their lodgings, hoping that they would be pleased with his preparations. And when Garter King of Arms went back to the Duke, he told him how impressed he was with the preparations, and with the aristocratic pomp of Saintré's retinue; he also told him about the house which had been so delightfully hung with tapestries and carpets, and which was already fully equipped apart from the table linen and bed linen, which was not yet in place. Then everyone praised Saintré to the skies. And so matters remained until the third day following, which was the first day of the month and the opening day of the jousts.

The opening of the *pas d'armes*

On Sunday May 1, the day the *pas* was to open, the Duke of Buckingham mentioned earlier attended Mass and came to the lists with a fine large retinue, and on the gable end of his house he fixed his pennon, *England a bordure argent*; his rallying cry was "England! Saint George!"

THE AUTHOR: And when time came to start the *pas*, the two judges, Champagne King of Arms and Garter King of Arms, with their heralds, were escorted to their stand so as to have a better view of the jousts for their adjudications.[115] Then began the first joust, fierce and intense and highly honorable for the two adversaries, but despite [177] the fact that the Duke of Buckingham was slightly wounded in the hand at the last course, he was judged to have broken his lance more cleanly and so won the diamond.

On the second day, the challenger was the Earl Marshal, who also had his pennon ceremonially fixed to his gable end: it was *England, with a label of three points argent*, and his rallying cry was "England! Saint George!" He bore himself most honorably, but Saintré was judged to have broken his lances more cleanly, and so won the diamond.

On the third day Lord Cobham presented himself in high estate; he bore *gules, on a chevron Or three lions sable*, and his rallying cry was "Saint George! Cobham!"; his pennon was displayed on the rooftop of his house. At the seventh course, he and his horse were borne to the ground, because of which he paid the ruby.

On the first day of the second week there came Lord Engorde[116] in great estate; like the others, he displayed his pennon which was *ermine, on a chevron gules three bezants Or*; his rallying cry was "Saint George! D'Engorde!" He won the diamond.

On the second day of the second week there came the Earl of Warwick, in great estate; he too displayed his pennon which was *gules, a fesse Or between six cross-crosslets Or*, and his rallying cry was "Saint George! Warwick!" He lost the diamond.

On the third day of that week there came Lord Clifford in very fine array. He displayed his pennon, *chequy Or and azure, a bordure ermine*; [178] his rallying cry was "Saint George! Clifford!" He lost the diamond.

On the first day of the third week there came in fine array the Earl of Huntingdon; he too displayed his pennon, which was *azure semé of cross-crosslets fitchy and a chief Or,* and his rallying cry was "Saint George! Huntingdon!" He lost the ruby.

On the second day of that third week there came in fine array the Earl of Arundel, who also displayed his pennon, *gules, a lion langued and armed argent*; his rallying cry was "Saint George! Arundel!" He lost the ruby.

On the third day following there came in fine array Lord Beauchamp, who displayed his pennon as before, *gules a fess Or*; his rallying cry was "Saint George! Beauchamp!" He lost the diamond.

On the first day of the final week, there came in fine array and great estate the Duke of Norfolk, who also displayed his pennon, *party per pale Or and vert, a lion gules armed argent, a fess Or overall*. His rallying cry was "Saint George! Norfolk!" And he won the diamond.

On the second day of the final week, there came in great array Lord Burghersh,[117] who displayed his pennon, *gules a lion the tail forked Or*; his rallying cry was "Saint George! Bruce!" He lost the ruby.

The third and last day of the *pas* there came in great array the Earl of Cambridge, who displayed his [179] magnificent pennon: *England, a label of three points compony argent and gules*. His rallying cry was "England! Saint George!"

THE AUTHOR: In this last joust, the judges were in a quandary, for both lances were broken so cleanly that it was impossible for them to distinguish the winner. They decided initially that neither of the two should win the prize. But finally they agreed that neither should lose what was due to him, and ordered that instead each should present a prize to the other, and that the Earl should be the first to do so, since Saintré had been first to break his lance. And thus, overall, Saintré lost three jewels and won eight—out of a total of eleven—and the twelfth he both won and lost.

THE AUTHOR AGAIN: I shall not describe in detail the deeds of arms or the blows struck, for it would take me too long to write; I shall simply say that all did very well and some better than others, and, thanks be to God, without any deaths or serious wounds. And so the challengers, as they parted, showed as much or more respect and admiration for each other as if they had been brothers. And each of them, without fail, presented each other with gifts: not just the prizes won but also rings, cloth of gold, silks, suites of tapestry, coursers, hackneys, gold and silver plate, and many other things. All this meant that they parted very satisfied.

And after the *pas* were complete, Saintré gave a supper for all. And at the parting of the combatants, he gave Garter King of Arms not only two hundred gold *francs a cheval*, but also his own first caparison, which was of crimson satin heavily embroidered with gold and bordered with sables. [180] To the other heralds he gave their house, their stand, and a hundred *francs* each. To the English trumpeters, buglers, and minstrels, he gave a total of two hundred *francs*. To Champagne King of Arms, who was one of the judges, he gave not only three hundred *francs* but also his final caparison of the *pas*, which was of finest crimson satin figured in silver all lined with sables, and three hundred *francs*. And to the other French heralds and pursuivants he gave the house and two hundred *francs*. To the trumpeters and minstrels of his own retinue, who were very numerous, he gave three hundred *francs*. And there was not one knight, squire, herald, or any other of his retinue who did not receive a gown in Saintré's livery—not to mention the gifts which he gave to certain individual knights and squires who had been his escort, and which would not have disgraced one of the princes of the realm. And thus everyone parted from him very much gratified.

THE AUTHOR: And when on his return Saintré presented himself to the King, he was greeted with God knows what honor and delight, as he was by the Queen, and indeed, to be brief, by the whole court. As I have said, I shall say and write nothing of Madame's reception of him, for everyone must use their own imagination, remembering the love she bore him and the honor that was done to him by all at court. And at this point I shall leave aside all the honors paid to Saintré, and the love between him and Madame, and what transpired between them over the next fifteen months before Saintré was to be subjected to another challenge.

How Messire Niccolò de Malatesta, knight, and Galeazzo of Mantua, squire, came to bear arms at the court of France[118]

[181] Fifteen months after Saintré's return, there arrived in Paris two young noblemen from that part of the Italies that we call Lombardy, one a knight, the other a squire, with a splendid retinue; they had just taken part in a *pas d'armes* of their own devising in the presence of the Emperor, against

the Seigneur de Wallenberg who bore *ermine an escutcheon gules*, and against the Seigneur d'Estandebourg who bore *argent three torteaux gules*. The Emperor, struck by the ferocity and intensity of the combatants, much to their honor, on both sides, had ordered that the combat be abandoned. This meant that their original *emprise*, which had specified that one or other party concede, was still in force.

THE AUTHOR: After they had arrived in Paris and were lodged at the Sign of the Bear by the Porte Baudet,[119] one of the King's heralds recognized one of theirs and realized who they were and why they had come; he hastened to notify the King, in the presence as it happened of the Queen and of Madame. Then Madame hurriedly sent for Saintré, and forbade the herald to tell anyone else his news. And when Saintré appeared, she speedily explained to him about the Lombards who had arrived in Paris in great pomp in order to perform deeds of arms; she asked him if he was courageous enough to be one of those who would take up the Lombards' challenge. "Courageous enough?" he said, "Alas, my lady, what have you seen to suggest that my heart is less courageous than it has been so far?" "Go on, then," she said—to make a long story short—"before anyone else can take up the challenge. I believe it would be useful for you to send word quickly to your brother-in-arms Boucicaut, to ask him if he would wish to be the second challenger." [182] And when Saintré heard this pleasing news from Madame, he made sure to thank her most humbly, then went to find Boucicaut and said:

"Brother, in the name of God and Our Lady, I bring excellent news. There are currently lodged at the Sign of the Bear, by the Porte Baudet, two noble gentlemen from Lombardy, with a sizable escort, who are the bearers of an *emprise* and have come to Paris in order to have it lifted. What do you say? Shall we be the ones to free them from their vows?"

"Free them?" said Boucicaut, "Brother, you and the news you bring are both most welcome; I agree most wholeheartedly. And to make sure that we are the first to present ourselves, let us go immediately to the King to ask for his leave."

This the King gave only very reluctantly, and in answer to their fervent appeals—specifying that first they should ascertain who the Lombards were and what precisely was their *emprise*.

At this the young men commissioned Guyenne King of Arms, a wise and competent herald, to go and discover the information needed, and he returned to report that they were first a knight named Niccolò de Malatesta, a great and noble baron from Ancona,[120] and second a Lombard squire, of very good birth, named Galeazzo of Mantua; each of them was wearing on his left elbow a heavy gold bracelet set with fine gemstones; they proposed to wear the bracelets in six Christian realms (they dared not trust a Saracen kingdom) unless and until they were able to find two knights or squires of noble blood and reputation, like themselves *sans reproche*, who would be willing to fight them on foot, with poleaxes and arming swords* only, until one or the other combatant was thrown or disarmed. [183]

This Galeazzo of Mantua, I believe, was later to become a highly renowned knight who fought Messire Jean le Meingre, Marshal of France,[121] *a outrance*,* in the presence of the last Duke of Padua; very soon thereafter, the Venetians laid a long siege to the city and conquered it,[122] and had Galeazzo imprisoned and then strangled to death: this was regarded throughout the Italies as a great loss, for Galeazzo was thought of as the father and the protector of all displaced nobility.[123]

THE AUTHOR: But to come to my subject. When Saintré and Boucicaut were informed of this welcome and pleasing news, they hurried, as you might expect of hearts so amorous and so valiant, to the King. They explained to him all the details, reiterating their ardent wish that he would give them permission. And the news of the arrival of the Lombards and of the King's consent soon spread throughout the court, with the result that no other requests for permission were made.

At this point the two brothers-in-arms took a good retinue and, on the pretext of seeing the visitors and welcoming them, went to have the terms of the *emprise* explained to them in person. And when the time came that the King asked to see them, Saintré and Boucicaut went to fetch the Lombards with a large entourage; the King, the Queen, and all the lords made them very welcome. What more need I say? There, in the presence of all, Saintré undid Messire Niccolò's bracelet and Boucicaut Galeazzo's, and the King declared the date for their encounter.

When the day arrived, the King, the Queen, the lords, Madame herself, and everyone else were seated in their stands, and the combatants entered their pavilions; [184] to be brief, I shall pass over the ceremonies and the pageantry. The King had offered to make Saintré a knight at each of the latter's former combats, and did so again now, but Saintré demurred: he said he would never have himself knighted other than when fighting under the King's banner, or on crusade against the Saracens. And when the combatants, in their pavilions, had sworn their solemn oaths, and when they had emerged

from their pavilions, and when the Marshal of the lists had made his procla-
mation, all four of them—they had so far been seated on stools facing each
other—set off like lions unchained. The battle was hard and ferocious; for a
long time it was impossible to tell who was having the best of it.

And then, as they duelled, Messire Niccolò by great misfortune knocked
Saintré's poleaxe from his hand, and it fell to the ground. I need scarcely say
how dismayed were Madame and all of Saintré's supporters. But then, being
a squire of intelligence and courage, and without so much as a backward step,
Saintré immediately drew his arming sword and held it over his head with
both hands. And every time that Messire Niccolò raised his poleaxe, Saintré
moved in closer to him until in the end he managed to snatch his sword,
which he threw away. But in the end Messire Niccolò, having the advantage
of his poleaxe, moved forward and thrust the spike of his poleaxe into one of
the slits of Saintré's visor; Saintré was somewhat shaken by this.

Then, seeing that his axe point was well embedded, Messire Niccolò,
wanting to destabilize his adversary, put every effort into jostling Saintré with
his arm—but Saintré was on his guard and held firm; he moved forward and
put out a foot, stabbing with his sword held short in both hands, [185] and
as he thrust at Messire Niccolò's poleaxe he put him off balance. And then
he stabbed so sharply that Messire Niccolò fell to the ground on hands and
knees.

At that Saintré lifted his foot as if to kick him in the side and tumble
him to the ground, but he did the honorable thing and refrained. Then he
went to the assistance of his brother Boucicaut, who had forced Galeazzo
back more than a lance's length. And while Saintré had his back turned,
Messire Niccolò, who was still holding his poleaxe in one hand, got to his
feet and ran after Saintré, but the King had him held back. And then Galeazzo, now fighting both adversaries, was thrown to the ground and surrendered. And in this way, their *emprise* was most valiantly accomplished, on both
sides.

I shall be brief and pass over the honors done to them, the gifts given,
and the tributes paid, as much as or more than to others; I shall simply say
that the visitors were much gratified, amazed at such honors, and marveled
at a court whose nobility and luxury were beyond description. And thus they
took leave of the King, the Queen, the lords and ladies, and bade farewell to
Saintré and to Boucicaut and to the many others who gave them escort. And
here I shall leave off speaking about them and about other events at court, to
address a different subject.

THE AUTHOR: News of this duel soon spread everywhere, and especially to the court of England, which paid particular attention to the conditions laid down for Saintré's *pas d'armes*. Baron Tresto,[124] a lively and enterprising young knight, heard that the rules of engagement specified that in the aftermath of the *pas*, [186] if any knight or squire of name and reputation *sans reproche* wished to challenge him, Saintré, to further deeds of arms on foot or on horseback, that provided God would keep Tresto from danger or from any other legitimate impediment, he, Saintré, would accede to the request and engage in such arms, in the presence of his sovereign lord the King or of his representative.

Then Baron Tresto determined that he would indeed challenge Saintré head to head, with all four weapons, until one or the other of them surrendered, or lost all four arms. And thus it was done. Then, to be brief, the duel was fought fiercely in the presence of the King, the Queen, the lords, and Madame, so fiercely indeed that Saintré dropped his poleaxe—a loss that in the long run served him well, for at that point he drew his long-sword, which he carried on a hook on his sword belt to his right, and wielded it and covered himself most valiantly. And as they fought fiercely with each other, Baron Tresto accidentally stood on the fluke* of his axe head as it lay on the ground, and it pierced his foot deeply. He recoiled, trying to shake free of the poleaxe. Saintré pressed after him fiercely, but the King, wishing to safeguard the honor of both of the combatants, cast down his baton, and both combatants were brought up short and made to exit the lists side by side, on horseback. Then Baron Tresto was presented with great gifts and given the warmest of receptions. At that he took his leave and returned to England. And I shall now say no more about all these deeds of arms, and the many others in which Saintré took part later, for it would take too long, and I shall turn to other matters.

THE AUTHOR: Saintré was by now in high favor with the King, the Queen, the lords, and Madame—[187] indeed, with everyone; he was the best loved and most honored squire in the whole of France because he was so courtly and so unpretentious, and also because of his generosity—always an advantage. For he never showed the slightest sign of arrogance at the King's affection for him, or at anyone else's, or for the honors he received. And it was at this stage in his career that news came of the death of his father, by which he became universally known as the Seigneur de Saintré.

THE AUTHOR AGAIN: It happened that that same year the voyage to Prussia[125] was held. So Madame said to the Seigneur de Saintré:

"My only love, you are the object of all my thoughts and my love for you is so generous, so complete that I want you to be known as the best and most valiant man in the world, despite the fears that I so justifiably have for you. But for this one time, and never again, I want to put your safety at risk. So far, in all your knightly doings, and although the King and others have repeatedly asked you, you have not wished to be dubbed knight; you have excused yourself by saying that you would never allow yourself to be knighted other than in service against the Saracens or under the King's own banner. I'd have wished that this latter could be the case, for it would have given the King pleasure, and your deeds in his service would have been set to your account. But I take comfort from the fact that no good deed passes unnoticed—and so I propose that you should become a knight as did your ancestors; that is, that you become a knight in the most holy and honorable way, on the most holy expedition to Prussia, and in that most holy battle to be fought against the Saracens. We wish you to take part in great estate, in honor of His Majesty, who will grant his help, as indeed shall we." [188]

When Saintré heard Madame's most virtuous and noble proposition, he fell to his knees and said: "Ah! My most supreme and noble goddess, you who can and must command me, you to whom I owe all obedience from now until the world's end, I thank you with all the humility I can muster for your loyal commission, for your advice and your command; with God's help, with the help of Our Lady and of the True Cross, hoping ever to be at their service, I shall obey and abide by your command, hoping that you will have news of me that answers to your every wish." And having said this and more, he bade her farewell.

Then he went to the King and entreated him night and day until he was given permission to take part in the crusade. The King, who by now loved the Seigneur de Saintré more than anyone other than the princes of his own blood, gave him most generous support. Moreover, wishing to do him honor in this holy endeavor undertaken, with haste and against the Saracens, in the service of God and of the faith and of the Christian creed, he decided to give him command of five hundred lances,[126] all of them of the nobility, each lance bringing two further men at arms, and of three thousand bowmen, as well as of the lords who would take part, with men of their own, at their own expense; these latter would be a total therefore of two hundred lances, with their attendant bowmen. And under Saintré's banner would be placed, from each of the King's twelve provinces, fifty more lances. When the news spread, untold numbers of lords and nobles from across the kingdom and across the rest of Europe came to enlist, and the King answered their entreaties and gave permission for there to be one hundred and sixty banners, the command of which he gave—[189] as we said—to Saintré. And when Saintré, who could not decline the command, had thanked the King most humbly, he gathered all the lords to one side, and said, laughing:

"My lords, you have seen that the King, by his grace, and despite all my protestations, has done me the honor to give me a command that would best have been given to one of the princes of the realm; what he has done is just what was expressed by a little monk, as the story tells us:

"Once upon a time a lord, booted and spurred, was making his way with all his entourage to a neighboring abbey to hear Mass. And when Mass had been said, five or six of the youngest novices from the seminary flocked over to unbuckle his spurs. When the lord found the boys attacking his feet, he asked what was going on. His men said: 'It's the custom in churches like this for the novices to ransom the spurs that anyone wears in the church choir.' Then the lord gave the novices an *écu*, and called over the youngest and the most angelic looking of all the boys and said: 'I want to know who is the cleverest[127] of all of you.' Then the little boy said, quickly: 'My Lord, the one that's cleverest is whichever one our Lord Abbot says.' And everyone remembered his response because of course it's true. And you could say the same thing of me, because although I'm the least qualified of all of you, I must nevertheless, as the little boy said, be thought the cleverest of all of you because that is what the King has commanded."

Everyone laughed at this amusing little story, and agreed that the King would know what was best—and so, to abide by the King's command and for love of him, [190] all of them expressed themselves happy and content. And I shall now leave aside these matters and set out the list of lords, barons, and knights banneret* who took part in the expedition, and whose blazons were as follows:[128]

THE AUTHOR: And first, those of the March of France:

The Seigneur de Montmorency, who bears *Or, a cross gules between five eaglets azure*, whose battle cry is "God help first the Christian!" The Seigneur de Trie, who bears *Or, a bend azure*, whose battle cry is "Boulogne!" The Seigneur de Rosny, *Or, two bars gules*, whose battle cry is "Rosny!" The Seigneur de Forest, *gules, six martlets argent*. The Seigneur de Vieux-Pont, *argent, ten annulets gules*. The Vidame de Chartres, *Or, three bars and an orle of six martlets sable*, whose battle cry is "Merlo!" The Seigneur de Saint-Brison, *azure, fleurs de lis argent*. Le Bouteillier, *quarterly Or and gules*, whose battle cry is "Les Granges!" The Seigneur de Marolles, *bendy of six, argent and gules.*

Those of the Beauvaisis, in the said Ile de France

The Count of Clermont, *gules, two barbels addorsed Or between two crosses recercelé Or fitched at foot,* whose battle cry is "Clermont!" The Seigneur d'Offémont, *similar, a label of three points Or,* whose battle cry is "Offémont!" The Seigneur de Gaucourt, *ermine, two bars endorsed gules,* and whose battle cry is "Gaucourt!" The Seigneur d'Espineuse, *ermine, an escutcheon gules.* And many other knights and squires from the said March of the Beauvaisis. [191]

Those of the March of Champagne

My lord Jean of Champagne, *azure, a bend argent, double cotised potent counter potent, a label of three points gules,* whose battle cry is "Passavant!" The Count of Rethel, *gules, three rake's heads with six tines Or,* whose battle cry is "Rethel!" The Count of Brienne, *azure, billety a lion Or.* The Viscount of Rosel, *vairy Or and azure, two bars gules.* The Seigneur de Châtillon, *gules, billety a lion surmounted by a bendlet Or,* whose battle cry is "Châtillon!" The Seigneur de Conflans, *azure, billety a lion surmounted by a bendlet Or, with a baton sinister Or.* The Seigneur de Roussy, *Châtillon, an eagle sable,* and whose battle cry is "Châtillon!" The Seigneur de Joinville, *azure three horse-brays in fess Or, bound in saltire argent, on a chief ermine a demi-lion gules crowned Or,* and whose battle cry is "Joinville!" The Seigneur de Marne en Brie, *gules, three torteaux Or,* and whose battle cry is "Mareuil!" And many other knights and squires from Champagne.

Those of the March of Flanders

The Seigneur de Gavre, who bore the arms *Flanders, a label of three points gules,* whose battle cry is "Flanders! The Lion!" Messire Henry of Flanders, who bore the arms *Flanders, a bendlet compony argent and gules,* whose battle cry is "Flanders! To the Copplet!" Messire Jean du Gavre, who bore the plain arms of Gavre: *gules, three lions argent, crowned and armed Or,* whose battle cry was "Gavre!" The Seigneur de Rodez, who bore *azure, a lion Or langued gules and armed argent,* whose battle cry [192] was "Rodez!" The Seigneur de Ghistelle, *gules, a chevron ermine,* whose battle cry was "Ghistelle!" The Seigneur de Commines, who bears *Or, an escutcheon sable diapred, and an orle of roses gules,* whose battle cry was "Commines!" The Seigneur d'Halluin, *argent, three lions sable crowned, langued and armed Or,* whose battle cry was "Halluin!" And many other knights and squires of Flanders.

Those who were of the March of Aquitaine

The Count of Périgord, who bore *argent, a mill rind vert, surmounted by a bend gules,* and who cried "Périgord!" The Count of Bigorre, who bore *Or, two lions passant gules, crowned argent,* and who cried "Bigorre!" The Count of Ventadour, who bore *chequy Or and gules,* whose battle cry was "Ventadour!" The Viscount of Cahors, who bore *sable, three lions argent,* whose battle cry was "Cahors!" The Viscount of Limoges, who bore *ermine, a bordure gules,* whose battle cry was "Limoges!" The Seigneur d'Albret, who bore *argent, a lion gules crowned azure, langued and armed sable.* The Viscount of Combronde, who bore *Or, two lions passant gules,* whose battle cry was "Combronde!" The Seigneur de Lesparre, *lozengy Or and gules,* whose battle cry was "Lesparre!" The Seigneur de Villars, *quarterly Or and gules,* whose battle cry was "Villars!" The Seigneur de Harpedaine, *gules, a harp Or,* whose battle cry was "Harpedaine!" The Seigneur de Cadillac, *gules, a lion argent within an orle of plates.* The Seigneur de Barbesan, *azure a cross Or,* whose battle cry is "Sau a Barbesan!" The Seigneur de Montmirail, who bore *barry argent and sable, a lion* [193] *gules,* whose battle cry was "Montmirail!" The Seigneur de la Trémouïlle, *Or, a chevron gules between three eagles azure.* The Seigneur de La Sale, *barry undy of eight argent and gules,* whose battle cry was "Mars!" And many other knights and squires, French, from Guyenne.

Those from the same March but who enlisted with the English, and who, on that blessèd day, will wish to honor and ride under the King's standard. And first:

The Count of Béarn, who bore *Or, two cows gules horned azure, collared and belled argent,* whose battle cry was "Béarn!" The Captal de Bueil, *Or, on a cross sable five escallops argent.* Le Loup de Foix, who bore *Gules, a wolf Or langued and clawed and denté argent.* The Seigneur de Montferrand, *Or, four*

pallets gules, a bordure sable, whose battle cry was "Montferrand!" The Seigneur d'Auras, who bore *Or, a lion azure surmounted by a bend argent,* whose
battle cry was "Auras!" And a number of other knights and squires of the
March of Aquitaine.

Those of the March of Anjou, including Touraine and Maine

First, from Anjou: the Viscount of Beaumont, who bore the arms *France,
a lion Or, langued and armed gules,* whose battle cry was "Beaumont!" Messire
Hue de Craon, who bore *lozengy Or and gules, a bordure argent,* whose battle
cry was "Craon!" The Seigneur de Maulevrier, who bore *Or, a chief gules,*
whose battle cry was "Maulevrier!" The Seigneur de Matefelon, who bore *gules,
six escutcheons Or,* whose battle cry was "Matefelon!" [194] The Seigneur
d'Avoir, who bore *argent, a lion azure, a label of five points azure,* whose battle
cry was "Avoir!" The Seigneur de Châtel-Fremont, who carried the standard,
and who bore *gules, a cross moline Or,* and whose battle cry was "Châtel-
Fremont!" The Seigneur de Bueil, who bore *azure, a crescent argent between six
crosses crosslet fitchy Or,* whose battle cry was "Bueil!" The Seigneur de Monjean,
who bore *Or fretty gules,* whose battle cry was "Monjean!" The Seigneur de
Beauvau, *argent, four lioncels gules crowned azure, langued and armed Or,* whose
battle cry is "Beauvau!" And many other knights and squires of Anjou.

Those of Touraine, in the said March of Anjou, who were there

The Seigneur d'Amboise, who bore *paly of six pieces Or and gules,* and
whose battle cry was "Amboise!" The Seigneur de Mailly, *undy Or and gules,*
whose battle cry was "Mailly!" The Seigneur de Pressigny, who bore *paly per
fess counterchanged with four cantons, the first and fourth gyronny of the first
and second, the second and third barry per pale counterchanged of the same,* and
whose battle cry was "Pressigny!" The Seigneur de l'Isle, *gules, two leopards
argent, langued and armed azure,* and whose battle cry was "L'Isle Bouchart!"
The Seigneur de Montbazon, who bore *gules, a lion Or,* and whose battle cry
was "Montbazon!" The Seigneur de Sainte More, who bore *argent, a fesse
gules,* and whose battle cry was 'Sainte More!" The Seigneur de Mermande,
who bore *Or two fesses sable,* and whose battle cry was "Mermande!" The said
Seigneur de Saintré, who bore *gules, a bend Or, a label of three points Or,* and

whose battle cry was "Saintré!" And many other knights and squires from the said Duchy of Touraine and the March of Anjou. [195]

Those of the County of Maine. And first:

The Seigneur de Laval,[129] who had himself dubbed knight on the expedition, who bore *Or, on a cross gules between sixteen eaglets displayed azure, and charged with five escallops azure,* and whose battle cry was "Laval!" The Seigneur de Tucé, who bore *sable, three fesses argent gemel,* and whose battle cry was "Tucé!" The Seigneur de Sarcel, who bore *vert, a lion argent.* The Seigneur de Cormes, *argent, three fesses gemel sable.* The Seigneur des Echelles, who bore *gules, three roses argent.* The Seigneur de la Forest, who bore *argent, a chief indented sable.* The Seigneur de Beauchamp, who bore *argent, in chief a danse gules, within an orle of six martlet gules.* The Seigneur de Montfort, *gules, two leopards Or armed argent.* And many other knights and squires of the said County of Maine and the March of Anjou.

Those of the March of Ponthieu, also called "Poyers"

The Viscount of Quesnes, who bore *argent, a cross gules fretty Or.* The Seigneur de Rambures, *Or, three bars gules.* The Seigneur de Brimeu, *argent three eagles gules, membered azure.* The Seigneur de Pinquegny, who bore *barry argent and azure, a bordure gules,* and whose battle cry is "Pinquegny!" The Seigneur de Cambronne, *barry of eight Or and gules.* The Seigneur de Créquy, *Or a cherry-tree gules,* whose battle cry is "Créquy!" The Seigneur de Baconne, *gules crusily and two barbels addorsed Or.* The Seigneur de Linières, *argent, a bend gules,* whose battle cry [196] is "Linières!" And many other knights and squires of this March.

Those of the March of Vermandois

The Seigneur de Hangest, who bore *Or, a cross gules,* whose battle cry was "Hangest!" The Seigneur de Genly, *argent, on a cross gules five escallops Or.* The Seigneur de Moy, *gules, a fret Or,* whose battle cry was "Cercelles!" The Seigneur de Flavy, *ermine, on a cross gules five escallops Or,* whose battle cry was "Hangest!" The Seigneur de Roye, *gules, a bend argent,* whose battle cry was "Roye!" And many other knights and squires of this March.

Those of the March of Corbie who were present

The Seigneur de Saucourt, who bore *argent fretty gules,* whose battle cry is "Saucourt!" The Seigneur d'Hérilly, who bore *gules, a bend fusil Or,* whose battle cry was "Hérilly!" The Seigneur de Mailly, *Or three mailles vert,* whose battle cry was "Mailly!" The Seigneur de Rubempré, *argent, three bars gemel gules,* whose battle cry was "Rubempré!" The Seigneur de Miraumont, *argent, six torteaux gules,* whose battle cry was "Miraumont!" The Seigneur d'Aubigny, *argent a fesse gules,* whose battle cry was "Aubigny!" And many other knights and squires of this March.

Those of the March of Normandy

The Seigneur de Châtel-Gontier, son of the Count of Le Perche, who bore *argent, two chevrons gules,* and whose battle cry was "Le Perche!" The Seigneur d'Ivry, who bore *Or, three chevrons gules,* whose battle cry was "Ivry!" The Seigneur de Marny, *sable,* [197] *a cross couped argent,* whose battle cry was "Marny!" The Seigneur de Graville, who bore *azure, on a fesse argent crosslets Or,* whose battle cry was "Graville!" The Seigneur de Forges, *azure, six torteaux Or, a chief argent,* whose battle cry was "Forges!" The Seigneur de La Haye, *argent, three escutcheons gules,* whose battle cry was "La Haye!" The Seigneur de Braquemont, *sable a chevron argent.* The Seigneur de Thionville, who bore *argent two bendlets gules, an orle of escallops gules.* The Seigneur de Ferrières, *gules on an escutcheon ermine a fesse gules, the whole within an orle of horseshoes Or,* whose battle cry was "Ferrières!" The Seigneur de Gamaches, *argent, a chief azure surmounted by a bendlet gules,* whose battle cry was "Gamaches!" And many other knights and squires of Normandy.

Those of the Marches of Berry, Bourbonnais, and Auvergne

The Count of Sancerre, who bore *azure, a bend argent double-coticed potent counterpotent Or, a bordure gules,* whose battle cry is "Passavant!" The Viscount of Villemur, who bears *argent, a lion azure,* and whose battle cry was "To the fair one!" Monseigneur Philippe de Bourbon, who bore *Or, a lion gules within an orle of escallops azure,* whose battle cry was "Bourbon!" The Seigneur de Châtel-Morant, *gules, three lions argent crowned and armed Or,* whose battle cry was "Châtel-Morant!" The Seigneur de la Tour d'Auvergne, who bore *France, a tower gules,* whose battle cry was "La Tour!" The Seigneur de Montagu, who bore *gules, a lion ermine,* whose battle cry was "Montagu!" The Seigneur [198] de Chalençon, who bore *gules, three lions' heads erased Or,* whose battle cry was "Chalençon!" And many other knights and squires of the said March.

Those of the March of Brittany who were present

The Count of Lisle, who bore *gules, a cross cleché, voided and pommetté, Or,* whose battle cry was "Lisle!" The Vicount of Labellière, who bore *quarterly of argent and gules,* and whose battle cry was "Labellière!" The Seigneur de Châteaubriant who bore *gules, semy of fleurs-de-lis Or,* and whose battle cry was "Châtcaubriant!" The Seigneur de Rais, who bore *Or, a cross sable,* and whose battle cry was "Rais!" The Seigneur de Malestroit, *gules, with torteaux Or,* and whose battle cry was "Malestroit!" And many other knights and squires of that March.

Those of the March of Artois

Messire Louis d'Artois, who bore *Artois, gules a lion Or armed azure,* whose battle cry was "Artois!" The Count of Saint-Pol, who was dubbed knight for the occasion, who bore *argent, a lion tail forked and crossed in saltire gules, crowned and armed Or.* The Seigneur de Fiennes, who bore *argent, a lion sable,* whose battle cry was "Fiennes!" The Seigneur de Béthune, who bore *argent, a fesse gules,* whose battle cry was "Béthune!" The Seigneur de Renty, *argent, three axe heads gules,* whose battle cry was "Renty!" The Seigneur de Creseques, *azure, three bars coticed Or,* whose battle cry was "Bourbourg!" The Seigneur de Bailleul, *fretty azure and Or,* whose battle cry is "Bailleul!" The Seigneur d'Inchy, *barry of six, Or and sable,* whose battle cry is "Inchy!" The Seigneur de Humières, *Or fretty sable, a label of three points gules.* And many other knights and squires of this March. [199]

Those of the Marches of the Duchy and County of Burgundy

The Count of Burgundy, who, although he was not the King's subject, to honor the King offered to ride under his standard, and who bore *azure, a lion Or,* whose battle cry was "Châtillon!" The Count of Auxerre, who bore *gules, a bend Or,* whose battle cry was "Auxerre!" The Seigneur de Montagu, *azure, a lion argent,* whose battle cry was "Montagu!" The Seigneur de Vergy, *gules, three cinquefoils Or,* whose battle cry was "Vergy!" The Seigneur de Saint-Georges, *gules, a cross Or.* The Seigneur de Charny, *gules, three escutch-eons argent,* whose battle cry was "Charny!" The Seigneur de Chassenay, *gules, a fesse Or.* The Seigneur d'Anthoigny, *sable crusily, two barbels addorsed Or,* whose battle cry was "Anthoigny!" And many other knights and squires of these provinces of Burgundy.

Those of the Barrois and of Lorraine, who to honor the King offered to ride under his standard

The Seigneur de Pont-à-Mousson, who bore *Bar, a label of three points argent,* whose battle cry was "Le Pont!" The Seigneur de Pierrefort, who bore *Bar, a bordure gules,* whose battle cry was "Pierrefort!" The Seigneur de Dum, who bore *Bar, a bordure ermine,* whose battle cry was "Dum!" Messire Ferry de Vaudémont, who bore *barruly argent and sable,* whose battle cry was "Vaudémont!" The Seigneur de Bauffremont, *vairy Or and gules,* whose bat-tle cry was "Bauffremont!" The Seigneur d'Apremont, *gules, a cross argent,* whose battle cry was "Apremont!" The Seigneur de Thollon, who bore *Vaudémont, a baton gules.* The Seigneur de Ruppes, who bore *Bauffremont,* [200] *a bendlet azure.* The Seigneur des Armoises, who bore *gyronny of twelve Or and azure.* The Seigneur de Ludres, *bendy of six Or and azure.* And many other gentlemen.

Those of Lorraine and Barrois, all together. And first:

Lord Nicholas of Lorraine, who bore *Lorraine, a bordure indented azure,* and whose battle cry was "Prigny!" The Count of Chiny, *barruly Or and gules, a lion sable,* and whose battle cry was "Chiny!" The Count of Clermont en Bassigny, who bore *gules, a stag argent.* The Count of Grand-Pré, *barruly Or and gules.* The Seigneur de Grancy, who bore *argent, a chief gules.* The Seigneur de Brey, *chequy Or and sable.* The Seigneur d'Archimont, who bore *sable, a bend argent, two cottices similar.* And many other knights and squires from the Marches of Germany, who are known as Ruyers.

Those of the March of the Dauphiné, who offered their service to the King, and were present

The Seigneur de Clermont, who bore *gules, two keys*[130] *in saltire argent,* whose battle cry was "Clermont!" The Seigneur de Valbonnais, *gules, semé of fleur-de-lis Or,* whose battle cry was "Valbonnais!" The Seigneur de Sassenages, *barruly of argent and azure, a lion gules crowned Or,* whose battle cry was "Sassenages!" The Seigneur de Maubec, who bore *gules, three lions passant guardant argent,* whose battle cry was "Maubec!" The Seigneur de Mont-Chenu, *gules, a bend engrailed argent,* whose battle cry was "Mont-Chenu!" The Seigneur de Châteauneuf, [201] *argent a chief gules,* whose battle cry is "Châteauneuf!" The Seigneur de Bellecombe, *Or, a bend sable,* whose battle cry is "Bellecombe!" The Seigneur de Mollard, *Or, a lion vair.* The Seigneur de Châteauvillain, *gyronny of eight argent and sable.* The Seigneur de Gière, *vert, on a chief gules a demi-lion Or.* And many other knights and squires to serve the King in battle under his standard, along with more than one hundred and sixty banners.

But here I will leave this most powerful nobility of lords, barons and banners, and talk about the piteous and mournful departure of Saintré and of all the French lords, when they left the King and the court.

THE AUTHOR: And when the time of departure came, Saintré and all his forces were ready, with their arms and armor and all their baggage loaded into carts and other wagons, and all their archers and bowmen were drawn up wearing red jacks* with a white cross. Then Saintré, and all the noblemen of the party, all also dressed with their men in their own livery—a most imposing sight—heard a solemn Mass sung by the Bishop in the Cathedral of Notre Dame in Paris; they had themselves confessed, and the Bishop gave them the papal absolution for their sins. Then, in the presence of the King, Saintré's banner was blessed, as were all the other banners, and the whole party followed the King to a dinner. And at two o'clock, when all were assembled, they filed into the presence of the King, who was in the great hall. The Queen, the lords and the ladies were also all present for the leave-taking.

And when all had fallen to their knees, the King said to Saintré:

"Saintré, in this expedition I charge you [202] with the safeguard of my banner, which symbolizes my own person; I charge you also with the command of the lords and other nobles here present who will be of your company, and I commend them to you as if they were my own person."

And then turning to the other lords there present, he said:

"My friends, you are all noble and scions of noble houses that have brought forth so many valiant men whom you have so often emulated with your own valor. Now that you go to fight in the service of Our Lord Jesus Christ, a service in which you may win the salvation of your souls and everlasting admiration, I commend to you our sacred faith, my banner, and your own honor. Men may fight, but God gives victory to his own. There is no doubt therefore that, if you and other Christian princes and lords and other combatants have God's grace, your mission will go better, however great the forces the Saracens muster against you—there will be more of them than one can imagine. And for my part, I swear by my faith that were it not for the great affairs of state that occupy me, I would be in your company. But I beseech you all, from the greatest to the least, that you act as friends and brothers, free of envy and resentment, free of quarrels and disputes, for it is these things that have so often in the past broken up companies such as yours, and left them dishonored and overwhelmed."

And then he took his banner and gave it to the Baron of Châtel-Fremont as bearer. And then he said: "Now, my friends, as your king and your father, I shall give you my blessing." Then he made the sign of the Cross, and said:

"In the name of [203] the Father, the God who created us, and of the Son, the God who redeems us, and of the Holy Spirit, the God who illumines us, the One True God in three names and three persons, may you go out, may those whom he wishes to take to himself remain, and may you return with your souls and your honor unscathed. And I beg you all that, win or lose, you behave honorably, warning that in the contrary case you should not return."

And at these words, weeping and much grieved, saying "God speed, my friends," he touched each hand. Then you might have heard all hearts sighing, you might have seen all eyes weeping, for no one, man or woman, could speak for emotion.

Then the combatants went to the Queen, who was overcome with tears and had withdrawn a little with her ladies. Then Saintré, on behalf of all, spoke as best he could, and said: "Our sovereign lady, what might be your own commands?" The Queen turned to them all and wordlessly touched the hand of each of them.

Then the combatants went to the three royal brothers and spoke the same words. Then the Duke of Anjou said:

"Saintré and all the rest of you, fair cousins and our good friends, you have heard the words of our lord the King. Go forth and act joyously, and you cannot fail to succeed."

Then they turned to Madame. I need not speak of her: however hard she tried, her own emotions and the great passion she felt as she looked at Saintré meant that she was near to fainting, and would have fallen had he not caught her. [204]

Then they turned to the other ladies and damsels, who were all grieving together as if their lovers were already dead, saying to each other:

"Alas for us all! Never again shall we see so fine and joyous a company gathered together as we do here!"

The officers of the court wept aloud, lamenting the departure of Saintré, and saying:

"Alas! Now we see departing the young man who gave us counsel, who gave us comfort in adversity, who succored us in time of trouble, and we do not know if we shall ever see him again!"

Then those present reached out to him from all sides, offering prayers and vows; they could only with difficulty be persuaded to let him go. And then they retired to rest for that day.

THE AUTHOR: And when the morning of the following day dawned, the trumpets began to sound for the horses to be saddled. Then all the company went to church, and when they had heard Mass, each mounted and made ready to depart. There were the three royal brothers, the Dukes of Anjou, Berry, and Burgundy, and all their retinues, who were to escort the King's banner out of the gates of Paris; there also were the remaining knights, squires, and townspeople, so many of them that there seemed scarcely a soul left.

The departure of the banners

The first to depart were the pursuivants, two by two, all on horseback, wearing their tabards with the front and back over the arms. After them came the heralds, also two by two, wearing tabards emblazoned with the arms of their lords. After them came the kings of arms of the different provinces and fiefdoms, also two by two, having been vested with their coats of arms just as they set off. [205] After them came a large number of trumpeters and buglers, two by two. After them, riding alone, came Montjoie King of Arms of France, wearing the royal arms. After him came the Seigneur de Châtel-Fremont carrying the King's standard, and flanked by the Dukes of Anjou and Berry. After them came the Duke of Burgundy on the right, with Saintré on his left. After Saintré came the first three banners, France Ancient as well as France Modern,[131] as specified in the royal ordonnances and in the ancient records of successive Montjoie Kings of Arms of France; these books were designed, following visitations from Montjoie himself along with the kings of arms of the provinces, to ensure the integrity of the blazons and to avoid disputes and clashes between local lords and ladies. And after these three banners came the three lords whose blazons they showed. And thus, three by three, in perfect order, the expeditionary army paraded through Paris.

The departure of the army and its admirable organization was regarded as a most splendid spectacle, so pleasing was the sight. For this reason, throughout the day, not a single shop or stall was opened, just as if it had been Easter Day. But as the army paraded through the city, many ladies and damsels, townsmen and their wives, and people of all sorts, crowded to their shop fronts and windows to watch the noble company ride by. And then you might have seen all the spectators sigh and lament and weep, out of regret and pity, and not one of them could refrain from clasping his or her hands and crying at the tops of their voices: "Ah, fair squire Saintré, may God give you grace, and may you and your company return joyfully [206] and laden with honors!"—all the while promising to God masses, pilgrimages, vows, and the giving of alms. And when the army was somewhat outside Paris, Saintré and the other leaders begged that the King's brothers return to the city, and at that point they took their leave. And here I shall say no more about their leave-taking, or about the distress felt by the King, the Queen, the King's brothers, the ladies and the damsels, and the whole court—especially, of course, Madame, who launched herself into constant pilgrimages, almsgiving, and prayers, as well as secret sorrowing and weeping. I return to Saintré and his army, who were delighted to have arrived safely in the city of Thorun, in Prussia.

THE AUTHOR: Saintré, along with his men at arms and his archers, made good progress and arrived in the said city of Thorun in Prussia where the expedition was to assemble. And there they found the prelates, the princes, and the lords whom I shall now list, and who had come to salute the King's standard; they were delighted when they saw so noble an array, with so many banners and an army so numerous and so well equipped, especially considering that there were some five or six thousand combatants, that it would be difficult to find better.

THE AUTHOR: As concerns the King of England, because he had too many great affairs in train, he wished neither to come himself nor to send an army, but he was persuaded, with difficulty, to give permission for the following lords to take part; here are their names:

The Earl of March, who bore *azure, three fesses Or, overall an inescutcheon argent*, and whose battle cry was "La Marche!" The Earl of Northampton, who bore *azure, on a bend argent three mullets gules*, [207] and whose battle cry was "Northampton!" The Earl of Suffolk, who bore *sable, a cross Or*, and whose battle cry was "Suffolk!" Lord Cobham, who bore *gules, on a chevron Or three lions sable*, and whose battle cry was "Haston!" Lord Clifford, who bore *chequy Or and azure, a bend ermine*, and whose battle cry was "Clifford!" Baron de Lisle, who bore *Or, two chevrons sable*, and whose battle cry was "Lisle!" Lord Molyneux, who bore *sable, on a chief argent three lozenges gules*, and whose battle cry was "Molyneux!" Lord Rokeby, who bore *argent a chevron sable*, and whose battle cry was "Rokeby!" These eight lords formed a body, with one hundred lances and three hundred archers.

In order to counter the great forces assembled by the Saracens, the four Christian Kings of Spain, that is Castile, Aragon, Portugal, and Navarre, had sworn an alliance to make war by land and sea on the neighboring Saracen Kings of Granada, Morocco, and Bellemarine.[132] Nevertheless, they had assembled and sent an army of quite marvelous size, as follows:

The prelates, princes and other lords who were present, and in the first place[133]

The Duke of Brunswick representing the Emperor, who was prevented by illness from being present; the blazon on the Duke's banner was *Or, an eagle displayed double-headed and membered sable*. He was in command of all the princes and lords designated to accompany him: that is to say, the Duke of Austria, [208] the Duke of Bavaria, the Duke of Brabant, the Duke of Stettin, the Duke of Lemburg, the Duke of Luxemburg, the Duke of Mons, the Marquis of Metz, the Marquis of Brandenburg, the Count of Hainault, the Count of Estaimbourg, the Count of Le Mont, the Count of Nassau, the Count of Espehem, the Count of Montgellin, the Count of Württemberg, the Count of Sone, the Count of Berneberg, the Count of Maine, the Count of Vuido, the Count of Muert, the Count of Wallenstein, the Count of Guerles, the Count of Holland, the Count of Zeeland, the Count of Sene, the Count of Oste, the Count of Cille, the Count of Puilly, the Count of Augsburg, the Count of Lost, the Count-Marquis of Blankenburg, the Count of Luido, the Count of Wittenburg, the Count of Saulme, the Count of Vernemburg, the Count of Limbourg, the Count of Sallebrune, the Count of Richecourt, the Count of Vuardence, the Seigneur d'Enghien, the Seigneur d'Hanrech, the Seigneur d'Antoing, the Seigneur de Luynes, the Seigneur de Fontaines, the Seigneur de Bossu, the Seigneur de Barbençon, the Seigneur de Hamalde, the Seigneur de Lalaing, the Seigneur de Trazégnies, the Seigneur d'Avène, the Seigneur de Hoorne, the Seigneur de Condé, the Seigneur de Robertsart, the Seigneur de Marquette, the Seigneur d'Oisy, the Seigneur du Quesnoy, the Seigneur de Clermont, the Seigneur de Saint Vaast, the Seigneur de Crépy, the Seigneur de Fontenay, the Seigneur d'Esmeriez, the Seigneur de Jeumont: all these were from Hainaut.

Those present from Hasbain in the County of Loos[134]

The Seigneur d'Aigremont, the Seigneur de Rumines, the Seigneur de Moireaumes, the Seigneur de Landry, [209] the Seigneur d'Estonnenost, the Seigneur de Duras, the Seigneur de Flemalle, the Seigneur de Baugines, the Seigneur du Cerf, the Seigneur de Montgardin, the Seigneur de Galles, the Seigneur de Salles, the Seigneur de Semalle, the Count of Namur, Messire Robert de Namur, Messire Antoine de Namur, the Seigneur de Rochefort, the Seigneur du Peel, the Seigneur de Haudemont, the Seigneur de Huffalise, the Seigneur d'Argentel, the Seigneur de Wassebech, the Seigneur de Dou, the Seigneur de Ville, the Seigneur de Harpain, the Seigneur de Sulp, the Seigneur de Barressies, all Ruyers* depending on Hasbain.

The Ruyers present from the duchies of Limburg, Luxemburg, and Blanquebourg

The Count of Mons, the Seigneur de Rodemach, the Seigneur de Fauquemont, the Seigneur de Toumenge, the Seigneur de Lescle, the Seigneur de Humbeghe, the Seigneur de Heussedenge, the Seigneur de Lampast, the Seigneur de Ramsberg, the Seigneur de Blassemare, the Seigneur de Coblenz, the Seigneur de Richeespee, the Seigneur de Wissenbourg, the Seigneur de Zarmalle, and the Seigneur d'Estelles.

Those present who were German, Ruyers from Bavaria

The Seigneur de Sesmalle, the Seigneur de Pallengest, the Seigneur de Naudes, the Seigneur de Lisigny, the Seigneur de Houdines, the Seigneur de Walemberghe, the Seigneur d'Estaudebourg, the Seigneur de Hellens, the Seigneur de Rodon, the Seigneur de Maudresset, and the Seigneur de Boncourst.

Those present who were Germans from Brabant[135]

The Seigneur de Mechelen, the Seigneur de Grimbergen, the Seigneur de Wezemaal, [210] the Seigneur de Rotselaar, the Seigneur de Warsselar, the Seigneur de Rollye, the Seigneur de Brauch, the Seigneur de Souberf, the Seigneur de Marbais, the Seigneur de Horn, the Seigneur de Halle, the Seigneur de Walhain, the Seigneur de Pietersheim, the Seigneur de Gosseberghe, the Seigneur de Bellelare, the Seigneur de Diest, the Seigneur de Her, the Seigneur de Durs, the Seigneur de Briqueval, the Seigneur de Huldenberg, the Seigneur de Hamsseberghe, the Seigneur de Ruppellau, the Seigneur de Grez, the Seigneur de Dimpleu, the Seigneur d'Anvers, the Seigneur de Wandres, the Seigneur de Roy, the Seigneur de Dinghehem, the Seigneur de Vuandres.

Those present who were Ruyers from Holland and Zeeland

The Marquis de Jullier, the Seigneur de Heemstede, the Seigneur de Brederode, the Seigneur de Dierbre, the Seigneur de Waltrellen, the Seigneur de Hornes,[136] the Seigneur de Hondrues, the Seigneur de Lek, the Seigneur de Polanen, the Seigneur d'Egmond, the Seigneur de Herlaar, the Seigneur d'Abzcoude, the Seigneur de Lisestain, the Seigneur de Lavore, the Seigneur de Raderonde, the Seigneur de Vuoste, the Seigneur de Tornebor, the Seigneur de Baudebourg, the Seigneur de Lalesque, the Seigneur de Hondekerk, the Seigneur de Kattendijk, and the Seigneur de Rhomas: all these gentlemen, thirty thousand horse, twelve thousand archers, and twenty thousand foot, were ready to fight in God's service, and had answered the summons of the Emperor.

The prelates from the Germanies who were present, and first:

The Archbishop of Cologne, with three thousand horse, two thousand archers, and three thousand foot. The [211] Archbishop of Trier, with three thousand horse, two thousand archers, and three thousand foot. The Archbishop of Mainz, with two thousand horse, one thousand archers, and fifteen hundred foot. The Bishop of Passau, with two thousand horse, a thousand archers, and fifteen hundred foot. The Bishop of Liège, with two thousand horse, a thousand archers, and fifteen hundred foot. The Grand Master of the Teutonic Order in Prussia, and all the knights of the Order,[137] with four thousand horse, two thousand archers, and five thousand foot.

Also present was the Despot of Romania, representing his brother the Emperor of Constantinople, under the Emperor's standard and in command of three thousand horse and three thousand foot. Also there was the Count of Zilch, representing the Emperor of Trebizond, under the Emperor's standard, and in command of two thousand horse and two thousand foot. Also there was the Duke of Lesto, representing the Emperor of Bulgaria, under the Emperor's standard, in command of fifteen hundred horse and two thousand foot. These three dignitaries had arrived together.

There also was the King of Bohemia in person, bearing *gules, a lion argent, armed and crowned, queue nowed, fourchée and crossed Or*; with him were the Duke of Saxony, the Marquis de Blandebourg, the Count Palatine, the Count of Grave, the Count of Marque, the Count of Wautebourg, the Seigneur de Rissembourg, the Seigneur de Ressembourg, the Seigneur de Wassembourg, the Seigneur d'Estremembourg, the Seigneur de Plommellau, the Seigneur de Donru, the Seigneur de Brunech, the Seigneur de Flamenqueton, the Seigneur de Bussvelt, the Seigneur de Misque, the Seigneur de Denstone, the Seigneur de Wectemberghe, and many other knights and squires: this was a force of ten thousand horse, six thousand archers, and eight thousand foot. [212]

And there also was the Duke of Lithuania, representing the King of Poland, and bearing *gules, a horse argent thereon a man in complete armor Or, in the dexter hand a sword argent with hilt and pommel Or*. With him were the Duke of Craponne, the Duke of Orrighe, the Duke of Suodvich, the Marquis of Nasse, the Count of Wellendech, the Count of Surtemberghe, the Count of Craiere, the Seigneur de Loissellench, the Seigneur de Chisselich, the Seigneur d'Endach, the Seigneur de Briquembourg, the Seigneur de Lisemberge, the Seigneur de Nulz, the Seigneur d'Enterg, the Seigneur de Salberg, the Seigneur de Don, the Seigneur de Morg, the Seigneur de Parghe, the Seigneur de Sausserg, the Seigneur de Samblourg, the Seigneur de Sumig, the Seigneur de Warssvich, the Seigneur de Plom, and many other knights and squires amounting to eleven thousand horse, eight thousand archers, and ten thousand foot.

THE AUTHOR: Also present was the Duke of Musgrave, under the King of Hungary's standard: *barry of eight, gules and argent*. He had a great company of dukes, princes, marquises, counts, viscounts, barons, knights banneret, knights bachelor, and other knights and squires whose names, to be brief, I shall not mention: in all, there were twelve thousand horse and twenty-two thousand foot. In the whole Christian army therefore there were some one hundred to one hundred and twenty thousand horse, which included thirty to forty thousand well-equipped knights and squires, and beyond that some one hundred and forty thousand to one hundred and fifty thousand archers and other good warriors.

THE AUTHOR:[138] On the Saracen side, however, was the largest army assembled since the time of Mohammed, [213] for it included all the sultans, kings, and lords of the three principal regions: that is, of Asia Major, which has six provinces, India, Persia, Syria, Egypt, Assyria, and Asia. That part of India is bordered by the southern sea that some called the Black Sea and others the "Mer Battue" because it is constantly rough, day and night, because of the seven thousand five hundred and forty-eight islands there, one of which is very large and has ten cities. The major city is called Gelbona, and in that city are great quantities of gold and precious stones, and there are more elephants there than anywhere else on earth. That island was formerly converted to Christianity by Saint Thomas the Apostle, but the greater part of the country is today peopled by infidels.[139]

THE AUTHOR: Those from the second region of the Saracens were from Persia, or rather Turkey, which has several provinces: that is, Africa, Media, Persia, and Mesopotamia; in this last was the great city of Nineveh, which it takes three days to cross, and which is now called Babylon. And in that city were built the foundations of the Tower of Babel, which itself is four thousand paces across, and there too are the provinces of Chaldea, Araby, Sheba, and Tarsus. And in Tarsus is the Mount Sinai to which the angels took my lady Saint Catherine's body, which now lies in the church of Sainte Marie de Rubo, very close to Mount Sinai.[140]

THE AUTHOR: Those from the third region of the Saracens were from Syria, in which we find the provinces of Damascus, Antioch, and Phoenicia, where once were found Tyre and Sidon; there too [214] is Mount Lebanon, from which springs the River Jordan, and there also are the cities of Palestine, of Judea, of Jerusalem, of Samaria, of Gabeste, of Galilee, and of Nazareth. And in that land were the two cities of Sodom and Gomorrah that were swallowed up in the abyss because of their most abominable sins. And from the three regions I have described, there came to the great battle so many kings, so many lords, and so many warriors that the whole land was covered; their intention, as I have said, was to conquer the whole of the rest of the world. I shall name some of these Saracen lords later.

THE AUTHOR: And when the day set for the battle arrived, and when all the Christian lords were drawn up on the field, having early that morning heard a high and solemn sung Mass celebrated by the Archbishop of Cologne—this meant that they were all in a state of grace, as good Christians should be—and having heard absolution given by the Cardinal of Ostia, the papal legate, and having asked pardon one of another, those who wished to break their fast did so; then, when all of them had mounted their horses and taken their places in the ranks, Saintré, on his destrier, went to the King of Bohemia. Then, in the King's presence, he drew his sword, and, in the name of God, of Our Lady, and of Saint Denis, he asked and requested that the King confer on him the order of knighthood. The good King, who was very fond of Jean himself and all Frenchmen, was delighted to bestow on him the accolade and the order of chivalry, praying God that He would give Jean all the honor and the joy that he could wish. And from that time onward Jean was universally called the *Seigneur* de Saintré. At that point anyone who wished to be dubbed knight came forward. Many banners were raised at the point, and many points were clipped from pennons.[141] [215] And when this had all been done, and when everyone had returned to his post, then all the army made the sign of the Cross and rode off.

The battle order

In the name of God and Our Lady . . . ! It had been decided that the vanguard should be assigned to the banner of France, to the banner of the Teutonic Order (*argent a cross sable*), to those of the five prelates, and to those of certain German dukes, counts, princes, and barons, and to those of the English: that would be a total of some thirteen thousand horse, and would include four thousand of the finest knights and squires. The King of Bohemia and his cohort, which consisted of ten thousand horse, would be on the right flank of the army. The left flank was under the command of the Duke of Lithuania, bearing the standard of the King of Poland that had been entrusted to him, and in command of some eleven thousand horse. The banner of Our Lady was borne by Gadiffer de La Sale, as he had done once before, and the main body of the army, the center, consisted of the banners of the four Emperors—of Germany, Constantinople, Trebizond, and Bulgaria—along with those of the other dukes, princes, barons, and knights banneret: that provided twenty-five to thirty thousand horse, all excellent fighting men. The rear guard was assigned to the Duke of Musgrave, under the standard of the King of Hungary, and to his knights, around twelve thousand horse. The sixty thousand foot would be divided into two equal divisions, one on the left and one on the right flank, and would be stationed somewhat to the fore of the vanguard, and on its left and right flanks. They had strict orders not to break ranks and overtake each other, and those who were not armed with bows were each to carry a pavise* painted with a great white cross. And those on foot [216] with pavises were to halt whenever the banner stopped, and give cover to the archers. And when all sections of the army had been drawn up, and when all the men had broken their fast, and when they had been inspired for battle by their commanders and princes, so much so that no previous army had ever been in such good heart, then they advanced in step, in good array, across the plain of Bellehoch.[142] Very soon thereafter they met up with their scouts, who brought excellent news about the enemy's dispositions. And when the cavalry was about a league from the enemy position, it halted to allow the infantry to catch up, and assigned men to scout out the enemy's ranks; they reported that the enemy had no more than three divisions, drawn up in close formation, and with no cavalry to protect the two flanks, which were largely made up of the common people.

The battle order of the Saracens

The Saracens had established six divisions, that is, three mounted and three on foot; the infantry were to follow up the mounted knights and go into battle behind them to kill those who were unhorsed and to slash off the legs and feet of the Christians and their horses; in the vanguard was to be the Grand Turk of Persia, at that time a certain Abzin, whose banner bore *gules, with in bend a Turkish scimitar argent, emmanché azure, hilt and pommel Or*, who was so proud of and confident in his great forces—some thirty to forty thousand horse and more than one hundred thousand foot— that he had no respect for the Christians. And in the second division came Zizaach, who called himself Emperor of Carthage, and whose banner bore *sable, two horses' heads couped Or addorsed*, and Almoch, [217] Sultan of Babylon, whose banner bore simply *Or*, and Azachul, Sultan of Mabaloch. Their forces totaled sixty thousand horse and one hundred and sixty thousand foot. In the third division were the kings of Greater Armenia, Fez, Aleppo, and the Lord of Wallachia, named Bagazul; these lords had forty thousand horse and three hundred thousand to four hundred thousand foot, coming from Armenia, Barbary, Russia, Sarmatia, and Tartary, so many that all the earth was covered.

Here begins the battle

And when the two armies had advanced until they were about a bow-shot's length apart, the Turk halted his division to check the battle order of the Christian army and to allow time for his own troops and their horses to catch their breath. But then, when he saw that the vanguard was holding firm and that fire from the cannons and culverins,* longbows and crossbows on the two flanks of the Christian army was taking a great toll on his own forces, he decided to change his battle plan and sent to have the foot soldiers who were behind him divided into two sections, and ordered both sections to attack the two divisions of archers. But when the foot soldiers found themselves so desperately under attack, not one of them dared to advance, and all of them retreated. Then the Turk, in a desperate move, ordered his banners to advance, and the army rode at full gallop toward the vanguard, shouting their battle cries.

Then the French, shouting their own battle cry, "Jesus! Our Lady! Montjoie! Saint Denis!" ordered the King's banner to advance, and all the other banners followed suit and galloped forward at the best pace the destriers could manage; the two sides clashed together with such violence that the Seigneur de Saintré, [218] who was fully armed and mounted on his destrier, both horse and rider richly caparisoned in cloth of gold emblazoned with Saintré's arms, Saintré himself having an elaborate helmet crest designed to be visible to all, by great good fortune struck the Grand Turk with his lance through his beaver flap* so hard that the whole lance point penetrated the steel, and the force of the blow tossed the Turk from his horse, stone dead.

At that point the battle began, fierce and furious, for few of the Saracens had so far understood that their lord was dead. Then you might have seen men and horses tumble and fall in heaps, and heard deafening cries. But when the Seigneur de Saintré realized that he had lost his lance, he seized his sword and struck right and left so ferociously that none of the Turks dared to withstand him. But when he attempted to approach the Turkish banner, he was attacked on all sides with such brutality that had it not been for God's help, and had he not had rapid assistance, he would certainly have been killed. But the King's banner that followed him closely everywhere was

guarded by good and brave Frenchmen and others who fought with marvelous courage and made the enemy pay dear—although it would take too long
to name all the combatants and describe their deeds; after all, if I mentioned
the deeds of some and not of others, I would make myself resented, so I beg
all my readers to excuse my silence. On the other hand, I do need to say
more about the Seigneur de Saintré, whose particular story this is.

When the said Seigneur de Saintré had freed himself in this way from
the press, he spurred his destrier toward [219] the Turk who was holding the
banner, and struck him so hard with his sword that the banner fell to the
ground. The other Turks, who were fighting in expectation of reinforcement,
were defending themselves with the greatest courage. And as this ferocious
battle was raging, the two sultans rode up, but when they saw the Grand
Turk's banner on the ground they halted to discuss which part of the battle
they should enter and what they should do. The Turks, unable any longer to
withstand the Christian charge on foot and on horse, broke ranks and fell
back; at that point, the two sultans broke into a full gallop and came to their
support, summoning the third division to their aid and assistance.

At that point it was time to come to the support, aid, and assistance of
our vanguard, which was weary and exhausted; the King of Bohemia with
his army on one flank of the battle, along with the Duke of Lithuania with
his army on the other, charged with such violence that they swept up to the
enemies' banners, one of which was thrown to the ground. And when the
enemy foot, coming up behind, saw their banner on the ground, not one of
them dared to advance. When the commanders of the third division, the
Kings of Greater Armenia, of Fez, of Morocco, of Aleppo, and the Lord of
Wallachia, saw that the first two divisions were defeated although they had
not yet engaged the main body of the Christian army, nor the rear guard,
nor the two flanks of foot, they were greatly dismayed. However, since they
had after all come to give battle and since they still had a powerful army of
foot and horse, [220] they concluded that they should engage the Christians
as quickly as possible.

And when the main body of the Christian army saw the final enemy
division advancing toward them, the princes who were in command and who
had not so far engaged the enemy sent word to the rear guard that once they
saw battle engaged, they should move up quickly to take the enemy on the
flank, for on that open plain there was no cover, no woods or valleys where
an army could lie in ambush. This command was followed to the letter. And
once these commands were understood, all were ready for the attack: there

ensued a battle that was ferocious, punishing, and deadly, which might have
had terrible consequences for the Christians save that the rear guard, shouting
their battle cry "Our Lady!" or, in the case of the King of Hungary, "Saint
Lancelot!" advanced at full gallop, their lances lowered, striking to right and
left, while the archers on the flanks fired into the throng of that accursed
rabble. And when the Saracens felt themselves under close attack, they broke
and fled.

Then there was a great slaughter, for the enemy were as defenseless as
sheep. But the enemy horse resisted for longer, and might indeed have held
out for some time, given their sheer numbers, if the rear guard had not come
up and routed them more quickly than might otherwise have been the case.
In this attack their banners were thrown to the ground, and the few of them
who could by God's grace flee took to their heels. At that point there was
such slaughter that there had been nothing comparable since the Battle of
Pharsalus, where Pompey was defeated. There were killed the Emperor of
Carthage, the two Sultans of Babylon [221] and of Mabaloch, Bazul[143] the
Grand Turk, and the Lord of Wallachia; there were captured the Kings of
Morocco and Aleppo; and there were so many lords killed and captured that
I must cut short the story. The pursuit lasted more than six leagues, and only
when night fell did our men halt and take shelter in the marshes beside a
lake[144] and at the edge of a forest, and there they rested and rested their
horses, which were exhausted by the chase. They also tended to the wounds
of men and horses, until early the following morning when scouts went
round the battlefield to find the bodies of those who had died.

And when they got to the field, they found among the dead a great many
wounded Saracens who held up their hands in surrender, but all of them were
put to death. And then the scouts picked out all the Christians—recognizable
because of the different-colored crosses that they wore—and those who were
still alive were carried into the army positions and then into neighboring
towns for their wounds to be tended; and those who were dead were buried
with full honors and full mourning, and with all due solemnity. And the
French lords set an excellent example, for all of them dressed in solid black,
and they were much praised by all for the love that they showed their men.

THE AUTHOR: News of this most holy victory spread everywhere, as fast
as if it had been carried by Perseus on Pegasus the flying horse, and everyone
wrote home to his own lands to describe what had happened. Among all the
deeds of valor that had been performed, everyone made much of those of a
new young French knight called the Seigneur de Saintré; [222] the word

spread everywhere, and particularly the news that at the first attack, he had killed the Grand Turk and swept him off his horse, and that he had, through his remarkable bravery, done such feats of arms as to throw the banner of the Grand Turk to the ground, and that he had performed so many other marvelous feats of arms that it was impossible to list them.

THE AUTHOR: And when this most holy news became known everywhere, all true Christians gathered and ran to their churches, ordering the bells rung, in order to give thanks to Our Lord; foremost among the princes of Christendom, the King of France mounted his horse and went to the cathedral to give thanks to God and Our Lady, and to Saint Denis.[145] And very soon thereafter Anjou King of Arms, who had been present at the battle, came to the court to describe in person how matters had transpired, and the countless valiant deeds of the knights of his kingdom, living and dead, and especially those of the Seigneur de Saintré as they had been outlined in all the written dispatches. When the King had heard precisely what had happened, he said: "Ah, dear God be praised . . . ! Have mercy on those who have died in your service." And because of his delight in this excellent news, he gave the King of Arms his own gown and a reward of three hundred *écus*. Then there was universal rejoicing at court and throughout the city, as one might imagine—except of course for those ladies and damsels and others who had lost their loved ones. And here I shall leave aside these things, and return to the said Seigneur de Saintré. [223]

After the Seigneur de Saintré and his noble and chivalrous company had arrived at Saint-Denis, and had completed their devotions in the church, they were escorted into the city of Paris by the three dukes mentioned above, and by so many others that scarcely a single soul remained at court. And they rode into the city in the very same order in which they had ridden out, and dismounted in the courtyard of the Hôtel Saint-Pol;[146] only missing were the banners of the dead, and those of the Seigneur de Châtel-Fremont and of the others who were still lying wounded; the Seigneur de Maulevrier was chosen by common consent to replace Châtel-Fremont and carry the King's banner.

Then was the greatest honor paid and the greatest welcome given to all by the lords and others at court. And when the company came into the presence of the King and the Queen, and Madame and the rest of the royal household, they bowed low to the King. The King, to honor them and because of his joy in their victory, rose to his feet and took one or two steps forward, and then delightedly touched all their hands. And as the King made the rounds so that everyone could touch his hand, the Seigneur de Saintré and the others bowed to the Queen, to Madame, and to all the ladies present, who were jubilantly celebrating their return, except, again, those who had lost lovers and relatives.

When everyone had made their bows and the ladies and maidens had all been greeted with a kiss, the King sat back down on his throne and said to them all: "My friends, praise the Lord and his blessed Mother that you have returned in such honor and in such joy. May God pardon the souls of those who have not returned [224] and who—just as our holy faith would have us believe—have been saved. But so that our Lord may deliver their souls from the pains of purgatory and bring them to rest in his most glorious realm of paradise, we wish and command that at vespers we all assemble at Notre Dame, where we will have vespers and vigils said for the dead; and tomorrow, we shall order that the priest pronounce the liturgy and the Solemn Mass for the Dead. And from every altar of the church—for as many as there are priests to preside—the Requiem Mass will be recited. And I request that we all be there; we wish and command this service to be performed for thirty straight days; and beyond this, we order, in perpetuity, an anniversary Mass on the same day that these true martyrs spent their last days in the service of the Lord." And so it was done. And now I will cease to speak of these things and will tell how Madame, greatly desiring to speak to the Seigneur de Saintré, made her signal to him, and how he responded with his own.

THE AUTHOR: That evening, once all this had been done, the King, the Queen, my lords the King's brothers, and the ladies went to great lengths to entertain the knights, especially the Seigneur de Saintré. Madame was more reserved than the others; nonetheless, overjoyed as she was, she could not refrain from approaching Saintré and saying, "Seigneur de Saintré, after these ladies have entertained you, let's at least have our turn to see you. We remember when you were considered a most courteous squire. Could it be that your great exploits and the fact that you're now called 'Seigneur' and have been recently knighted have changed you?" [225]

As she spoke, she took her pin and gave her signal; the Seigneur de Saintré replied immediately with a smile, "My lady, whatever may have happened to me and despite what I've become since you last saw me, I'm still exactly the same person that I was before."

Then, since everyone was present, Madame and Saintré spoke of other things until it was time for supper. Once the tables had been cleared away, a few guests suggested dancing. But when the King and Queen heard this, they forbade singing or dancing out of respect for those who had died in combat, which was certainly no cause for joy. Instead, the King called for the spices and the parting cup, since everyone had to be at church early the next morning.

THE AUTHOR AGAIN: When the King was in his chamber, the Seigneur de Saintré laughingly said to him, "Your Majesty, to celebrate our safe arrival, I beg you to sleep with the Queen tonight."

The King, who was an extremely gracious prince and who dearly loved Saintré, replied with a laugh, "You've always been, and will be, very gracious—and always on behalf of the ladies! Out of great affection for you, I intend to do so."

Saintré, laughing, then approached the Queen and said, "You owe me at least a big thank-you."

"And why Saintré, should I be so grateful?"

"First thank me, Ma'am, and then I'll tell you."

"I shall not," she retorted. "You would just make fun of me."

"My lady, I promise that this is something that will please both you and the King as well as me; don't you trust me?" [226]

"Yes, I do," she said, "and since you say so, I'll say a hearty 'Thank you.'"

Then the Seigneur de Saintré said, "My lady, enjoy yourself, because I hope that tonight, if it hasn't already happened, you'll conceive a very fine son—for in honor of our homecoming the King has granted me that he will sleep with you."

"Well, how kind you are!" said the Queen. "It's only been two days since I slept with him. Pray tell me, what moved you to make this request of the King?"

"I'll tell you, Ma'am. As you know, whenever a lord or lady arrives while children are in school, it is customary, at the visitor's request, to let the children go play."

"Heh!" she said. "Saintré, Saintré, you're hiding the real reason. Pray tell me the truth, sworn on your arms and by your love." She took him by the sleeve and said, "You won't get away from me until I know."

Then the Seigneur de Saintré, laughing, called Madame over and said, "My lady, please come help me. You can see that the Queen here is trying to pressure me." So he told her all about what he had asked the King to do and about what he told the Queen.

Then Madame said to the Queen, "Oh, Ma'am, let him go, for he has told you the truth." "He has not," said the Queen. "He's hiding something else up his sleeve, for my lord the King told me yesterday that he was looking forward to his arrival to have a good word with him. The Seigneur de Saintré has dreamed up this scheme as an excuse to be somewhere else."

Madame, who feared that their laughter and signals might have raised suspicions—in the way that truth always gives rise to fear—in an attempt to cover up their intentions, said to the Seigneur de Saintré, [227] "Well now, sir. Would you really be trying to do such a thing? In my opinion, you must tell her the truth before she lets you go."

So Jean said, "Do you promise, my ladies, that if I tell you, you'll let me go?"

"Yes, certainly," said the Queen.

"And you, my lady, do you promise the same as the Queen?"

Then he told them, "Your Majesty, we only finished our exploits about a month or six weeks ago, which is why the King wants me to spend the whole night talking to him. But I would rather sleep and rest. That's the reason that I tried to get away from him, my lady."

"Ah," said the Queen. "This time I believe you."

Then Madame said, signaling to him once again, "Really, Ma'am, I think he's telling the truth this time. You can certainly let him go now."

THE AUTHOR: And when the most desired hour had come that Madame and her lover could speak together at leisure—what can I tell you?—there were kisses given and kisses returned, for they could not get enough of each other. There were the kinds of questions and answers that Love desired and commanded. The lovers remained in this most agreeable state of pleasure until they had to part. They could not return to such activities unless the Queen slept with the King, which they endeavored to do each time the King sought his own pleasures. What more can I tell you? Madame and the Seigneur de Saintré continued like this for fifteen months. But now I will stop talking about their love, which was so loyal and so secret that no love affair in the world has ever been more faithful and or so well conducted.

THE AUTHOR: It happened that fifteen months after the Seigneur de Saintré had returned from Prussia, on many occasions he mulled over a new idea, saying to himself, [228] "Alas! Look at how lacking in sense, in ideas, and in every good quality you are! You've never taken up any feat of arms that your very noble, sweet goddess hasn't set you up for. Now, really, I've come to the conclusion and I've decided that for love of her I would like to accomplish some worthy deed on my own account."

So he conceived a plan to engage five knights, of whom he would be one, and five squires—the most powerful and the best in arms that he could find in France. He would require them to be his companions and brothers for three years, wearing a visor on their light helmets—gold for the knights and silver for the squires—to which, between the two eye slits, would be affixed a precious diamond. The company would remain together until they found the same number of knights and squires to fight with them *a outrance,* each one defending his diamond, with their adversaries also putting similar diamonds at stake. He decided to tell no one about this plan until the last day of April, when he would make his request known to the knights and squires he had chosen.

Once he had deliberated about all this, he sent off to Florence a pattern of golden visors painted on linen, to be transferred and embroidered on white silk; this motif would be used to decorate their gowns and their horses' caparisons; and the same motif would appear embroidered on lengths of fine white damask; and in the same way, silver visors would be embroidered on the squires' gowns and on their horses' trappings. He also sent secretly for pure white horses, the most beautiful and spirited that could be had; he had these delivered to a certain secret place, where they were hidden away. Then he had ten of the most beautiful new hats made, plumed with ostrich feathers, embroidered with the same pattern, with gold embroidery for the knights and silver embroidery for the squires. [229]

Once the embroidered silk fabric had been received from Florence and the ten horses had been procured, Saintré had the gowns I described tailored to fit the bodies of people of similar build to those whom he would invite. And for the horses he had ten very lovely accoutrements made, with great white silken borders embroidered with alternating golden and silver threads—all of this done in the greatest secrecy.

When the last day of April came, he summoned to supper the Seigneur de Pressigny, the Seigneur de Bueil, the Seigneur de Mailly, and Messire Hugh de Craon, with himself as the fifth of the knights; he invited the Seigneur de Genly, the Seigneur de Moy, the Seigneur de Herly, the Seigneur des Barres, and the Seigneur de Clermont as squires; he entertained them all in fine style in his mansion. And when the tablecloths had been removed, before the tables had been removed, they all said grace. Then Jean called the servant who looked after his chamber and had him bring forth a little chest.

Then he dismissed everyone else from the room to go have supper, and he said laughingly to those who remained, "My lords and my brothers, please forgive me if I've been too presumptuous in the things I intend to say to you, for by my faith, I consider myself the least of those who are gathered here. What I have in mind and what I'm about to say to you has been conceived only to increase your honor, as all noble hearts should desire to do. I've chosen you above all others in the kingdom to be brothers and companions in a chivalric enterprise—to accomplish worthy feats of arms for the love of our ladies and for our own honor. Now then, my lords and brothers, what do you have to say about this?" [230]

At this, they all looked joyfully at each other to see who would have the honor of being the first to reply, each saying, "Answer him!" and "No, you answer him!"

At last, it was the Seigneur de Genly who spoke first. "Monseigneur de Saintré, each may speak as he wishes, but it seems to me that such a noble proposition deserves a prompt reply. For my part, with the help of God and Our Lady, I'll accept your offer, with thanks for having chosen me to be part of such a small, select group."

Then each of the others put himself forward as best as he could, although a few did not feel themselves worthy of Saintré's invitation. But so valiant, gentle, and courteous were his attentions, as you have heard, well beyond anyone's expectations, that there was no one who would not have given his life for him—and all the more so because the King esteemed him above all others, which made each knight or squire especially eager to please him.

Then, thanking them all as best he could, Saintré opened his chest and gave each one his visor, all made in the same fashion, and distributed the diamonds, telling them, "Now my lords and brothers, in the name of God the Father, the Son and the Holy Ghost, as well as the blessed Virgin, his daughter and mother, I give you these tokens to accept on condition that each of us wear these emblems on our left shoulder for three years. During those three years, we'll seek continuously to find an equal number of worthy knights and squires who will engage us in combat with thrusting lances and poleaxes, with swords and rapiers, to the point where one opponent will have lost all four weapons or have been brought to the ground. [231] And if God brings us defeat, we'll each be ready to give up the diamond from our visor; if our opponents lose, they'll each give up a diamond similar to ours. To be delivered from our vows, we'll send messengers to the King of the Romans, and then to England, and to wherever else we might find the best opponents; you can count on me to take care of this. I'll also approach our King for financial support."

Then they all outdid themselves in thanking him. "And to acquit ourselves honorably and accomplish our duty as best we can, I advise that each
of you go to see his lady, asking her to be the first to place your token on
your left shoulder, fixing it only by hand, without any other attachment,
until the day that we're all wearing them. But to make our exploit even more
novel,[147] I pray that you show up at four in the morning, when we'll go to
wake up the King and the Queen, who will be sleeping together, and, if it
pleases them, we'll lead them out to the May festivities."

Everyone was just as happy with this plan as they could be.

Then the Seigneur de Moy spoke up. "Alas! What if someone doesn't
have his lady's permission?"

"Well, my good brother Moy," said Saintré, "he'll have all the more
reason to beseech her earnestly for her grace and mercy. For unless she's the
haughtiest of ladies, she would never refuse such a worthy request." [232]

Then they all took leave of each other and went off to their ladies as
described. And now I shall stop talking about these lords and their ladies and
shall tell how the Seigneur de Saintré was received by his lady.

That night, which was the eve of the first of May, after the King had
taken the spices and the parting cup, the Seigneur de Saintré approached the
Queen and then called Madame, and said laughing to the Queen, "What
will you give me, Ma'am, if I arrange for you to sleep with the King tonight?"

"Ha, my lord," said the Queen, laughing. "I would give you no thanks
for it."

While laughing at her answer, Saintré made his signal to Madame, who
knew perfectly well why he wanted the Queen to sleep with the King. She
immediately answered him with her own signal.

When the King was in bed, the Seigneur de Saintré followed the customary practice for princes, princesses, lords, and noble ladies, which was that
their attendants brought holy water to their bed, the stewards serving their
lords, and the ladies-in-waiting their ladies. This practice is today considered
shameful by some people, and they perform it badly, influenced as they are
by the devil. Once the holy water had been administered, Saintré retired to
his room, where he waited until the highly desired hour that he and Madame
could be together. Then they kissed and kissed again, all the while playing,
conversing, and making up games that the God of Love ordered them to
play. [233]

And after they had been together like this for a long time, the Seigneur
de Saintré fell to his knees and said to Madame, "Ah, my goddess on high

without peer, as deeply and as humbly as I can, I beseech your grace, pardon, mercy, and compassion."

"For what reason, my dear?" asked Madame.

"My lady," he replied, "ever since I first became your humble serf and faithful servant, I have never been so bold as to undertake an *emprise* for you on my own. All the chivalric deeds I've undertaken or in which I've been involved have been at your command, following your counsel and good advice. And for this reason, I recognize that I have seriously failed and fallen short. But I know that it's better to act late than never, so I humbly beseech and entreat you, Madame, that with your hand on my left shoulder, you place this *emprise* that I carry as one of ten knights for love of you, just as all my companions have done with the good graces of their ladies, who are so and so, and so and so . . ." and he named all his companions, each in turn. As he spoke, he took from his sleeve his *emprise,* which was wrapped in a fine linen kerchief; he moved forward to kiss her as he presented it.

Madame was furious when she heard these words and refused to let him approach. She said, "So you have devised a chivalric *emprise* and publicized it without my knowledge and permission? Never as long as I live will I have any more love for you."

Was he stunned by Madame's reply? He certainly was, for he had no idea if she spoke in jest or in anger. [234] So he looked at her more closely, and when he realized that she was angry, he said, "Alas, my lady, this is sorry news, that I should be punished for trying to do a good deed, I who have loved you so long and so loyally, who have given my heart, my body, my honor, and my life to obey you. And now, just as I was about to act in your service, to increase your grace and my honor, must I lose the one to whom I have been so devoted? Alas, my most esteemed and incomparable lady, have mercy on your servant and find it in your heart to pardon me just this time. And if ever I should fail you again, may I be harshly punished."

Then Madame said to him, "Go immediately to your companions and call off your *emprise.*"

"Alas, my lady, how could I do that? Our undertaking is so far along that it's a matter of life or death if I don't pursue it. Please understand that if it were possible, I would do so, for you're the one to whom I owe the greatest obedience; therefore, my lady, on my knees and with my hands clasped, I beg most humbly that you pardon me gladly and willingly, and that you place my *emprise* on my shoulder. Don't worry about the rest. I have faith that God and Our Lady will bring us a favorable outcome."

At these words, Madame reluctantly took the token and placed it on his left shoulder and then half-heartedly allowed him to kiss her. Then, as it was growing late, he took his leave of her most humbly, and departed. And now I shall cease speaking about Madame and shall talk about the arrival of Saintré's nine companions, and of how they assembled at his home.

How the nine companions came before the King the next morning

[235] THE AUTHOR: The next day, the first of May, the nine companions arrived at Saintré's home by early morning. To make a long story short, after they had all heard Mass, the Seigneur de Saintré invited them all to his chamber. Then he gave each knight a silk gown, with the emblem embroidered with gold or silver, as you have heard. He had the ten plumed hats brought forth—beautiful and striking indeed—and then gave each one a golden or silver belt to fasten his gown, which amazed everyone. Then he called for the visors and attached them himself to the left shoulders of his companions; he laughingly asked how each had fared in obtaining his lady's consent. Alas! He spoke not a word about his own lady or about the hidden pain that he bore within his own sad heart.

When the moment came to sally forth from the mansion, there were the ten white horses, superb and frisky, that he had had secretly purchased. The horses were all adorned in the same silken cloth as the knights' gowns; and the saddle skirts were trimmed with silver visor motifs, golden for the knights and silver for the squires, as were the bridles. Then Saintré picked up three dice and called out, "To each his chance! Whoever rolls the highest will have first choice of a horse."

Each companion then thanked Saintré as best he could, and they all said to each other, "There has never been anyone like him."

And as each mounted his horse, he was provided with the same new spurs, which were golden for the knights and silver for the squires; the straps were of woven silk,[148] such as they used to wear in the good old days. [236]

Then you should have seen them sally forth from the mansion, the horses bounding forward and curveting, the men calling out, shouting, each one galloping along and rushing ahead—there has never been a more joyous spectacle! And so off they rode at a swift pace for the great court at Saint-Pol. Then each man's joy was redoubled, for they all knew very well that the King was in residence and already awake.

When the King heard the companions' ruckus, he woke the female attendants who were sleeping in his chamber so they could investigate the commotion. They went to the barred windows and immediately reported to the
King, "Ah! Sire! Sire! Come see this marvelous sight. We've never seen anything so beautiful."

The Queen, who was not asleep and was eager to see what was transpiring, said to the King, "Now, Monseigneur, let's go see what might be
happening."

Then the young ladies returned, so overcome with joy that they could
barely speak. The King and the Queen had themselves dressed, and then the
King, still in his nightcap, went to the great window, and the Queen
appeared at the latticed window. When the ten companions, who were singing and frolicking merrily, saw the King, they all ran toward him, and when
they saw the Queen next to him, they all cried out, "Sire! Sire! And you my
lady! We wish you a very fine day and a merry month of May." And the King
replied, "Good day, good day, my fine fellows."

Then the King and the Queen retired to finish dressing, and the ten companions dismounted and went to the chamber of the King, whom they found
accompanied by the servants who were dressing him. Then, on his knees, the
Seigneur de Saintré began to speak, saying [237] "Our sovereign prince, the
lords my brothers who are here and I, their companion, have today taken a
vow that with your kind leave and permission, we'll wear the *emprise* of arms
that you see here on our left shoulders for three years. You'll find further details
of our chivalric enterprise spelled out clearly in this letter. We very humbly
entreat you that it be your pleasure to permit us to undertake this exploit."

When the King heard the news and saw their *emprises* on their shoulders,
he was scarcely pleased, and so replied, "My friends, you're acting like someone who has married his cousin, and only asks for dispensation after the
wedding.[149] It's wrong for anyone to plan an exploit, and even worse to
execute it, without permission from one's lord or from someone empowered
to authorize it on his behalf. Strictly speaking, whoever does so, whatever
good may come of it, should be severely punished."

As he spoke, he took hold of their letter of arms, saying, "I shall see what
we have here. And as for you, Saintré, will you and your heart never cease to
undertake military exploits and expeditions? It seems to me that you have
done quite enough."

"Ah, sire," replied Saintré, "it's neither for my heart nor for my own sake
but rather for honor, in which you share, that we've been inspired to act."

And with this, the King was dressed and ready, and went off to Mass.

At these words, the King's brothers arrived and observed the ten companions smartly dressed and bearing their new *emprises*. They bowed before the knights and squires and then commended their deeds. But they added, "His Majesty is perfectly right about your *emprise*; even if you've now sought his leave and pleasure, you've misbehaved. It would be wrong of him to say otherwise. [238] We'll make an appeal to him when we see him."

The Queen appeared shortly after the King and the lords, and she received them with great joy; and afterward came Madame des Belles Cousines, who scarcely greeted them at all. Then everyone went off to High Mass; you should have seen the ladies, damsels, knights, and squires who looked on in amazement at the companions.

When the King was in his chamber, he called my lords his three brothers and showed them the letter of arms, and then asked for advice. To come to the point, it was concluded that the King would give them permission this time, but that they would incur the King's wrath and punishment if they or anyone else tried to embark on a similar enterprise without permission ever again. The companions all came forward in great humility to offer thanks to the King.

When the festivities had ended, Saintré and his companions worked ceaselessly to outfit themselves in fine form; they had matching gowns made for each of them for every day of the week, and had all their attendants and their horses dressed in the same livery, which was a beautiful thing to see. What more can I say? The entire kingdom was abuzz with the news. While they were preparing their wardrobes, Saintré and his companions ordered that a very eloquent letter of arms be drawn up, addressed to the Emperor's court, the highest court of all: the letter was given immediately to Normandy King of Arms to convey. But now I will stop talking about these matters for a while, to return to the rest of my subject.

How the King spoke to Saintré and what gifts he gave to his retinue

[239] THE AUTHOR: While they were outfitting themselves as you have heard, the King, who dearly loved Saintré, said, "Saintré, whatever moved you to undertake this exploit without my permission? Where are the sealed letters containing promises from Fortune, who has done so much for you in the past, assuring you that she would not abandon you? Furthermore, don't

you fear the wrath of Our Lord, who forbids us to undertake such vain deeds? And if he has enriched you so much, you should be all the more beholden to him, and you should beware of offending him, if you're a good Christian. However, since this exploit has become such public knowledge that you can't back down, I'll give you leave this time. But I forbid you ever to do such a thing again!"

"Ah, sire," said Saintré, "please forgive me."

"I forgive you with all my heart," said the King. "Now, where are you intending to take up arms?"

"Sire, we intend to announce our call to arms at the Emperor's court, and if we don't find anyone there willing to meet our challenge, we'll take our letter to England. We hope that one of these two courts will accept the challenge."

"Well, then," said the King. "What kind of equipment will you have, and how many people? Will you all have a common purse? If not, what will the arrangements be?"

When the King had the answers to these questions, he told Saintré, "I'll give you four thousand *écus*, and fifteen hundred *écus* to each of your companions." And the Queen gave him fifteen hundred *écus*, a length of deep crimson velvet and one hundred marks' worth of silver plate; she gave six hundred *écus* and a length of gray velvet to each of the knights, and to each of the squires a length of gray damask. And my lords the dukes each gave him fifteen hundred *écus* and forty marks of silver plate, and to all the others six hundred *écus* apiece. [240]

The time for departure came quickly, and when the day arrived, all the champions came in a group to take leave of the King and Queen, and of the lords and ladies. I shall skip over the fine speeches and words of thanks that were exchanged to speak about the secret laments, tears, and very anguished sighs that Madame made over her lover's departure. Although it displeased her more than ever, it was necessary for Saintré to leave. I shall now stop talking about their departure and their trip to the Emperor's court to speak of Madame's doleful existence—and about another, new event.

On Madame's great sorrow and her departure from the court

THE AUTHOR: Madame, abandoned by her lover, had no heart for finding pleasure in tilting, jousts, dances, hunts, or other entertainments. Whenever she saw pairs of lovers or couples enjoying themselves, grief flooded back into her heart. She became so immersed in this melancholy existence that she gave up eating and drinking for fasting, and sleeping for staying awake, so much so that little by little, to everyone's amazement, her rosy complexion turned sallow. Seeing Madame so ill-disposed, so pale and pensive, the Queen asked her repeatedly what the matter might be. "Ma'am," she replied, "it's nothing. As you know, we women are ill when we like."

"That's true," said the Queen, "yet we're often ill when we do not like. [241] But, as best you can, fair cousin, tell us what is wrong with you and where it hurts and what we can do to help—for you can be sure that we'll try to do our very best."

"Ah, my very sweet lady, I thank you most humbly." With these words, their conversation ended. But the Queen, who was very fond of Madame, did not hesitate to call for her physician, Master Hugh of Fisol, a most expert doctor and philosopher. Informed by the Queen about Madame's illness, he ordered her to remain where she was, so that he could visit her the following morning, and so the matter rested. The next morning, when Master Hugh had surveyed the situation he found her physically healthy—free from headaches, fevers, and other ailments. But her heart harbored sadness within that left her in mortal danger, unless a remedy could be quickly found: all the vital spirits emanating from the heart could be killed by that acute anguish, and they were already almost extinguished. Yet he comforted her as best he could and said, "My lady, with respect to your health, I find that your body is in fine shape, but your heart is not. Such an overwhelming secret sorrow lies buried there, that if you don't soon find a remedy, you'll fall into an illness from which it will be difficult to recover. Therefore, my lady, forget your sadness, and I'll take care of the rest."

What Madame told Master Hugh and how he comforted her

When Madame heard Master Hugh speak so accurately about her sorrow, she told him, "Master Hugh, woe is me! I have only one pain in my heart, and only your words can help me. [242] If indeed you were to offer me such comfort, I should be forever in your debt, and I would also give you a fine scarlet mantel."

When Master Hugh heard about the scarlet mantel, he replied very merrily, "Madame, please give your order. I'll do anything I can to help you."

"Truly, Master Hugh," said Madame, "we are most grateful for that. Physicians are like confessors: what I'm about to tell you will in no way dishonor you or embarrass you, and I pray that you keep it a secret."

"Madame, you may speak boldly, I promise never to breathe a word of what you tell me."

"Well, Master Hugh, I'd like to let you know that my heart's malady and distress come from nothing other than the desire to spend two or three months at our country estate. This is a matter of great urgency, for we haven't been there in sixteen years or more, and our affairs there have suffered from our absence. Yet I'm sure that if my lady the Queen knew that this was my own idea, she wouldn't be at all pleased with it."

"Just so, my lady!" said Master Hugh. "I'll see to this. Cheer up—you'll be able to leave; I know just the way to arrange for it. But you must remain in your room for three or four days and leave the rest up to me."

Master Hugh went to the Queen and said, "Ma'am, I have just seen Madame your cousin." "Alas," said the Queen, "dear Master Hugh, how is she doing?" "Madame, if I may speak in confidence, I see only one remedy." "Alas! What are you saying, and what remedy might that be?"

"For the love of God, Ma'am, she must relax and enjoy herself in her native region for two or three months." [243] "Ah, and if she went there, would she be cured?" Master Hugh replied, "Yes, I hope to God that will be the case, Ma'am. I'm going to think about what her diet should be and about what elixirs would provide some comfort."

The Queen immediately went to see Madame, whom she found lying in bed. The Queen comforted her cousin as best she could, telling her in particular that she would be cured if she retired to her own domain, as Master Hugh had suggested, and that for heaven's sake she should brighten up and get ready to go to wherever she pleased, so that she could recover her health and be cured. Madame sought no other medicine than to flee the dismay that she felt in her heart when she saw other lovers dancing, singing, playing, and conversing even as she realized that she could do none of these things until her lover returned; she was much consoled by the idea of her departure. To come to the point, as soon as she could, she took her leave of the King, the Queen, and my noble lords, the King's brothers; she said farewell to everyone and then left. But when she took her leave of the Queen, the Queen only gave her permission to be away for two months, and made her promise to return if she had regained her health by then. So Madame took leave and departed.

How Madame arrived at her manor house and how everyone came to celebrate her arrival

THE AUTHOR: Now, we must not divulge the name of the region, estate, or manor house to which Madame traveled. The story remains silent about these points for many reasons that will become evident later. But let us imagine that her principal residence was located one league from a well-known city and another league from an abbey that had been founded by her ancestors. And that Abbey was located another league from the aforementioned city, so that the city, Madame's residence, and the abbey were situated as if they were at the points of a triangle. [244]

On Madame's arrival and the joy and warm welcome of the local residents

THE AUTHOR: When the news of Madame's arrival in her manor house spread throughout the region, lords and ladies, squires and damsels, and townspeople and their wives all came to see her; their visits gradually caused her great sorrow to diminish. And now I'll leave this topic for a while to speak of Madame's stay, and I shall speak about the Abbey and about the Lord Abbot.

This speaks of Lord Abbot and his Abbey

THE AUTHOR: As I've said, this Abbey (which will remain unnamed here) had been founded by Madame's ancestors. They executed so many fine works there that it is today one of the ten most prominent abbeys in France. The Lord Abbot at the time was the son of a very rich burgher from the city; his father had bestowed so many gifts on the Abbey that through his own donations, through the entreaties of the local noblemen, and also through the influence of his friends at the Court of Rome,[150] his son was named abbot. This son was twenty-five years old, tall and strong, and talented in wrestling, jumping, casting the bar or throwing the stone, and playing tennis; there was no monk, knight, squire, or townsman who could beat him in tennis when he had the leisure to play. What more can I tell you? He devoted himself to all these activities lest he be reproached as idle. He distributed gifts so generously and freely that he was beloved and highly esteemed by all good fellows.

When Lord Abbot learned of Madame's arrival, he was delighted. [245]
He had one of his carts loaded with thick haunches of venison, with boars'
heads and sides of wild boar, with hares, rabbits, pheasants, partridges, fat
capons, poultry, pigeons, and a barrel of Beaune wine, and sent it to be presented to Madame, with his entreaties that she accept it. When Madame saw
this handsome gift, you need not ask if she was delighted; she commanded that
the bearer of gifts be warmly received and that Lord Abbot be thanked.

At this time, it was very nearly Lent, and the Abbey was busy with
confessions and pardons on Mondays, Wednesdays, and Fridays during Lent.
Madame, inspired by great piety, decided to go there, once the great press
and crowd of people had dispersed after the first two weeks. She let Lord
Abbot know that she would be at Mass in his Abbey to seek indulgences.

Lord Abbot, who had never met the lady, was delighted and ordered
that the high altar, the oratory, and the chapel where her ancestors lay be
adorned with relics, and on the other hand, he ordered that the market town
stock up on lampreys, salmon, and all other sorts of sea and freshwater fish
that could be found. Then he commanded that the stables be well outfitted
with everything necessary for the horses; and he also laid in foodstuffs of
various kinds and had fires lit in several rooms, for it was still the season for
fires. When Madame arrived and descended at the church steps, she was
welcomed by the principal officeholders, the most important monks from
the church who had come on behalf of the Lord Abbot and were on their
knees offering her all the wealth of the Abbey along with their services, for
which Madame thanked them profusely. After she had made her offering at
the high altar, Madame was led into the family chapel to hear Mass. [246]

As she came to end of the recitation of the Hours, Lord Abbot, who was
accompanied by the priors and monks of the Abbey, fell to his knees to say,
"Our most esteemed lady, you are most warmly welcome in your home. We
are overjoyed and delighted that God in his grace has allowed us to see you;
as our patroness and our founder, we offer you the abbey, its community of
monks, and all its wealth."

Then Madame said to the Abbot, "Lord Abbot, we thank you with all
our heart. If there were anything that we could do for you and for the rest of
the monastery, we would do it very willingly." Then Madame asked to see
the relics.

The Lord Abbot rose from his knees, and took such-and-such a head,
such-and-such a hand, and other bones of the holy relics that the abbey held
in abundance, and said, "My Lady, here lies the most valiant prince, our first

founder, who brought back these relics from his first conquest in the Holy
Lands—this head, this hand, and these bones—from my lords Saint So-and-
so and Such-and-such. And Monseigneur his brother gave this finger, this
jawbone, and this arm bone from Saint Such-and-such, and, to make a long
story short, your ancestors have given this great number of relics, and have
built this church and a great deal more of what you see here; the rest has
been done by the abbots who are my predecessors and by the neighboring
noble families whose ancestors lie buried within these walls."

After Madame had kissed the relics and had given a ceremonial cope and
two chasubles, and an altar cloth for the great altar, all made from fine crimson figured velvet and richly embroidered with gold, she thought she would
return home. As the carriage horses and other horses were being fed and
prepared for harnessing, Lord Abbot led Madame into his well-heated private
chamber to warm up. [247] The room was neat and very well appointed,
hung with tapestries, with good rushes on the floor and fine glass in the
windows. Then, being a jovial, good-humored, fine fellow, the abbot said to
everyone, "Let's all go out and leave Madame on her own to warm up and
relax a bit."

When Madame and the ladies and maidens of her retinue had warmed
up and relaxed, Madame asked if her carriages were ready. Then Lord Abbot,
who had already told his Steward that Madame would be dining with them
and that the meal was all ready, had asked him to see to it personally that
everything was in order.

At these words the Abbot came into Madame's presence, and led her
into his charming private parlor, which was as well furnished as if it had been
a formal reception room, with magnificent hangings and tapestries, and rush
matting on the floor; the windows were glazed, and there was a blazing fire,
and three trestle tables had been set up, covered with pristine table linens,
and there was a sideboard with an abundance of elegant dishes and platters.

And when Madame saw that the tables had been set up, she said to the
Abbot: "Lord Abbot, do you intend to dine so very early?"

"Dine?' said he, "Goodness, my lady, surely it's time? Look at the clock!"
(which he had carefully wound forward by an hour and a half, so that as he
spoke it chimed twelve).

Madame, hearing noon strike, was in a hurry to leave, and when the
Abbot saw that she wanted to do so, he said to her: "My lady, by heaven,
you shan't leave before you have dined!"

"Dined!" said Madame, "I certainly can't stay, I have far too much to do."

"Well now, Steward," said the Abbot, "and you, Madame's ladies, will you allow Madame to refuse my invitation?" [248]

At that the ladies and maids of honor and the Steward too, who had not yet broken their fast and were feeling hungry, aware that they would eat much better at the Abbey than they would with the everyday fare at home, begged Madame, winking and nudging each other, to grant the Lord Abbot's very first request to her, and so insistently that Madame consented. At that the Lord Abbot was delighted; jovial and pleasant, he spiritedly thanked Madame, on bended knee, as did her ladies. And the horses were returned to the stable yard, and the entire company was overjoyed—even those who had already broken their fast.

"Now, my lady," said Lord Abbot, "we are in the holy season of Lent and in a house dedicated to penance, so you must not be surprised if your reception is meager and the service poor; after all, we did not know of your visit until late yesterday evening."

"Lord Abbot," said Madame, "we are certain that we shall be more than comfortable."

Then the Lord Abbot ordered water to wash the guests' hands, and the servants brought pure rosewater warmed, which delighted Madame and her retinue. Madame wanted the Lord Abbot, as a churchman, to wash his hands first, but the Lord Abbot steadfastly refused, and begged Madame to be the first to wash: she was so insistent that he finally went to the sideboard to wash his hands.

Then the table was readied, and Madame begged the Lord Abbot to take his seat; he replied: "My lady, you are the mistress and the abbess of this house; please be seated and I will manage everything."

Once Madame had been seated, Madame Jeanne, Madame Katherine, and the Seigneur de Gency, who were with her, sat at the other end of her table; at a second table were seated one of the priors from the Abbey, and Isabel with Messire Geoffrey de Saint Amant opposite her, and the other maids of honor and one or two squires. [249] When they were seated, the Lord Abbot spread a white napkin over his shoulder, went to the sideboard and served Madame and all those at table with sops in white hypocras,* then with Lenten figs baked in sugar.

Madame begged him to join them at table, but he declined and said: "My lady, may it not displease you, I prefer to join my Steward, so that on this occasion I can be the one to serve you."

But once the Lord Abbot and the Steward had come and the first course was on the table, Madame said to the Abbot: "Really, Lord Abbot, if you won't take a seat, we shall stand."

Madame wanted the attendants to pull out the tables so that he could sit, but the Abbot demurred and said: "God forbid that the tables should be disturbed on my account." Then he had a stool brought and placed opposite and a little below Madame's chair, and sat down. And he ordered his attendants to bring white wine from Beaune, then red wines of three or four different vintages, and all the company was served.

Well, what more can I say . . . ? All those present responded to the Lord Abbot's admonitions to eat and drink well, so much so that Madame had not fared so well for many a long day, and as she drank, Madame looked at the Abbot and the Abbot at Madame, and his eyes and hers, archers of their hearts, shot darts back and forth, heart to heart, between them, so much so that their feet, concealed by the heavy floor-length tablecloth, began first to nudge, and then to tread on each other.

Then the burning darts of love struck each of their hearts in turn, so that both of them lost their appetites—but the Abbot, charmed by this new pursuit, became the most jovial of the company and proposed toasts to all and sundry. [250] What more can I say . . . ? Never was an abbot so jovial: now he would pick up his stool and go and sit with the ladies for a while, now he would stand by the maids of honor and beg them to eat up and enjoy themselves, now he would drink a toast to Madame's serving maids—and then he would go back to Madame and sit cheerily opposite her.

And then the arrows of desire would fly once more, thicker and faster, and foot would tread foot more enthusiastically than ever. Of the good fare that they were given—wines, various dishes, lampreys, salmon, sea fish and freshwater fish of every variety—I shall say nothing further for the moment, because I want to come to the rest of the story, which is highly pleasing.

How Madame and the Lord Abbot conversed
and how she thanked him

When the tables were raised and the Steward and all the others had gone to dine, Madame thanked Lord Abbot for the fine feast he had laid on, and step by step, speaking all the while, they reached the other end of the room, where they chatted and diverted themselves until everyone had finished eating. And while the last of the diners finished eating, Madame's bed was prepared with fine linens for her rest. Once the Steward finished eating, Madame called for her carriages.

"How is this, my lady?" asked Lord Abbot. "Do you intend to break with the fine customs of the house?"

"And what might those customs be?" [251]

"My lady, they are such that whenever ladies or damsels of honor come to dine, they and their retinue must lie down afterward, either to sleep or to remain awake, whether it's winter or summer. And if they have had supper here, I give up my own room to them for the night, and I go off to sleep somewhere else. Therefore, Madame, you really ought not to refuse to respect the customs of your own abbey."

Lord Abbot and the ladies urged Madame so insistently on this point that Madame graciously agreed to uphold the custom. So Madame entered his room, and the wine and spices were prepared. The door was closed, and Madame went off to rest until vespers.

How Lord Abbot was praised

When the ladies and maidens were on their own, Isabel began to speak. "You're not saying anything, my lady, nor are you other foolish women, about Lord Abbot's fine hospitality and about how he has entertained us and treated us so generously to fine wines, excellent dishes, and good fish."

"He certainly does seem to me to be a good man," said Madame.

"What do you mean, a good man? I've never seen such a generous monk in my entire life."

"And you, my lady," said Lady Katherine, "you who had to be begged to stay on!"

"Ha!" said Isabel. "I understood by his entreaties that things were going well and that he was putting his heart into it."

Then all the young ladies spoke at once, as ladies are in the habit of doing, praising the generosity, good humor, and handsome demeanor of the Lord Abbot with such excitement that they could not calm down.

Madame, already so infatuated with the Abbot that she had forgotten her sorrows, replied tersely, "He is a very good man."

And while they were speaking so enthusiastically about Lord Abbot, the bells rang out for vespers. [252] The ladies had to get up to attend vespers without having slept a wink.

Once vespers had been said and Madame prepared to mount her carriage, Lord Abbot took her by the hand and she said, "Abbot, where are you taking me?"

"If you please, my lady, I would like to take you to have a little refreshment, for it's time for a bite."

And as he spoke, Lord Abbot took her by the arm and clasped her hand firmly with his own; he led her to the lower ground-floor chamber that was so well hung with tapestries, where the fire had been lit, where the sideboard and the tables were set with salads; watercress in *sauce vinaigrette*; platters of roast lampreys, served *en croûte* and well sauced; great poached soles, fried or roasted with orange verjuice; red mullet; salmon roasted, poached, or *en croûte*; huge pikes and fat carp; platters of crayfish; thick fat eels served in aspic; platters of different foods smothered in white, red, and golden aspic; Bourbonnais tarts; curd tarts and almond creams, heavily sugared; pears and apples, both fresh and cooked; shelled, sugared almonds; green nuts in rose water; as well as figs from Melicque, the Algarve, and Marseille; raisins from Corinth and Orte, and many other things I'll skip over to come to the point—all of it laid out according to the instructions for a banquet.[151]

How Madame enjoyed a hearty snack

Madame, who was fasting and who intended to take nothing other than spices and wine, observed the tables so generously provisioned. The treacherous God of Love had assailed her so hard during dinner that his amorous darts had completely sated her. [253] But Nature now intended to strike back, giving Madame such an appetite that she hardly had to be asked to eat. When the other ladies saw Madame and Lord Abbot seated face to face in the middle of the table, all of the ladies, or at least most of them, allowed themselves to be coaxed and persuaded by the Abbot's prayers; they also intended to obey Madame and to keep her company. So they seated themselves at either end of the table and along the two sides. To make things even merrier, four or five monks sat down along with them. You should have seen how much they all ate and drank, rising to the occasion!

What more can I tell you? Never has such a crowd of people celebrated with such joy and merriment. But at last, with deep sighs of regret, Madame had to leave Lord Abbot. As she mounted her carriage, Lord Abbot and the priors thanked Madame most humbly and commended the church and the monastery to her.

Madame replied, "We shall see you more often, for we intend to seek out your indulgences more frequently than we have in the past" (which made everyone very happy). "But as for you, Lord Abbot, we beg you to spare us the abundance of nourishment you offered, for you've certainly been most extravagant, and we don't intend to indulge ourselves any more."

"Very well, my lady, but enjoying sops with *poudre de duc** and sops dipped in white wine, hypocras, muscatel, grenache, malmsey, or Greek wine, as much as you please, taken after Mass to warm up a bit—surely you're not forbidding me to serve you these things?"

"Yes, I am," she replied, "for we have every intention of fasting during Lent."

"Fasting? My lady, this wouldn't be breaking your fast! And, besides, I promise to absolve you of any infraction." [254]

With these words, the Lord Abbot mounted his horse and rode with Madame for a while, and then took leave of her.

How Madame and her ladies sang the praises
of the Lord Abbot to each other

When Lord Abbot departed and returned to his Abbey, the ladies began to outdo each other singing his praises. Isabel, the merriest, was the first to speak, saying with a laugh, "Ah, Madame! How I hate it when you refuse such good meals. No one should turn down the good things that come one's way."

Then Lady Jeanne said, "Well, really now, Isabel, you're wrong. Since Madame intends to come here often, does she need to stay for dinner each time?"

Then Lady Katherine said, "You're both wrong. There's no reason why Madame should stay to dine each time she comes, but I also see nothing wrong in occasionally accepting the Abbot's invitations. Because, for heaven's sake, he's inviting her in good faith, and, if I'm not mistaken, he does so willingly and has the wherewithal to do so, I believe, none of which does any harm. What do you say, Madame? Am I not right?"

Madame, who had listened to everything they had said, replied, "One should take only the wool from the lamb, which is why I'll stop at sops in *poudre de duc*, hypocras, and the other delicious foreign wines; all this should be enough to satisfy us. But we certainly hope to earn all these indulgences, or at least most of them, since we don't know if we'll be able to return on another occasion."

And at last they reached home.

Madame, her heart inflamed by this new love, spent the entire night lamenting, moaning, and sighing, so deeply did she desire to see the Lord Abbot and to be able to converse with him again. [255] And Lord Abbot, assailed by the same attacks of Love and by the sweet and loving glances that they had cast upon each other, had no rest either, for the sighs and desires of burning love kept him from sleeping all night long.

When the next day finally dawned, Madame told her ladies that in order to truly earn the indulgences of the Abbot, who was a prelate and seemed like a very pious man, she intended to make her confession to him. Then Lady Jeanne said, "Madame, that would be a good idea; I myself did it yesterday."

Then Madame bade young Perrin from her entourage to mount his horse; she sent him off with the order that Lord Abbot come immediately to her side.

Lord Abbot was diligent and quickly obeyed Madame. He bowed before Madame, in front of all her ladies, and Madame said to him in front of everyone, "Abbot, so that we may more worthily earn your indulgence, we would like to make our confession before a priest."

"Ah, my lady, now you are with God; and who, my lady, is your confessor, so that he may be given the proper authority, if need be?"

Then Madame said, "There is no one who is more worthy or suited for the task than you."

"Ah, Madame, you think that only because of my crozier—as for the rest, I am as ignorant as anyone."

At these words, Madame went into her boudoir, handsomely decorated with tapestries, where a fire had been lit, and the Abbot followed her very devoutly. [256] The door was closed. And for two hours Lord Abbot tenderly heard her confession, and the lady, contrite and remorseful, repented of her

Fɪɢ. 5. Brussels, Bibliothèque Royale, MS 9457, f. 160r:
Madame and the Abbot retire to a bedroom.
Reproduced by permission of the Bibliothèque Royale.

good deeds and her loyal love. They played the game honorably and fairly without any baseness.

As they took leave of each other, Madame went to her jewel chest and took out a very beautiful deep red Balas ruby ring set in gold. She placed it on the Abbot's middle finger and said, "My dear heart, my only thought, and my true lord, I retain you as my only love and wed you with this ring."

Then the Lord Abbot thanked her as humbly as he could, thinking to himself of the well-known proverb that says, "Whoever renders half a service will get no thanks." So he gave Madame her absolution, kissed her very sweetly out of charity, and took leave of her. And as he passed through the room, he said with great solemnity to the ladies and maidens, "Let no one go in until she calls. My sisters and my friends, I commend you to God until the next time."

Madame remained alone for a bit, in order to regain the color that she had lost doing penance. Her ladies and maidens and all the others went off to hear Mass. When the clock struck eleven, Madame called Jeanette, who dressed her in her simplest gown; Madame donned her largest kerchief for a headpiece, so as to best conceal her face. And in this modest attire Madame emerged quietly from her room, her head and eyes lowered. She went piously to Mass and then had dinner, and so passed the day.

The following day, Wednesday, another day of penitence, Madame returned to the Abbey to seek pardon. [257] Lord Abbot, full of joy, served an abundance of sops in wine, and supplied hypocras and various kinds of foreign wines, kippered herrings, soups, and other dishes for the companions; to top it off, he had a good thought for the horses.

Once Madame had heard Mass, Lord Abbot took her by the arm and led her into his chamber, where a fine fire glowed, and the entire luncheon had been prepared. After Madame had eaten well, the Lord Abbot took her aside and said, "Madame, while your ladies are enjoying themselves, let me show you my new building projects." Then the two of them left the room in such a way that the ladies would not know how to find them. As they left the secret room, Lord Abbot gave Madame a length of fine black velvet, which she later sent for in secret.

Then Madame came back into the great reception hall where everyone was assembled, and when her ladies arrived Madame scolded them as if she were very angry, "Now, where have you been? I told you to follow me, and I thought that you were doing so, but you evidently preferred to sit by the fire and enjoy your sops in wine rather than accompany me!"

"Ah, my lady! By my faith, we were not able to follow you quickly enough to be able to find you."

"My lady, please," said Lord Abbot. "Forgive them just this time."

Madame then offered her profuse compliments for the buildings that the Abbot had shown her; she went off to get into her carriage, and then took her leave of Lord Abbot.

What more can I tell you? [258] No week of Lent went by that Madame did not go off with great devotion to seek indulgences. Many times she went without a great retinue to dine in private, to enjoy intimate banquets and suppers. And after a nap, she went to hunt foxes, badgers, and other pleasures in the woods. And just so did Madame pass the entire Lenten season very joyously.[152]

About the first time the Queen wrote to Madame

And so it happened that the term of two months by which Madame had promised to return to the Queen came and went without the Queen receiving any news or letter from her cousin. This astonished the Queen, who sent the following letter:

"To our dearest and most beloved cousin, etc.

Dearest and most beloved cousin, Considering your promise to return to us, we're amazed that two and a half months have passed without a single bit of news since your departure. We implore you by your faith to keep your word immediately, since we so desire to see you. And if there's anything that we can do for you, we'll be very glad to do it, as our loyal secretary, Julien de Broy, will tell you—you can trust him just as you would trust us. Dearest, beloved cousin, may Our Lord protect you. Written in our city of Paris, the 8th of April.

Bonne."

How Madame, understanding perfectly the letter's intent, responded to the Queen without hearing the formal letter of credence[153]

[259] THE AUTHOR: The above-mentioned Master Julien de Broy, the Queen's secretary, arrived while Madame was receiving her pardon at the Abbey. He found her seated at the dining table, where he expected to be well received as one of her special friends at court, and he presented the Queen's letter. Madame felt nothing but displeasure at his arrival; she said very little as she took the Queen's letter and read it. She rushed through dinner so that she could be rid of him as soon as possible, and then rose from the table. She went straight to her room to pen her response, and then said to Master Julien, "Come to see me immediately after dinner."

Lord Abbot, who was a courteous gentleman, welcomed Master Julien warmly and sat down beside him to chat. While he was dining, one of the Lord Abbot's huntsmen approached, reporting that he had found an enormous stag, accompanied by ten or twelve hinds—it would be a great diversion to go see this. The Lord Abbot then said, "I'm sorry that Madame is not here, but we'll wait until tomorrow, at the risk of missing it altogether."

"How so?" asked Master Julien of the Abbot, "Is Madame willing to go hunting?"

"Is she willing?" replied the Abbot without thinking. "Why yes, she hunts two or three days a week, either on horseback or foot, in one hunting party or another."

"Ah, my Lord Abbot, so you have a good supply of dogs and hounds?" asked Master Julien.

"A good supply? I should say so, and very fine birds, as fine as belong to any prelate in France, I dare say."

"Holy Mary!" said Master Julien. "That does indeed do you great honor."

As they spoke together, Master Julien observed that the Abbot's finger bore the beautiful, large red Balas ruby that he had seen Madame wear; although he said nothing, he thought about it nonetheless. [260] When he had dined and gleaned what he wanted from his conversation with Lord Abbot, he took his leave, thanking him heartily. Then he mounted his horse and went to Madame as she had asked; he delivered his message with the formal letter of credence, as it had been written. Madame, who was eager to be rid of him, handed him her letter of response to the Queen, which read as follows:

"To my most revered and sovereign lady, the Queen.

My most revered and sovereign lady, I commend myself to Your Grace through your secretary, Master Julien de Broy, as humbly as I can. I've received your letter and read the content, and I beg you as humbly as I can to forgive me for my broken promise. My illness has made it necessary for me to stay here until now, although, thank God, I am beginning to get much better. After I take care of a little business with my people, I'll be at your side immediately, to keep my pledge. For the rest, the Holy Spirit knows that I will be delighted to follow any orders and commands that you please as best I can, my most revered and sovereign lady; may he bring you all the delight you may wish. Written in my hand the 11th day of April.

Your very humble and obedient, etc."

How Madame gave her letter to Master Julien and gave him her letter of credence

[261] In her great haste to be freed of Master Julien as soon as possible, Madame gave him her response, along with her own letter of credence, as it pleased her. She gave him an adequate welcome, offering him wine but nothing else—even though at court he was one of her most loyal and intimate friends, which is why the Queen had sent him. But Madame was so eager to see him on his way that she didn't even inquire about the King, the Queen, or any of the lords and ladies at court, but said simply, "Farewell, Master Julien."

Having heard about the hunting parties organized by Lord Abbot and Madame, Master Julien could scarcely resist thinking about what might really be going on between them. He took leave of Madame, and rode to where he could take rest for the night, riding for some days until he reached the Queen, who said as soon as she saw him, "Is Belle Cousine coming back, Master Julien?"

He replied coldly, "She commends herself humbly to your grace, Ma'am, and says that you will see her shortly." He then presented the letter with his credence and then wisely said nothing more about the matter.

The Queen was not satisfied with either the letter or the credence. She asked Master Julien, "Is she in good form?"

"In good form?" said Master Julien."I've never seen her in better form, Ma'am."

"And whatever can she be doing that's keeping her so busy?"

"To tell the truth, Ma'am," said Master Julien. "I don't know, for I only spent an hour with her before I was rushed away . . . and I wasn't able to speak with Lady Jeanne, Lady Katherine, Isabel, or to any other man or woman there, except to hear them say 'welcome' when I arrived, and 'God bless you' when I left."

"But how can this be, for you who are one of her closest friends?" [262]

Then he told about how he had gone to seek pardon at the Abbey, where he found Madame and the Lord Abbot, face to face, at a table with very few people present; how he presented his letter; and how Madame gave him a very cold welcome after reading it. Indeed, Madame had had the tables cleared immediately and had her horses prepared for the trip back to her estate. He told how the Lord Abbot invited him to sit and dine, and how the huntsman brought news of having discovered the great stag and his hinds, in the forest where Madame was to go hunting. He told her about several other things. But about the red Balas ruby that he saw on Lord Abbot's finger, he wisely said not a word.

When the Queen heard all this, she fell silent from that point on. She forbade Master Julien to say anything to anyone about it, in order to protect Madame's honor; she remarked that everyone needed to amuse themselves from time to time. With these words, the Queen pensively took her leave, unable to believe that Madame had conducted herself so badly or that she had meant to misbehave or do anything wrong. The Queen decided to wait a month and a half before sending Madame another message or letter.

That month and another one passed without Madame returning to the Queen or sending her any letter at all. Astonished by this, the Queen had another letter drawn up with the same message as the previous one. The horseman from her stables who carried the letter was enjoined to return quickly; he rode so fast that he found Madame with Lord Abbot in the fields, where he presented the letter. [263] Madame, who was supposed to share supper with Lord Abbot there in the fields, penned a response saying that she would soon be at the Queen's side. Then the horseman took his leave without drinking or eating anything or scarcely saying anything else, and he made great haste to return.

The Queen received the letter and read it. She also learned that Madame had been found in the fields with Lord Abbot. She very regretfully drew her own conclusions. She thought that she would no longer write to Madame but would instead let Madame remain away as long as she wished.

Madame was stricken with mortal sadness at the thought of leaving her handsome Father Abbot, and told him, "My only love, for as long as I can stay away and delay my return, rest assured that I won't give up your most desired company."

What more can I say? A good part of the summer was spent in hawking and hunting with falcons, pursuing game, and in many other pleasurable diversions.

Now I shall stop talking about the great pleasure Madame and Lord Abbot took in each other's company, and I shall return to speak of the Seigneur de Saintré and his companions.

How the Seigneur de Saintré and his companions came to the court of the Emperor, and how they were released from their vows, with great honor, by the following lords, all of them noble in name and arms: they were:

The count of Estainbourg, who bore *gules a chief argent*; the count of Espenchein, who bore *chequy of Or and gules*; the Seigneur de Estonnenosse, who bore *argent with torteaux gules*; the lord of Flouraille, who bore *argent a saltire gules;* the Seigneur de Semalle, who bore *or a cross vert*; the Seigneur de Huffalize, who bore *azure a cross Or*; the lord of Wallebech, who bore *argent an escutcheon vert*; the Seigneur de Huppain, [264] who bore *gules three lozenges argent*; the Seigneur de Tongre, who bore *vairy a fesse gules*; the Seigneur de Seulp, who bore *gules a cross argent*.

When news reached the Emperor's court that ten French barons were approaching with a challenge to arms, a great commotion arose about who would take up the fight. When the lords and barons mentioned above were chosen, they all went together before the Emperor to beg to be allowed to engage themselves, which the Emperor willingly granted. Then each knight began to prepare and equip himself as necessary. All ten made their gracious response known to the French men; each one of them made certain to offer the King of Arms cloaks, rings, and silverware. Before long, the French quartermasters arrived to secure their accommodations, followed by the French knights and squires themselves, who arrived within the week. As befits a very wise prince, the Emperor had his lords come before him and asked if they had agreed upon their chosen adversaries; he had the names of the French knights written just as they had been named in the letter. To prevent disagreement, he had them draw lots to decide who would oppose whom, a solution that satisfied everyone.

How the French arrived and were received with great honor

THE AUTHOR: When the Seigneur de Saintré and his splendid retinue were about a half a day from the city of Cologne, the appointed place where the Emperor and Empress had come to witness the armed combats, [265] they let their people know that they were coming and that they would be there by supper. Upon learning of their arrival, the Emperor commanded his cousin the Duke of Brunswick to escort the Seigneur de Saintré, and he selected nine other counts to escort each of the others, as well as various barons, knights banneret, knights, and squires, all very noble men who were accompanied by great retinue, and just so was it done.

As the French approached the city, the Emperor ordered that the two counts and eight barons who were designated to challenge them be all dressed the same as the French were, and that they go to meet them with their great retinues, and so it was arranged. This festive welcome conferred great honor on Saintré and his companions. Then, just as the Emperor had commanded, the Emperor's courtiers rode to the left of their companions, despite the protestations of the French, and the French counts rode on the right. And so, in this beautiful formation and in fine company, Saintré and his men were conducted through the city to their lodgings, passing right in front of the palace where the Emperor and Empress resided. I shall skip over all the other ceremonies and ordinances of heralds, trumpeters, and minstrels, as well as the warm welcome and honors that everyone exchanged during the two weeks that Saintré and his men spent there.

How the battle took place and the Emperor's arrangements

THE AUTHOR: The eighth day after their arrival was the appointed day for the encounter. The lists had been prepared, and the Emperor was at his viewing stand accompanied by his court and by other princes and barons who had come to witness feats of arms. [266] The Empress was seated at left in the viewing stand as above, accompanied by many princesses and other ladies of great standing. The Emperor mandated the first call to arms, calling first for the Seigneur de Saintré and then for his nine companions, who appeared at the second call. And so it was also with the Germans, who, to make a long story short, came forth with splendid large retinues.

When all the challengers were installed in their pavilions and had taken the customary oaths, the Emperor had them sally forth from their respective positions, wearing their heraldic tabards—a beautiful spectacle to behold.

Saintré appeared in the midst of his men. Then the rules of engagement were proclaimed. Each French knight made a great sign of the cross with the pennon he held in his hand, then kissed the pennon and handed it over to his squire. Each man, fully armed, lowered his visor, taking up his shield in the left hand and his thrusting lance in the right. In a gracious, joyful manner, the knights lined up against each other, waiting for the Emperor to release them to do their duty and fight.

Then both sides attacked, raging like lions; two Frenchmen were wounded in the first meeting of lances, but not so badly that they stopped fighting. Three Germans were wounded, one with a foot that was pierced with a lance. Then the real battle began, so fierce and arduous that it was a marvel to behold. The fighting stormed on entirely on the German half of the field; such a ferocious fight with so many combatants had never been seen. As the long battle continued, the Seigneur de Saintré ceaselessly pushed his own adversary into retreat. [267]

When the Emperor saw the valiant deeds of all the knights and realized that neither side was likely to give way, he cried out, "Alas, how can my heart have permitted so terrible an ordeal?" Then he quickly lowered his baton with a "Hold!"

At that, everyone was stopped in his tracks and retreated to the pavilions on each side. Then the Emperor had them all gathered before him and made them remove their helmets and gauntlets. He ordered that the wounded be treated and required all twenty combatants to hand in the prizes that they owed if they lost. After the prizes were brought forward to him, the Emperor then handed them over to the Imperial King of Arms and stipulated that each knight be awarded his due; the King of Arms pronounced the following words:

How the Imperial King of Arms conferred
the prizes and spoke to the winners

THE AUTHOR: When the Emperor had finished speaking, the King of Arms went down to the battleground and appeared before the combatants, saying, "My lords, counts and other lords, German and French, all who are assembled here, the most Christian and victorious prince and our very sovereign lord, the King of the Romans and Emperor you see before you, has commanded that I proclaim that all of you, on each side, German and French, have fought today so honorably and fulfilled your duty so nobly that no one could have done it better. You have fought so well that it's scarcely possible to tell who had the upper hand, which is why the Emperor wishes, judges, and commands that, on each side, each knight, with the greatest courtesy and cordiality, bestow the prize on his opponent as if he had earned it. [268] But since you, my esteemed French lords, have most valiantly and consistently advanced into the German territory, the Emperor wishes, judges, and commands that the German lords bestow your prize on you first, and that you will award them their prize afterward. In that manner, your very beautiful ladies will not lose the rewards promised to them. And he orders that you proceed in pairs through the lists, and that you, my esteemed French lords, ride through the lists on the right, to honor you and your feats of arms."

Then everyone knelt to thank the Emperor, and they bestowed their prizes on each other with great honor, sallying forth from the list as ordered. They then all took leave of each other and went to disarm in their lodgings, remaining there until nightfall when they took supper with the Emperor.

And the following day, they dined with the Empress—both Emperor and Empress received them generously and with great honors. And the knights on both sides dined and supped with one another until the fifteenth day after their arrival, when they dined once again with the Emperor. Then they took their leave of the Emperor, the Empress, and the other knights and ladies, who gave them cloth of gold and lengths of silk, silverware, fine destriers, and many other beautiful gifts. They also bestowed gifts on their adversaries, and vice versa.

After everyone had taken leave of each other, the French mounted their horses and were escorted by several lords with great ceremony for a good league. Then with great honor and courtesy, they all cordially took leave of each other. And for many days afterward everyone who had been present, knights and ladies, praised the French knights for their courteous behavior, their valiant deeds, and the splendid style and equipment of their retinue. [269]

The Germans said to each other publicly that if the Emperor had ever so slightly delayed in calling them back and ending the fight, they would surely have lost: for one knight had been badly wounded in the foot, incapacitated so badly that he could no longer fight, and two of them had lost so much blood that they nearly fainted, and besides that they had lost a great deal of ground, so that the day was really won by the French. Now I shall stop talking about their feats of arms and about their very joyous trip home; I shall talk about their arrival before the King.

How the Seigneur de Saintré and his companions arrived in Paris before the King

THE AUTHOR: When the Seigneur de Saintré and the other noble companions, passing through Luzarches to the Church of Saint Cosmas and Saint Damian[154] as pilgrims, reached Saint-Denis in the evening, news of their much anticipated arrival traveled far and wide; the King, the Queen, the lords and ladies were all delighted. At the King's orders, a host of noble knights rode out to meet them: my lords the Dukes of Berry and Burgundy, the king's brothers, who rode on either side of Saintré, and also the counts of La Marche, Flanders, Clermont, Rethel, Brienne, Le Perche, Beaumont, Armagnac, and the young heir to the county of Auvergne, each appointed to accompany one of the companions.

Then they all assembled before the King, who welcomed them very warmly, as did the Queen, and the other lords, ladies, and maidens, all from the court. To shorten the tale, after everyone had made their bows and courteously greeted each other, and the excitement had subsided a bit, [270] the Seigneur de Saintré, surprised and amazed that he did not see Madame, the one whom he desired to see most in the world, drew aside to speak to his cousin, Madame de Sainte-Maure. In the midst of their conversation, as if it were an afterthought, he said, "Goodness, my cousin, now that I come to think of it, I wonder if Madame is ill, since she isn't here?"

"Madame?" she said. "She certainly is in bad odor with the Queen; she has really fouled her own nest.[155] About three or four weeks after you left, she was overcome by such a violent illness that she seemed to shrivel up; the Queen's doctor decided that she would develop consumption or die if she didn't return to her own lands. So the Queen gave her leave for two months, and after two and a half months, when she hadn't returned, she sent word by means of a letter carried by her faithful servant Master Julien de Broy. Two months later, she wrote to her again, and Madame once again replied, 'I'm coming, I'm coming,' but she has yet to return."

When Monseigneur de Saintré heard that Madame was so ill, he thought about everything she had said before his departure: how her heart would never know joy until he returned. Realizing that she had probably gone away to forget the pains of love, he was happier than ever. So he decided to pay her a visit before she learned of his arrival—for he knew that she would return to court as soon as she heard he was there, and he wanted to have a chance to talk to her privately and at leisure. [271] He thought about this for ten or twelve days, and then said to the King, "Sire, if you please, I very humbly beg you to grant me a few days' leave—perhaps eight or ten days—so that I can visit my mother, who has called for me to come home."

The King said, "How is this, Saintré? You can't remain with us? But since it's your mother who has called for you, we'll give you leave for a month."

After the Seigneur de Saintré thanked the King, he spent all night preparing, equipping his people and himself as well as his horses, so that he could more lovingly please the one who held his entire heart in thrall. Then he took leave of the King, the Queen, and the noble princes. He rode constantly until he reached a place one league from Madame's domain. There he dined, then dressed himself in a crimson silk doublet embroidered in fine gold, and scarlet hose embroidered with fine, large pearls, in Madame's colors and device; he donned a cap in fine scarlet silk that was fashionable at the time, on which a very beautiful, precious jewel was fastened; he was accompanied by two knights and twelve squires from his household, all well dressed in similar outfits bearing Madame's device. Thus attired, Jean went off to see Madame at her home. When he reached the door, he asked the porter to inform Madame that the Seigneur de Saintré was there. The porter replied, "Actually, Madame left this morning for the Abbey to hear Mass and then to stay for dinner."

So off he went to the Abbey, where he learned that Madame and Lord Abbot after dinner and a nap had left to go hawking for game. [272] He found out which way they had gone and, after riding some distance, he called four or five of his retinue and told them, "Set your spurs in that direction, you this way, you that way, and if you see any ladies on horseback, come right back to me."

So each one went off riding across the fields, and, before long, one came hurrying back, saying, "My lord, I've seen about twenty horses, with six or eight ladies among the riders, all dressed up."

Then the good knight, who as yet had no inkling of Madame's treacherous love, rode as fast as his horse would carry him, thinking he could not see his beautiful, beloved lady soon enough. As soon as he saw her, his heart overflowed with joy. Splendidly dressed as he and his men all were, he spurred his fine, frisky steed in her direction. Then one of Lord Abbot's monks saw them and went off to tell the Abbot.

When the Lord Abbot, who was riding right next to Madame, saw the horses gallop up, he was not sure who it was. He thought it might be relatives of Madame who had heard about their love and wanted to thrash him for it; so he turned tail and dug his heels into his mule, his hawk on his wrist, and he rode up to three monks who were carrying huge bottles and all the provisions for a meal, and turned away as best he could as if he dared not approach Madame, and in this way virtually abandoned her. [273]

Madame, seated on her sturdy hackney, riding with her hawk on her wrist, wanted to see who was approaching; she waited quietly with all her attendants. And when her people recognized that it was the Seigneur de Saintré, she said, "The Devil take you all! Do you have to get so excited over a man?"

And as she spoke these words, the Seigneur de Saintré, his heart overflowing with joy, jumped down quickly from his horse. When Madame saw him dismount, she said so loudly that several people overheard it. "Alas, sir, you're certainly not welcome here."

The Seigneur de Saintré, who had not heard these words, knelt before her with the greatest joy, touched her hand and said, "Ah, my most esteemed lady, how are you?"

"How am I? Do you have to ask about something you can see perfectly well for yourself? Can't you see that I'm on my horse, holding my hawk?"

Then she swung around on her hackney and called her hounds for the hunt, as if she took no account of him and was contemptuous of him.

When the Seigneur de Saintré heard Madame's cruel response, he did not know what to think or do, other than to reach out, offering an embrace and a kiss to each of Madame's ladies and maidens as they passed by. Then he got back on his horse and rode after Madame; each of her attendants rode up to bow before him and greet him. When he came to Madame, he said to her very dejectedly, "Alas, my lady, why such a cold greeting for one who has loved so you deeply and has never disobeyed you? Alas, my lady, why? Are you doing this on purpose or is this to test me? Has anyone told you that I have been other than loyal? If that's the case, you'll soon realize the truth."

Madame, who was annoyed by his presence and by everything he said, replied, "Don't you have another song to sing? If you can't say anything else, then say nothing at all." [274]

While this was transpiring, Lord Abbot, assured that he was in no danger, asked the Steward through one of his monks who this knight might be. When Lord Abbot learned that it was the Seigneur de Saintré, he came forward to greet him. "My most honorable lord, I would like to extend a warm welcome to you and your fine company. Upon my word, you're the lord I've most wanted to meet in all the world."

The Seigneur de Saintré understood by these words that he was speaking with the Abbot, and he said to him and to those monks standing behind him, "Lord Abbot, I'm delighted to meet you and your companions."

"My lord," said the Abbot, who by now was quite reassured, "what do you think of the fact that my most esteemed lady has had the patience to spend time with her poor monk, and also to go hunting with him?"

"As a worthy, honorable woman," said the Seigneur de Saintré, "Madame has found an honorable, enjoyable way to pass the time; she has always been devoted to Holy Church."

With these words, Lord Abbot edged away, step by step, leaving Madame and Saintré together. Since vespers had rung, Lord Abbot went home and ordered one of his monks to let the Steward know that he should tell Madame that they would retain the Seigneur de Saintré for supper. The Steward told Madame what the Abbot had demanded. Madame, who had not heard clearly the first time, asked him what he was saying. He repeated it so loudly that the Seigneur de Saintré could hear, and when Madame had understood, she thought for a moment and then replied, [275] "Tell the Abbot that he can do as he likes, but not to badger him to get him to accept."

The Seigneur de Saintré, who had heard everything and understood very well what it meant, thought to himself that they wouldn't have to press him too hard and that to see this farce to the bitter end, he would readily accept the first invitation. Madame, who was quite annoyed by the appearance of her first love, said that she was exhausted and would return home. Lord Abbot, who was most accommodating, was already there and had prepared everything for their arrival.

The Seigneur de Saintré had dismounted and tried to help Madame dismount, but she asked one of her attendants. When everyone had gotten off their horses, the Seigneur de Saintré tried to take leave of Madame, but just as she was extending her hand, the Lord Abbot, in a show of courtesy, said to Madame, "Are you letting him leave us?"

"I'll let the two of you decide that."

"Well, Monseigneur de Saintré, won't you dine with Madame? I insist that you stay."

And the Seigneur de Saintré said to Lord Abbot, "Lord Abbot, I wouldn't wish to disobey or to refuse your first invitation."

Then the Seigneur de Saintré retained only two squires, a servant, and a page and sent the rest of his retinue into town to eat; he told them, through the Steward, that they should come back to Madame's house soon afterward. Then the tables were set and supper was prepared. Madame washed her hands alone first, and Lord Abbot and the Seigneur de Saintré washed afterward. [276] In consideration of rank and honor, Lord Abbot was seated at the head of the table, facing Madame and leaning back on the bench, then Madame was next to him, and then the Seigneur de Saintré, Lady Jeanne, and Lady Katherine.

Then, the guests were all served a salad, to which Madame and the Abbot helped themselves gladly, after which large platters piled high with hare, partridge, and plump pigeons from the manor were served, along with excellent wines from Beaune, Tournus, and Saint-Pourçain. When their bellies were full and their tongues began to loosen, the Abbot began to revive and said, "Ho! Monseigneur de Saintré, wake up, wake up! I drink to your thoughts; whatever is on your mind? You're doing nothing but daydream."

The Seigneur de Saintré turned to him and said, "My Lord Abbot, I'm tussling with so many delicious meats and fine wines placed in front of me that I have no time to do anything else."

"Monseigneur de Saintré," said the Abbot, "you know, I have often wondered how it can be possible that you noblemen, knights, and squires, who take up arms so often, claim that you have been victorious each time you return from a fight."

Then he turned to Madame and said, "My lady, isn't that so?"

"Yes indeed, Lord Abbot," said Madame. "You're right, how can this be? Dear sir, tell us your thoughts on the matter."

"My lady," said the Abbot, "do you really want me to tell you my thoughts on the subject? I will only be so frank by your leave and command. I don't know if Monseigneur de Saintré will resent it, but since you wish to know, my lady, my thoughts are as follows:

[277] "There are many knights and squires at the court of the King and Queen and at the courts of many other lords and ladies, and squires as well, who claim to be such loyal lovers of ladies that to gain your favors, if they don't have them already, they'll weep and sigh and moan in your presence, feigning such sorrow that you poor ladies, with your kind, tender hearts, take pity on them and are inevitably deceived when you accede to their desires and fall into their traps. And then off they go, from one lady to the next, accepting the challenge to defend a garter, or a bracelet, or a roundel, or a turnip—or goodness knows what trifle. And then the same knight will pro-claim the very same thing to ten or twelve of you, 'Ah! my lady, I carry this token for love of you.' And you poor ladies! How you are duped by your lovers, among whom many have no loyalty at all for their lady. But then the King, the Queen, and all the lords of the land praise them and esteem them and bestow favors generously upon them, which they use to their advantage. Isn't this so, my lady? What do you have to say to this?"

Madame, who was delighted by what she had heard, replied with a smile to the Abbot, "Who has told you this, Lord Abbot? I for one do think this is so." And she pressed the Abbot's feet with her own as she spoke.

"I'll tell you something else, my lady. When these knights and squires go off to accomplish their exploits and take leave of the King, if it's cold weather, they keep themselves warm by the stoves in Germany, amusing themselves with strumpets all winter long, and if the weather's warm, they take themselves off to the delightful kingdoms of Sicily and Aragon—where the meats and wines are so fine, where there are fountains and good fruit and beautiful gardens—and all summer long they feast their eyes on beautiful women, while gentlemen receive them with generous hospitality and honors; [278] then they find an elderly minstrel or town crier with an old tabard and give him one of their old gowns to go proclaim at court, 'My lord has been victorious! My lord has been victorious! My lord has been victorious and earned first prize in combat.' And you poor ladies, haven't you been abused and duped? My heavens, I do pity you."

Madame, who could not have been more delighted than by these words, turned her head a bit and said to Saintré, "What do you have to say, Seigneur de Saintré?"

The Seigneur de Saintré, very much dismayed by the accusations and insults that the Abbot was leveling against men of good birth, said to Madame, "Should you care to speak up for men of good birth, you know very well that the very opposite is true, my lady."

Then Madame said, "We have seen some for whom that is not the case, but how much do we know about the others? For our part, we agree with the Abbot." And in speaking these words, smiling and winking at the Abbot, she trod on his feet.

"Ha! my lady," replied Saintré. "You're speaking very freely at the moment; I pray that God may enlighten you about such things."

The Abbot asked, "Enlighten? How might Madame be better enlightened than by the truth?"

"The truth?" retorted Saintré. "Lord Abbot, I shall say nothing about what Madame has said. She can speak as she pleases. But I shall respond to you, who have insulted knights and squires, that if you were the sort of man to whom I were able to respond, I would have words with you. [279] But given the respect I owe to your office and to God whom you serve, I shall say nothing more now; perhaps we shall return to the subject at another time."

Lord Abbot, who was consumed by the flame of love, said sarcastically to Madame, "My lady, it is for your sake that I am threatened in your very own home."

And as he said this, Madame and the Abbot continued as before to spar with their feet under the table; when the Abbot saw her smile and wink, he realized that the game pleased Madame no end, and he continued, "Ah,

Monseigneur de Saintré, I am not a warrior or man of arms who can fight you in combat; I am a poor, simple monk who subsists on what little we have for the love of God. But if there were any man, whoever he may be, who would contradict me in this quarrel, I would wrestle with him."

"You would do that?" said Madame. "You would be so bold?"

"Bold, my lady? I risk little more than a fall; but I trust by God and by the power of my good, well-founded argument, that I'll win. Let's begin! Is there a man here who wants to defend all these warriors?"

Hearing the Abbot's outrageous taunts, which seemed to pierce him through the heart, and all the more because of the favor that Madame was showing the Abbot, the Seigneur de Saintré wished he were dead.

Madame, who saw that the Seigneur de Saintré was speechless, turned to him and said, "Ha! Seigneur de Saintré, you who are so valiant and have accomplished so many wonderful exploits, so they say, won't you dare to wrestle with the Abbot? If not, I'll surely have to agree with him."

"Ah, my lady," he said, "you know that I've never been a wrestler and that these monks are masters at it, as they are at tennis and at casting bars and throwing stones and iron weights, [280] and at all the other sports that they do in their leisure—which is why I'm well aware, Madame, that I cannot beat him."

"I entreat you to do so," said Madame. "Your refusal will be flagrant; I promise that if you don't do this, I'll reproach you everywhere, and I'll consider you a very cowardly knight."

"Ah! What are you saying, my lady? I've accomplished much more than this for a certain lady. But since this is the way things are, I shall do as you please."

"What does he say?" asked the Abbot.

"He says that he will not fail you in this venture and that he has done far more difficult things."

"He does? We'll see about that."

So without waiting for the tables to be cleared, the Abbot jumped up joyfully from the table, with Madame and the Seigneur de Saintré rising afterward, to everyone's amazement. Then the Abbot took Madame aside privately and led her into a beautiful meadow, where the sun had just set, and said, "Madame, please be seated beneath this beautiful flowering hawthorn; you shall be our judge."

And Madame sat down, as delighted as could be, and gathered her ladies-in-waiting around her; no matter how much they might pretend otherwise, there were few who were pleased by the events they were observing.

Then the Abbot did something that Saint Benedict, Saint Robert, Saint Augustine, and Saint Bernard, all prelates of the Church, would never have done as long as they lived: he stripped down in public to his doublet, unlacing his hose (which in those days did not attach) and rolling them down below his knees. [281] He then was the first to present himself before Madame; after his bow, he spun around, laughing as he leapt in the air, showing off his fat thighs, hairy and furry as a bear's.

After undressing at the edge of the field, the Seigneur de Saintré came forward, wearing hose richly embroidered with large pearls. He bowed before Madame, concealing the bitter sadness that had come over his heart.

Then Saintré and the Abbot stood before each other, but before the fight began, the Abbot turned toward Madame, bending one knee to the ground, and said derisively, "My lady, with joined hands, I beg you to commend me to Monseigneur de Saintré."

Madame, who knew well how strong the Abbot was, spoke with a smile to the Seigneur de Saintré. "Ah! Sire de Saintré, I commend the Abbot to you, and I beg you to show restraint with him."

The Seigneur de Saintré, who realized that she was mocking him, said, "Ah! My lady, I would have greater need to be commended to him."

Having said these things, the Abbot and the Seigneur de Saintré grappled each other and turned around several times; next, the Abbot extended his leg and hooked it inside that of Saintré, then suddenly pulled himself back and shoved his opponent away, head over heels, and knocked him down on the green grass. As he held Saintré beneath him, the Abbot said to Madame, "My lady! My lady! Please commend me to the Seigneur de Saintré!" [282]

Then Madame, who was laughing heartily, said, "Ah! sire de Saintré, consider the Abbot commended to you!" But she could scarcely speak from mirth and laughter.

The Abbot then stood right back up on his feet laughing before Madame as she said, "Once more! Do it again!"

At this, the Abbot said to Madame loudly enough so that Saintré and everyone else could hear, "My lady, what I have just done was in defense of my argument, with God and love as my witness. But if the Seigneur de Saintré wished to claim that he loves his lady more loyally than I love mine, you see before you a simple, weak monk who would challenge him to a fight."

"You would do that?" she asked.

"Would I do it? Yes, by God, I would fight against all those who would take me on."

Then Madame, laughing, said to Saintré, "What do you say, my fair lord? Is there anyone with the heart of a gentleman who would not respond to that?" "My lady," said the Seigneur de Saintré, "there is no gentleman at heart who would not respond in his own manner and in the way that's appropriate for such a case."

"You're making excuses," said Madame. "That's just how you tried to excuse yourself in the other challenge. It's right to reproach the heart of a gentleman who dares not defend his loyalty in a wrestling match. And I firmly believe that anyone who looked for loyalty in you would find very little of it."

"Alas, my lady" said the Seigneur de Saintré, "why do you say this?"

"I say it because you're aware that you're wrong, and that's simply how it is."

Then the Seigneur de Saintré said, "I see very well, my lady, that I'll have to wrestle again and that there's no reasonable argument with which I can dissuade you. Since you wish it, I am happy to oblige." [283]

The Abbot, who had overheard all these things, replied in jest, "Ah! My lady, I don't dare fight, for if it weren't for the good cause I defended, he would have flipped me over and thrown me down the first time; I found him so strong that it's no wonder that he has vanquished so many people. But because I'm defending a righteous argument, I want to uphold it, so let's back up and fight! Back up!" he called as each of them drew back, while the Abbot, who was beside himself and beyond any sense of self-control or reason, began to cry out, "Ha! Loyalty! Defend yourself!"

And with these words he tried to trip Saintré up again, almost but not quite throwing him down, but then they turned and twisted so violently that with another leg sweep stronger than the first one he knocked the Seigneur de Saintré down flat, and then he said, "My lady, as our judge, tell me if I have done my duty. Who is the most loyal?"

"The most loyal?" asked Madame. "You are, since you've beaten him."

Poor Seigneur de Saintré did not know what to say; he was overcome by the fight and by the great pleasure that Madame had taken in it, and particularly in the fact that he was weaker and less expert in wrestling. Then each man went off to get dressed. The two squires who had remained to serve Saintré thought that they would die of sorrow when they saw the Lord Abbot and Madame sneering and making fun of the Seigneur de Saintré, who was such an honorable and valiant knight that one could not find his equal in the kingdom of France.

And they said to him "You will not be a man if you do not avenge this great insult." [284]

To which Saintré replied, "Don't concern yourselves with this; have patience as I do, and let me handle the situation."

The Seigneur de Saintré, who had in such a thoroughly unjust manner and because of her great disloyalty lost the love of a lady whom he had served so long and so loyally before, behaved with great composure as if none of this were of any consequence.

Then forcing a happy face, he delighted the Abbot and Madame even more when he said, "Alas, Madame, what a great shame it was that such a fine, powerful body as that of my Lord Abbot did not take up arms to defend some border against the enemies of the realm; for I scarcely know two or three knights, as powerful as they may be, whom he would not have vanquished."

Hearing such praise, the Abbot leapt up and pranced up and down before Madame and her companions. Then he ordered that wine and cherries be brought forth as refreshments.

On the emissaries from the monastery

After all this had taken place, the priors and elderly monks of the monastery, greatly displeased by the Abbot's way of life—and all the more so after hearing about the wrestling match and about the mockery made by Madame and the Abbot (who furthermore made no pretense of religious devotion or practice but rather led a miserable, dissolute life)—decided that two of them would go to speak to the Abbot at the monastery, offering the following words: [285]

The emissaries from the monastery

"Reverend Father in God and our most esteemed lord, the priors and administrators of your monastery, *una voca dicentes*,[156] having made their most humble and appropriate recommendations, send us before you. They have learned that you have invited our most esteemed lady on several occasions to share dinner and supper and to join in other entertainments. Insofar as she is our patron and founder, the entire monastery is delighted by that—and all the more so because a knight such as the Seigneur de Saintré was present at supper; we have heard so many fine reports of his recent exploits and he is so close to our lord the King. But that you went so far as to engage him in a wrestling match, beating him several times, and making fun of him—all this is inappropriate for anyone in the rank of prelate or monk to do in the very public manner that you have done it. Our rules and statutes forbid such behavior; the entire order is extremely angry and dismayed. We implore you to comport yourself, from now on and until his departure, in a way that brings no blame to either yourself or the monastery or in any other way. The monastery advises you that if any news should reach us that would bring disfavor to the house or might cause any inconvenience whatsoever, the administration absolves itself of any responsibility and will hold you entirely to blame. Please forgive us for this unwonted procedure."

Lord Abbot's response and the reparations he made

After hearing the administration's latest pronouncement, the Lord Abbott replied to the emissaries: [286]

"Brothers, go to the house and tell them that I was only acting in good fun; they need not worry about it further. Before the Seigneur de Saintré leaves, I'll make sure that everything ends on a good note."

How the Abbot appeased Saintré

THE AUTHOR: While the emissaries from the monastery were delivering their speech, wine and cherries were brought forth. They all drank to each other's health in the best of spirits. After everyone drank his fill, the Abbot took the Seigneur de Saintré aside and said to him, "Monseigneur de Saintré, God has provided me the opportunity to invite you once to my home, which can be your home as well if you wish. I appeal to you by your goodness to honor both me and Madame by coming to dinner again tomorrow: I beg you not to refuse. It would bring us the greatest pleasure if you would accept."

Saintré's response and the Abbot's entreaties

SAINTRÉ: "My lord Abbot, I thank you as deeply as I can for the meal and your kind hospitality the first time; I thank you also for your invitation to dinner tomorrow. But, to tell the truth, I have business elsewhere in town and unfortunately can't accept."

"Alas, you can't?" said the Abbot. "My lord, if anything I did in good fun upset you, I beg your forgiveness. [287] My lord, I've a very fine mule, the finest in the realm, I dare say, and I have one of the best falcons in the world for hunting herons and other game on the river, and I have three thousand *écus*, like the Pope or the King: that's everything I have. I pray and entreat you to accept one, two, or all three of these gifts so that I'll remain in your good graces and you'll forgive me."

THE AUTHOR: The Seigneur de Saintré, who had no need either for money, a bird, or a mule, thanked him very graciously; to placate him, he said, "Lord Abbott, I don't ride a mule; I would accept your three thousand *écus* if I needed them; and as for your falcon, I'll accept it if you keep it for me—should anyone ask to use it, tell them that it belongs to me. But I beg you not to refuse my own special request."

"What might that be?" asked the Abbot. "My lord, command me, by my faith, and I shall follow your orders if I can." "You will?" "Yes, by my faith." "Then I ask that you and Madame come to dine with *me* tomorrow."

"That's your request? I promise you on her behalf and mine that we'll grant you this pleasure, on the condition that it be an informal dinner among friends."

THE AUTHOR: Then the two went off in good spirits to Madame, and the Seigneur de Saintré made his request. [288] When Madame heard it she refused immediately, saying that she had too much to do, and that the Seigneur de Saintré was pleading in vain. But the Abbot took her aside and said, "My lady, you must come, for I've sworn and promised for both of us; you would bring me great shame and displeasure if you made me a liar. Also, my dear, he might think badly of our love—you should know that you need to watch out for these dashing gallants as you would be beware of fire. That's why you should come, my lady—because I can regain his friendship; otherwise, I'm afraid he'll hold the wrestling match against me."

Since she could neither avoid nor refuse the Lord Abbot's request, Madame replied, "If that's your wish, it's mine, too."

Then Lord Abbot called merrily to the Seigneur de Saintré, "My lord, my most esteemed lady here has refused your request because she's afraid you'll go to great lengths to prepare an extravagant feast, with great ceremony—but I assured her you would do no such thing."

Then the Seigneur de Saintré said, "My lady, and you, my Lord Abbot: as honest people of the court, we'll leave the great feasts to you people of the Church; for our part, we'll very gladly do without them. We would rather serve a few good dishes and some fine wine, if we can manage it; and we trust that you and Madame will find the meal to your liking."

After these words, hackneys and horses were readied, and Madame and the Seigneur de Saintré thanked Lord Abbot and took their leave until the following day. Madame rode through the fields as fast as her horse would carry her. [289] As the Seigneur de Saintré galloped alongside her, from time to time he drew near her and said, "Alas, my most revered lady, how have I offended you? Is there anyone in the world who would dare to claim that I have not loved you most loyally and served you with all my might?"

"Ah! my lord," said Madame. "Listen to you talk! You certainly proved your loyalty in that wrestling match. Say nothing more about it; just leave me in peace."

The Seigneur de Saintré, who knew perfectly well what was going on, no longer cared to curry Madame's favor; nor would he ever again agree to love and serve her if she asked him. But he wanted to show her how wrong she had been to treat him so badly, without letting on that he knew anything about her new love.

Once they had arrived at Madame's estate, before she dismounted she said, "Now be off with you, Seigneur de Saintré, for I have a bit of work to do, as do you." And so they took leave of each other until the following day.

The Seigneur de Saintré, much preoccupied with all these new events, resumed his journey with the few people he had with him. He proceeded straight to the town where his people were, without stopping until he found his whole company gathered as he had ordered. Then he called his Steward and informed him that Madame and the Abbot were coming to dine at his home the following day. He ordered the Steward to procure the finest foods and best wines available for a magnificent meal and to provide generously of the same food for the rest of their company. On the other hand, he ordered him to settle accounts and pay their host appropriately, for the horses as well as for the fine hospitality; [290] Saintré promised the Steward that once everything was paid for, he would offer him ten *écus* for his service and two *écus* for the servants and the maidservants at the inn; he also ordered that his horses, his trunk, and most of his retinue be gone by daybreak. He wished to retain only twelve of his men. And all this was done just so.

Once Saintré had dismounted at his lodgings, he called his host and took him aside, saying, "My dear fellow, is there any gentleman or townsman who might be the same size as this squire you see before you?" He pointed to one of his men as he spoke.

"Yes, my lord, I should think there are plenty," replied the host.

"But do you know if they have a full, fine set of armor?"

"Yes, they have a full set of beautiful equipment."

Then Saintré asked for the name of the one who was best equipped with armor and demanded that he be brought before him, and so it was done.

When the townsman had arrived and bowed to the Seigneur de Saintré, who in turn greeted him graciously, the latter said to him, "Jacques, who is the man in town with the finest armor?"

"My lord," replied Jacques, "there are many; although I may not be as noble, I am as well armed as the best, with five or six sets of fine armor as full and fine as any townsman or nobleman in the area."

"Is that so?" asked Saintré. "By my lord Saint James, then you're all the more deserving of praise and esteem. Since you've a set of armor tailor made for your body, could you find me another one that would fit the knight you see before you? " He pointed to a knight with a similar body type.

"My lord, I'll provide you with armor that is so fine and well made that you'll be delighted. [291] But what type of helmets would you like: bascinets, salad helmets* with beaver, or full helmets?"

"Jacques, I would like bascinets as well as two matching poleaxes. And don't worry about your expenses; I'll see to it that you won't suffer any losses."

"Losses?" said Jacques, who was delighted to have made Saintré's acquaintance. "My lord, all that I have is yours, and your wish is my command. When would you like to have all this?"

"I would like to have the things immediately; but you must bring everything concealed in trunks or sacks, so that no one can see them."

Jacques went home straightaway and had brought back in secrecy two fine sets of armor with axes, which pleased the Seigneur de Saintré no end.

When the next day broke and after the Seignuer de Saintré had heard Mass, after all his baggage and retinue had departed except for the dozen men he had retained, after dinner had been prepared and the tables set, he mounted his horse along with his attendants, and rode out to meet Madame. Having ridden about half way, he found Madame and the Abbot together in the fields, and they graciously greeted each other. Lord Abbot spoke first, saying, "Well! Speak of the devil! Are your ears not burning, Monseigneur de Saintré?"

"I don't know," replied the Seigneur de Saintré. "I was thinking of the great feast that awaits you. I hope that you have not eaten, Madame, nor you, Lord Abbot."

"Yes, we have," replied Madame. "On account of this foggy weather, we've had some sops in hypocras and *poudre de duc*."

"May that serve you well, my lady, and you too, my Lord Abbot."

As the three conversed together, Madame was turned constantly only toward the Abbot. [292]

When the Seigneur de Saintré saw that his words were lost on Madame, he guided his horse toward Lady Jeanne, but she told him to ride behind, after which he approached Lady Katherine and then Isabel, who both told him the same thing: everyone was forbidden to speak to him. So the Seigneur de Saintré returned to ride with Madame, and they soon came to his lodgings. Then the Seigneur de Saintré took Madame by the arm and led her and her ladies into their rooms, and he guided Lord Abbot to another room. And as soon as everyone had settled in their chambers, Saintré told the Steward that they would come immediately to the table as soon as the horses were saddled and bridled in the stables, and ready to mount. Then, to make a long story short, dinner was ready.

When Madame and Lord Abbot had washed their hands, the Abbot was seated at the head of the table as befits a prelate, and Madame, who did not wish to be far from him, was seated a little further on. Then the other two ladies were seated at the lower end, but the Seigneur de Saintré could not be entreated to sit down. Instead, with his napkin on his shoulder he went back and forth serving fine wines and fine foods of many kinds in generous portions. What more can I say? It's hard to describe how delighted the Abbot was by the Seigneur de Saintré's hospitality. When their bellies were full and everyone's thirst was well quenched, the Seigneur de Saintré asked the Abbot if he had ever worn armor.

"Armor?" asked Lord Abbot. "No, not really."

"By God!" exclaimed Saintré. "It would be a fine sight to see you in arms. [293] What do you think, my lady? Isn't that the truth?"

"Indeed," said Madame. "I think, in fact I'm certain, that if he were armed, anyone who would make fun of him would get his comeuppance."

"My lady, I don't know who would make fun of him, but I can say that I've never seen a man who would be finer to behold in arms."

And then he told Perrenet, his personal servant, to do what he had been instructed to do. So Perrenet installed a table at one end of the room, and placed a huge set of armor upon it, without an axe or a sword.

When Lord Abbot observed the fine, glistening armor, in which he took great pleasure, and when he heard himself so highly praised, he thought that the Seigneur de Saintré would generously offer him the suit of arms, which he had doubtless brought out for that express purpose; the Abbot decided that if he were asked to arm himself, he would not refuse.

FIG. 6. Brussels, Bibliothèque Royale, MS 9457, f. 183v:
Saintré and the Abbot arming themselves.

Reproduced by permission of the Bibliothèque Royale.

Then, to show how much he admired the outfit, he began to sing its
praises.

"Since it's so much to your liking," said the Seigneur de Saintré, "if it
fits you, then you should really have it."

"Have it, my lord?"

"Yes, Lord Abbot, and have even better than that, if you wanted to ask
me for it."

"By my faith! For the love of Madame, I'll neither eat nor drink until
I'm armed."

Then he cried, "Remove the tables, we've already eaten more than
enough!"

Lord Abbot joyfully put on the doublet; the Seigneur de Saintré immediately took up an awl as well a good supply of laces and attached the Abbot's
armor completely from head to toe; he set the bascinet, firmly clamped, on
the Abbot's head and then fitted the gauntlets on his hands. [294]

When the Lord Abbot was completely armed, he turned back and forth
admiring himself and said to Madame and her ladies, "What do you have to
say about seeing a monk in armor? Isn't he a fine sight to see?"

"A monk? There aren't many monks like that."

"Oh, God! If only I had an axe and someone willing to fight me."

Then he jokingly said, "Ha! My lady, this gear weighs more than mine does,[157] but it will do for me, since I've earned it."

And as he uttered these words, Saintré said to him, "You haven't earned it yet, but you'll pay for it soon enough."

And he had another suit of armor brought forth, with which he armed himself completely.

When Madame heard these words and saw Saintré arm himself so quickly, she feared what was about to happen, and said, "Sire de Saintré, just what are you intending to do?"

"My lady," he replied when he was ready, "you'll soon see."

"I'll see what? You fool: do you mean to fight with an abbot?"

Lord Saintré, now completely armed, ordered his men to guard the door so that no one could enter or leave the room. He announced to the ladies, maidens, monks, and all others who were present: "Stand over there by the door, without moving or saying a word. Whoever does otherwise, I'll split his head open!"

Then you should have seen the women and monks tremble in fear, weeping and cursing the hour that they had all assembled there.

Then Saintré went up to Madame and said, "You agreed most graciously to be the judge of the wrestling match between the Abbot and me; now I beg most humbly that you adjudicate the kind of fight I've learned to fight, and that you make this request on my behalf to Lord Abbot." [295]

"I don't know what request you are talking about," said Madame. "If you do him any harm, I'll consider it harm done to me, and I'll take him under my protection."

Then the Seigneur de Saintré went up to the Abbot and said, "My Lord Abbot, at your request and at Madame's, I have fought twice with you; I am still stinging from the two somersaults I did as a result, but there was no way I could excuse myself from acceding to either her request or your own. So now I implore and beg you, for the love of the lady you love so loyally, to fight in the way that I've learned to fight."

"Ah! Monseigneur de Saintré," said the Abbot, "I don't know how to fight in armor."

Then the Seigneur de Saintré said, "You'll go through with the fight or you'll go through the window."

Seeing how determined Saintré was to fight, Madame said harshly, "Lord Saintré, unless both of you remove that armor immediately, as I command, you'll provoke my fury. If you don't, you stupid fool, we shall have you punished severely, every bone in your body."

When the Seigneur de Saintré heard himself insulted and threatened in favor of her beloved Abbot, he exclaimed, [296] "Oh, you treacherous, disloyal lady, such and such as you are, I have served you longer and more loyally than any man could serve and please a lady, only to have you abandon me and dishonor yourself by falling treacherously and dishonestly for a lecherous monk. And so that you won't abuse or threaten me or anyone else ever again, I'm going to do something that you'll never forget and that will serve as an example to all other ladies."

Then he grabbed a lock of hair protruding from her headdress and raised his hand as if to strike her. But he restrained himself from hitting her, having remembered all the good things which she had done for him and for which he could be blamed. She wept as if she had fainted in sorrow, and he made her sit down on a bench, from which she dared not move.

Then he ordered that the arms be brought forth—two poleaxes, two swords, and two daggers. He girded on the Abbot's sword and gave him a choice of axes and daggers, saying, "Lord Abbot, Lord Abbot, remember the insults you levied against knights and squires who travel the world seeking feats of arms to increase their honor; now's the time to pay for that! So now, Lord Abbot, defend yourself!"

Then he lowered his visor and had the Abbot's visor lowered and moved forward to attack him.

When Lord Abbot saw that he had no choice but to fight back, he raised his axe with such force that if he had struck Saintré—owing both to his own strength and power and to the fact that he was taller—he would have knocked him to the ground or wounded him, as Madame certainly wished. But by the will of God and by his expertise in armed combat, Saintré covered himself and withstood the blow. [297] That done, Saintré dug into his opponent with the spike of his axe and forced him to retreat to a bench in front of Madame; he knocked him over backward, and the Abbot fell so hard that he nearly blacked out, as he cried "Mercy! Have mercy! Mercy, my lady! Ah! Monseigneur de Saintré, for God's sake, have mercy!"

Then Saintré, still seething with rage because of the insults and nasty slurs described earlier, had every intention of bringing his opponent's life to an end. As he raised his axe, he remembered the verses where Our Lord speaks in the Old Testament in Deuteronomy, the fifth book of the Bible, which say: *Quicunque fuderit sanguinem humanum, fundeter sanguis illius.*[158]

And again the Lord says during the Passion, *Qui gladio percussit, gladio peribit*. And again, he says to David, *Non edificabis michi domum, quia vir sanguinium es*. And furthermore through the mouth of David, he says: *Vir sanguinum et dolosi non dimidiabunt dies suos*. And again through the mouth of David, he says: *Virum sanguinum et dolosum abhorabitur Dominus*. And again in the same way, he says: *Si occideris, Deus, peccatores, viri sanguinum, declinate a me*. And he has recommended so many other acts of pity, mercy, and compassion and commanded and demonstrated these through his own actions, that the Seigneur de Saintré restrained himself from pressing for death.

But in any case, either in pursuit of vengeance or by following the divine will that would have permitted his punishment for such an obviously manifest sin, he threw down his axe, took his dagger in his hand, raised the Abbot's visor and then said, [298] "Now, Sir Abbot, recognize that God is the true judge here, since neither your strength nor your false, wicked, and injurious speech has prevented your punishment. In the presence of she who has made you so arrogant and for whom you have lied so dishonestly and so calumniated knights and squires, your very false tongue will pay for it."[159] Then Saintré drove his dagger through the Abbot's tongue and both his cheeks, and left him in this state, with the words, "Lord Abbot, now you have most loyally earned your suit of armor."

Then Saintré had his own armor removed; when he had removed his armor, he saw Madame, with disheveled hair and her headdress askew, and he said, "Farewell, to the most treacherous woman who ever lived."

As he uttered these words, he observed that she wore a belt of blue fabric with a gold clasp. He unfastened the belt, saying, "My lady, how dare you wear a blue belt? The color blue signifies loyalty, yet you are truly the most disloyal woman that I know; you shall wear this belt no longer."

Then he unfastened the belt and took it off her, folded it, and placed it next to his heart. He went over to the ladies and damsels, the monks and all their other people, who were all bleating like sheep in the corners of the room, and told them, "You are witnesses to all that has been said and done, which, to my great displeasure, has caused me to do what I did; I beg you to forgive me for the discomfort this has caused you, may God bless you."

Then the door was opened, and Saintré went downstairs and said to the host, "The Lord Abbot may keep the large suit of armor if he wants it. As for the small suit and the two axes, return them to Jacques and tell him to come to me quickly. [299] Good host, are you well satisfied?"

As he spoke, he mounted on horseback and said farewell to the host. And now I shall stop talking about Saintré, who went back to the court. I shall tell about Madame and the Abbot, and their people, who remained stunned and in a state of great sorrow and melancholy—have no doubt about it.

How Madame and Lord Abbot remained with their people

THE AUTHOR: After Madame had straightened herself up again and all the ladies had cried enough and Lord Abbot was disarmed, they called for the surgeon. You should have seen them weep and curse their lives that this armed combat had ever been fought. Lord Abbot, who was unable to speak, was undressed and made to lie down, and then it was time for Madame to depart and leave her lover. And anyone who heard her laments, tears, and sighs over the state of the Abbot would have thought that she had lost all her friends and closest relatives.

Her ladies said, "Alas, my lady, we couldn't help but think as he was suiting himself up in that armor that harm would befall him for having attacked the honor of gentlemen."

"Indeed," said another, "and for having abused the Seigneur de Saintré and hurt him so badly, the revenge was well taken."

"Never mind," said Madame, "the Abbot will have his revenge, as soon as he heals. And Saintré also tried to hit *me*, and he insulted me, and then he carried off my belt, like the thief and murderer that he is!"

Now I shall stop telling about Madame and the convalescence of Lord Abbot, who had given themselves two months of good time together, better than they had ever had before; their parting surely was very hard. [300]

How Madame returned to court

THE AUTHOR: All the while Madame and Lord Abbot continued to enjoy themselves in this way, the King on the one hand and the Dukes his brothers on the other expressed amazement several times that their Belle Cousine had remained away so long—which they mentioned at one point to the Queen. The Queen, very displeased, suspected some unfortunate news but kept quiet for the sake of Madame's honor. They begged the Queen to write to Madame and insist that she return. The Queen informed them that she had already done so and that, in fact, she had dispatched two messengers to her. Madame could certainly return whenever she felt like it, but the Queen would not ask her again.

The Dukes understood by the Queen's way of speaking that she was extremely displeased with Madame; so they wrote to her themselves, sending one of their trusted priests as emissary. Then Madame was forcibly compelled, much against her will, to leave her own "confessor" and to send word to the Queen as to the day when she would, without fail, be back at court. And so the fair priest and confessor bade her farewell, and she took her leave of him and returned to the court.

THE AUTHOR: Ah! False, wicked, and treacherous Love, will you always resemble Hell, who can never swallow enough souls to be sated? Will you never get your fill of torturing hearts and destroying them? God and Nature have given you such power that you have stolen and imprisoned the hearts of popes, emperors, empresses, cardinals, kings, queens, archbishops, dukes, duchesses, patriarchs, marquises and marchionesses, bishops, princes and princesses, abbots and abbesses, counts and countesses, and people of all other estates and lay and monastic orders. [301] You have stolen hearts from all of them, as many stories recount. You have used them very falsely and wickedly, and then in the end left them confused, abandoned, and dishonored for having completely lost their souls and their honor, unless God has mercy, as this story bears witness. But I shall leave all this to come back to my point, as follows:

THE AUTHOR: When Madame was ordered so peremptorily to leave, she and the Abbot were both so heartbroken that I could not describe their pain. Nonetheless, the Abbot promised that he would often go to visit her in disguise, and with this sweet hope, with great distress in their hearts, they took leave of one another. They would have enjoyed each other's company if it had not been for the separation.

How Madame returned to the court, and the warm welcome that everyone gave her

THE AUTHOR: Madame, pensive and sorrowful about her love, returned to court, accompanied by numerous lords, counts and barons, knights and squires, who had come to meet her; she made her reverence to the King, who greeted her quite warmly, and then she went to the Queen, who said, "It has taken you a long time to return. You seem to enjoy the country air."

Then she went to the Dukes, who greeted her warmly, and said, "We're very thankful that you've returned." [302]

And then the other ladies and damsels, knights and squires, all went to bow before her and to celebrate her return. And so things went for about a month.

Then it happened that one evening after supper, while the King and the Queen were in a lovely meadow with a great number of lords and ladies, the Seigneur de Saintré said to the Queen and to the other ladies, "Come sit here, and I will tell you a marvelous new story I've learned from a letter sent from far away."

"Do go on!" said the Queen. "For heaven's sake, let us hear it."

"My lady, please be seated."

And then she called Madame, "Fair cousin, and all you other ladies, let's all be seated to hear this bit of news that Seigneur de Saintré wants to tell us."

Then the Queen was seated, with Madame next to her, and then all the other ladies and damsels, along with a few lords, knights and squires who were present. Then the Queen said with a laugh to the Seigneur de Saintré, "Master of new stories, now begin to tell your tale."

How the Seigneur de Saintré, without naming names, told the story of Madame, Lord Abbot, and himself, and how he gave the belt back to Madame in front of the Queen and many other ladies and maidens

THE AUTHOR: The Seigneur of Saintré then began to tell his story in the best manner he knew, and said, "Ma'am, I've read a letter recounting a true story that recently happened in Germany, about a very noble, prominent lady, who took pleasure in the company of a very fine youth. She showered him with so much wealth, honor, and love over a certain length of time that she made a renowned knight of him; they loved each other so loyally, as the letter describes it, that there were never more loyal lovers nor a more hidden love." [303]

THE AUTHOR:
But Fortune, the traitor jade,
As Boethius's poem said,

Overcome with her deceit,
Wants her followers full of grief;
Surprises them more suddenly
Than would a wave far out to sea,
And changes their state in a trice,
So that the low become the highest,
And the highest are as nought:
For their tears he has no thought.
The more they weep and wail and moan,
The louder does her laughter grow.
Her greatest joy is, out of hand,
To make a beggar a happy man.

SAINTRÉ: "And so it was, Ma'am, with this poor unfortunate youth who so enjoyed his lady's grace that no lover had ever found better favor with his lady. It came to pass that by Fortune's will, both for the sake of her love and to increase his honor, he came to France to accomplish feats of arms, which would redound to his honor. But as these things were transpiring, the lady took up with a tall, fat, powerfully built monk who was the lord abbot of an important, wealthy abbey; they loved each other so much that she completely forgot about her very loyal lover and servant."

The Queen replied, "Her joy was ill conceived when she left the one who loved her so much for a monk." [304]

"Ma'am, so it was, for the letter that I've read doesn't lie. Now listen, Ma'am, and you shall hear the end of the story."

"Do tell," said the Queen. "Finish your tale."

Then the Seigneur de Saintré recounted the story word for word: telling first how the lover found the couple hunting; then how the Abbot ordered Madame to invite him for supper, the reply she made, and how the knight accepted immediately so that he could see the farce played out. He told how the Abbot and Madame mocked knights and squires who performed feats of arms throughout the realm; how she set up and adjudicated their wrestling match; he recounted how they wrestled dressed in their doublets and told about the great capers that the Abbot performed before Madame, as well as the laughs, jests, and mockery that they engaged in during the wrestling match, which the Abbot won. He told of the messengers who were sent from the monastery, and, to make a long story short, he described how the two men took up arms, how they fought, and how the Abbot fared. He told how

Madame spoke to the knight, insulting him and threatening him out of love for her new lover, and how the jilted knight laid hands on her headdress, as if he meant to strike her. He repeated all the words that the young man spoke to her and told how he removed her blue belt, since her disloyalty made her unworthy to wear that color.

After he had concluded, everyone blamed the lady (who they believed was from Germany) and held her in contempt; and the knight was greatly praised for his fight and his endeavors. This fine piece of news brought such joy to the court that people could scarcely stop talking about it. But Madame simply sat there, quiet as a mouse, listening to the whole story with a stone face without uttering a word. [305]

Then the Seigneur of Saintré said to the Queen and to all the ladies present, "Ma'am, and you, my ladies, the story demands that you judge whether the lady behaved properly or not. And you, Ma'am, I shall ask you first."

As the Queen had listened to the tale about an abbot and a lady, she suspected that it might very well be about her Belle Cousine, but since she had no inkling of the love between Saintré and Madame, she did not know what to think. So to see what Madame might be thinking, she asked Madame to make the first pronouncement. "Please excuse me, Ma'am, because I wasn't really thinking about what he said. If you please, speak first or ask the others, and although I don't think this matter deserves judgment, when you and all the others have spoken, I shall say how the case seems to me."

Then the Queen said, "Since it is our duty as Queen to begin, really, Saintré, if all this happened as you say, we'll declare that such a lady is treacherous and wicked, and we'll leave it at that."

SAINTRÉ: "Well now, Madame de Rethel, what would you like to say?"

"I would say the same thing as the Queen—and furthermore, I think the lady should be banished from all good society."

"And you, Madame de Vendôme, what do you say?"

"I declare, good friend, that she should be tied backward on an ass, her face toward the tail, and led throughout the town as a symbol of contempt."

"And you, Madame du Perche, what is your opinion?"

"The Queen and the other ladies have well expressed my feelings; [306] if I were to add anything, assuming that the tale is true, I'd say that such a lady should be stripped naked above and below the waist, completely shaved, then coated with honey, and then paraded through the city so that the flies will swarm all over her and bite her. She's a most treacherous lady, if she's still alive, to have abandoned such a perfect love servant, be he knight or squire, for a monk. And blessed be the lover who so punishes her!"

Then there was no lady or damsel who did not laugh and agree with all these opinions, which were also pronounced by Mesdames de Beaumont, de Craon, de Graville, de Maulevrier, and d'Ivry. The men present listened with great delight and said nothing. Just so, in Madame's presence, were these opinions uttered and the judgment on her disloyalty pronounced.

THE AUTHOR: After the Seigneur de Saintré had asked everyone and after they had replied in the terms that we have seen, or even worse, he turned toward Madame and, on bended knee, asked her opinion, as he had of the others. Madame, tongue-tied, did not know what to say, as the one who was at the very center of the story. But pressed by the Queen and the other ladies to give her opinion as the others had, she said, "Since I must speak, it seems to me that whoever the lover was, knight or squire as he may be, he was very ungracious to have unfastened the lady's belt and taken it away from her, as you described."

"Come now, my lady," replied Saintré, "you're not answering my question, which is whether the lady was right to have abandoned her loyal lover and servant. Can't you say anything besides condemning the lover for his bad manners in taking the belt away from the treacherous lady, who was in any case unworthy to wear blue?" [307]

With that, he drew the belt with the golden buckle from his sleeve, saying "My lady, I do not wish to remain ungracious any longer."

Then, on bended knee, before the Queen and her assembly of ladies, knights, and squires, the Seigneur de Saintré placed the belt in Madame's lap, ever so graciously.

When the Queen and her retinue witnessed this marvelous event, they looked at each other in amazement. As you can imagine, they were astonished that the story was about Madame. And you need not ask if Madame must have been ashamed, for at that moment she lost all joy and honor.

And so I come to the end of my tale, praying, requesting, and entreating all ladies and damsels, townswomen and others, from whatever station in life they be, that they all heed the example of this indolent noble lady who lost herself for Love. Let them reflect on the common saying: There is no fire without smoke, however deeply buried the fire may be. This means that there was never any good or evil, however secret, hidden, or obscure it might be, that has not been discovered in the end—for so has decreed the true, most powerful Judge of all things, from whom nothing should, or can, be hidden.

The just and good are rewarded; the wicked and sinners are punished, in body, in soul, and in reputation, as happened to the lady in this story and to many other men and women who have been punished for their unruly desires. [308] There can well be smoke without fire, which means that there are many false wagging tongues belonging to flatterers who blow smoke without fire—that is, there are those who spread false and wicked rumors about men and women that have no basis or reason. But their smoke doesn't arise from fire, that is honest proof. So these rumor mongers are damned and dishonored, and they lose their souls, their honor, and, often, their lives; they are shamed and mocked behind their backs.

THE AUTHOR: Here I shall bring to conclusion my book about this most valiant knight. Aside from the exploits that I've recounted, he engaged in many other battles on land and sea and fought in armed combat many other times. In particular, he was one of the sixteen knights and squires who fought in Cairo before the Sultan and vanquished twenty-two renegade Christians and thus upheld the faith of Our Lord. And he traveled extensively—it would take me far too long to tell all that he did.

When it pleased God to take his soul through Death, who spares no one, the day that Death closed the door on the light of his eyes, he was considered the most valiant knight who had ever fought in the kingdom of France. He finished his natural life in Pont-Saint-Esprit on the Rhone, having taken all the Holy Sacraments, just as all good, true Christians should do. And as his grave was dug in the earth, a little chest was found with a scroll in it that said:

"Here will lie the body of he who will be the most valiant knight of his time in France and further beyond." [309]

About which "further beyond" they say that it means he was the most valiant knight there was in the world at that time.

Out of love and respect for his worthy acts, I had the pleasure of going to his gravesite, and I have committed to memory the words, engraved in Latin, on the tombstone that lay on his grave:

Hic jacet dominus Johannes de Saintré, miles, senescallus Andegavensis et Senomanensis, camerariusque domini ducis Andegavensis, qui obiit anno domini millesimo CCC^{mo} lxvii° die xxv° octobris, cuius anima in pace requiescat. Amen.[160]

Now, most honorable, excellent, and powerful prince and my most esteemed lord, if I have failed in any way by writing too much or too little, which I might easily have done, considering that I am neither a wise man nor a cleric, if you please—and I speak as well to all men and women—do pardon me, for often one does the best one can without doing very well, which is no wonder, since I am and have always been rough and unrefined in my behavior, my deeds and my writing. But to fulfill the wishes of the one whose wishes are my commands, more so than for any other lord, I have composed this book called *Saintré*, which I send to you in the manner of a letter; I entreat you to accept it graciously. And therefore, at the present moment, my most esteemed lord, I write you nothing else, except that as humbly as I know how I commend myself to your very good and desired graces, wherever I may be, and I pray the Lord of Lords that he grant you full enjoyment of all your desires.

Written at Châtelet-sur-Oise, the sixth day of March, in the year of Our Lord fourteen hundred fifty-five.

NOTES

INTRODUCTION

1. Jeay, "Les éléments," p. 90.

2. As Dubuis concedes (*Saintré*, trans. Dubuis, pp. 13–14), many modern readers may be tempted only by the love story.

3. Medieval readers seem to have enjoyed lists and enumerations; see Jeay, *Commerce des mots.*

4. Kristeva, pp. 22–23.

5. This manuscript may be viewed online at Gallica, http://gallica.bnf.fr/ark:/12148/btv1b6001339w.r = antoine + de + la + sale.langEN (acc. November 2013).

6. For a detailed description of this manuscript that emphasizes its composite quality, see Jeay, "Une théorie du roman."

7. The most complete account of La Sale's life story, culled in large part from autobiographical fragments within his works, remains Desonay, *Antoine de La Sale.*

8. The first two trips are told in *Le Paradis de la Reine Sibylle*; for the story of the selfless woman who tends to her leper husband in Pozzuoli, see *La Sale*, pp. 134–36. On the way that La Sale inserts travel narrative by an "unreliable narrator" into his pedagogic tomes, see Léglu.

9. See La Sale, *Le Réconfort* (ll. 904–1206).

10. The trajectory of La Sale's life and travels is provided by Lefèvre, pp. 295–98. We have adopted Lefèvre's dating for La Sale's biography.

11. See Szkilnik, "*Jean de Saintré* ou le rêve."

12. Parts of *La Salade* and fully three-fourths of *La Sale* are close copies of Simon de Hesdin's translation of Valerius Maximus's *Book of Memorable Deeds and Sayings*; see Lecourt.

13. *La Salade*, pp. 208–23. See the remarks of Lefèvre on this section, p. 137.

14. *La Salade*, p. 32; for the list in Simon de Hesdin, see Lecourt, pp. 43–44; for *Saintré*, see pp. 75–76.

15. The stories of the Sibyl's grotto and of the voyage to the Lipari Islands have been translated into modern French: see *Le Paradis*, trans. Mora-Lebrun. An edition of *Le*

Paradis de la Reine Sibylle, from the Chantilly manuscript dedicated to Agnès de Bourbon, is provided in Mora, *Voyages en Sibyllie,* along with a detailed study of La Sale's complex narrative and its many sources and analogues.

16. For two perspectives on La Sale's blend of fact and fantasy in his travels to these islands, see Léglu, and Mora-Lebrun, pp. 218–41.

17. See Lecourt.

18. Such is the opinion of the work's editor, Desonay, *La Sale,* p. viii.

19. Lecourt, p. 211.

20. *La Sale,* Prologue.

21. On the way that La Sale "signs" or marks his works with particular devices or signatures, see Lefèvre, pp. 69–82. His authorial consciousness develops throughout the course of his literary career.

22. Lecourt, pp. 200–203.

23. *La Sale,* p. 1.

24. *La Sale,* pp. xxxi–xxxiii.

25. On La Sale's likely sources, see the Otaka edition (1967) and Szkilnik, *Jean de Saintré,* pp. 19–41. On sources and analogues for particular passages, see the Otaka edition and our references to Otaka in the notes to our translation.

26. See Glixelli.

27. See Krueger, "Introduction," in Johnston, ed., *Medieval Conduct Literature,* pp. ix–xxxiii.

28. See Szkilnik, *Jean de Saintré,* pp. 19–41.

29. For the *Prose Lancelot* as a possible source for *Saintré,* see Taylor, "Pattern."

30. Szkilnik, *Jean de Saintré,* pp. 139–55.

31. See Lalande, "Le couple."

32. On *Saintré* as chivalric biography, see Szkilnik, *Jean de Saintré.*

33. On the life of Lalaing as a source for La Sale, see Poirion, p. 112; on *Saintré* as a source for Lalaing's biography, *Le Livre des faits,* see Szkilnik, *Jean de Saintré,* pp. 15–16, 22–25.

34. On the *nouvelle,* see Dubuis, *Les Cent Nouvelles nouvelles.*

35. *Saintré,* p. 206.

36. Who was brother to Louis of Luxemburg, in whose household Antoine was employed.

37. This sort of predetermined plot and complex *mise en scène* are typical of the tournaments of the fifteenth century: see Huizinga, *Waning;* Planche; Barber and Barker; Jourdan. René d'Anjou, La Sale's long-term employer, was an enthusiast: his tournaments included the *Pas d'armes of the Dragon's Mouth* (1446), and the *Pas d'armes of the Shepherdess* (1449); see de Mérindol.

38. *Turnierbuch,* st. 27; see Bianciotto.

39. Ed. Lefèvre, pp. 283–341; it survives in just two MSS.

40. For illustrations, see http://mandragore.bnf.fr/html/accueil.html. René's text is available with English translation at http://www.princeton.edu/~ezb/rene/renehome .html (acc. December 2013).

41. On tournaments see Heers; Vale, *War and Chivalry*; Contamine, "Les tournois"; Stanesco; Barber and Barker. Until the thirteenth century, such events were less closely prescribed (see Barker, *Tournament*, pp. 142–44).

42. Geoffroi de Charny, p. 86.

43. See Kaeuper, *Chivalry and Violence* pp. 161–88, and Vale, "Violence and the Tournament," in Kaeuper, ed., *Violence*, pp. 143–58.

44. Commonly regarded by authorities as the superior form of chivalric encounter: see Keen, *Chivalry*, 99–101.

45. See Vale, *Princely Court*, pp. 167–69.

46. "Drama," or "ceremony," but a *mistere* is also a "mystery play": see Planche; Jourdan. For discussion of other *pas d'armes*, see Stanesco, pp. 123–35, 198–206.

47. See Szkilnik, *Jean de Saintré*, pp. 114–20, and cf. *Livre des faits de Jacques de Lalaing*.

48. See Anglo.

49. Szkilnik, *Jean de Saintré*, pp. 71–94.

50. The "achievement" shows all the divisions which signify ancestry (see for instance, p. 76), along with supporters, crests, sometimes mottos; the "device," or badge, is a personal emblem.

51. See Vale, *Princely Court*, pp. 165–200.

52. Lefèvre, *Antoine de La Sale*, p. 299 (how tournaments are fashioned in terms of arms and helmet crests).

53. See Bianciotto; Heers; *Turnierbuch*.

54. On La Sale's own arms, see, exhaustively, Lefèvre, *Antoine de La Sale,* pp. 21–67.

55. See Lefèvre, *Antoine de La Sale,* pp. 264–74. Note that La Sale's blazoning can be faulty—but by this late date, heralds themselves are frequently rather approximate.

56. Or an "armorial," a manuscript recording, and illustrating, the arms of participants in a tournament, or from a particular court or region: see Pastoureau, and for examples *Rolls of Arms: Edward I (1272–1307),* ed. Gerald J. Brault (London: Boydell, 1997). La Sale seems, for instance, for his part, to have copied the names and arms of some of those taking part in Saintré's *pas d'armes* and crusade from those in the so-called *Armorial d'Urfé,* for a partial edition of which see http://www.armorial.dk/english/Urfe -en.pdf (we are grateful to Professor D'Arcy Boulton for this suggestion; cf. also Vaivre).

57. Geoffroi de Charny, p. 88.

58. Szkilnik, *Jean de Saintré,* pp. 95–112; Taylor, "La fonction."

59. Riley-Smith, pp. 251–54.

60. Riley-Smith, pp. 271 ff., and Christiansen; on La Sale's "crusade," see Knudson. The term "Saracens" is used throughout the Middle Ages to mean "non-Christian"; what is remarkable is the constitution of the "Saracen" army as imagined by La Sale.

61. Keen, *Nobles, Knights*, pp. 121–34.

62. See R. Cazelle, *Jean l'Aveugle, comte de Luxembourg, roi de Bohême* (Bourges: A. Tardy, 1947).

63. Almost certainly, again, transcribed from a roll of arms now lost; for a list of surviving examples, see http://www.armorial.dk (acc. July 2012).

64. Riley-Smith, pp. 276–81.

65. See Strubel.

66. Stanesco, p. 99.

67. Keen, "Huizinga, Kilgour."

68. See Taylor, "Image as Reception," and for the Brussels MS., see Johan.

69. For an overview of the history of Tressan's *Saintré,* see Speer, pp. 398–406.

70. For a complete account of these editions, see entry on La Sale in the Archives de Littérature du Moyen Age (ARLIMA): http://www.arlima.net/ad/antoine_de_la_sale.html (acc. December 2013).

71. Trans. Vance (1862) and Gray (1931).

72. Heraldry deserves a special note. The language of heraldry is precise, and very particular: it derives in part from Anglo-Norman, and many English terms therefore resemble La Sale's original French. We have translated, consistently, according to correct heraldic practice—with the invaluable help of Professor Jonathan D'Arcy Boulton, of the University of Notre Dame. Heraldic terms cannot be "translated" into modern English—nor can they easily be defined; in fact, they are best illustrated. As we say at the beginning of our Glossary, those who are interested should consult either the standard *Boutell's Heraldry* or Friar's *New Dictionary of Heraldry;* even more usefully, they could refer to a website which illustrates almost all the terms used here: http://www.heraldsnet.org/saitou/parker/Jpframe.html (acc. October 2013).

JEAN DE SAINTRÉ

1. The bracketed numbers refer to page numbers in the Misrahi and Knudson edition of *Saintré.*

2. Jean de Calabre (1426–70), son of René d'Anjou and putative heir to the throne of Sicily. La Sale was Jean's tutor from 1435 to 1455. See Bénet, *Jean d'Anjou.*

3. A French translation by Rasse de Brunhamel of Nicolas de Clamanges's *Floridan and Elvide* and the *Chronicles of Flanders* are included after *Saintré* in four manuscripts, three of which also name the fourth "treatise" as *Le Roman de Paris et Vienne,* which was to have appeared in the second volume. The author's (or scribe's) hand in BnF nouv. acq. fr. 10057 has scratched out mention of this work; no extant version of *Paris et Vienne* appears to have been produced for a companion volume. For editions of these and other works cited in the notes, see the Bibliography.

4. Son of Philip VI of Valois, John II or John the Good ruled from 1350 to 1364. In 1332, he married Bonne of Bohemia, who died in 1349. One of the couple's ten children was King Charles V (1338–80).

5. The historical Jean de Saintré (1320–68) was seneschal of Anjou and Maine; Froissart recounts his capture by the English at Poitiers; at the time he held to be "the best and most valiant knight in France"; Froissart, *Chronicles,* p. 138.

6. Bonne of Bohemia died before John's coronation and was thus never officially Queen. This is the first of several occasions when La Sale's historical facts are imprecise. On other historical errors or inconsistencies, see Lalande, "Le couple."

7. The citations and exempla about Roman widows are found nearly verbatim in *La Sale*, Book II, chapter XII, pp. 138–42.

8. 1 Timothy 5:3–16.

9. Virgil, *Aeneid* IV, 29–30.

10. Widely cited in the Middle Ages, St. Jerome's fourth-century *Adversus Joviniam* argues against marriage and in favor of virginity, often with an antifeminist bias. See Jerome, "Against Jovinian," in *Jankyn's Book of Wikked Wives*, ed. Hanna and Lawler, p. 172.

11. La Sale concludes his chapter on widows with this comic exemplum in *La Sale*, p. 140; it is drawn from Simon de Hesdin's MF [Middle French] translation of Valerius Maximus's *Memorable Doings and Sayings* (first century CE), a frequent source for *La Salade, La Sale*, and *Saintré;* see Lecourt, pp. 200–201.

12. The hero is often referred to as "le petit Saintré" in the opening scenes; the can be translated either as "young Saintré" or as "little Saintré," meaning small in stature, for Jean is both. The adjective "petit" disappears as Jean matures; by the end of the story, he has become "le Seigneur de Saintré."

13. Many of the classical authorities cited in this section are found in Diogenes Laertius, *Lives of Eminent Philosophers;* the Latin translation of this work was a treasure house of classical exempla and quotations for medieval authors. This particular saying is widespread in medieval florilegia. For further information on sources for La Sale's didactic citations, see Otaka, "Citations," in La Sale, *Jehan de Saintré,* ed. Otaka, pp. 343–48, as well as Dubuis's translation of *Saintré,* pp. 287–324.

14. When La Sale speaks simply of "the Philosopher," with no other identification, he refers to Aristotle, who was considered the preeminent philosopher and whose works were translated into Latin in the late Middle Ages

15. 1 John 3:15.

16. Ephesians 4:26.

17. One of the most widely transmitted medieval collections of wise sayings was attributed to Cato the Elder, a statesman in Rome, 234–149 BCE. The *Disticha Catonis,* which were actually composed in the fourth century AD and are not by the historical Cato, circulated in hundreds of editions in Latin and all the vernacular languages throughout the Middle Ages. The pithy moralizing couplets and aphorisms in the *Distichs* could be easily memorized and were standard schoolboy fare. For this citation in its classical context, see Cato, "The Distichs of Cato," in *Minor Latin Poets,* p. 604.

18. "Sens" can mean the capacity for understanding as well as moral sense or wisdom.

19. In MF, "maniere." Here as elsewhere "maniere" seems to refer to good conduct, more significant than polite "manners."

20. Cf. "Malo mori quam foedari" ("Death rather than dishonor"), the Latin proverb popular on coats of arms. The play on "fames" [hunger] and "fama" [reputation] is lost in translation.

21. Matthew 5:7.

22. Ecclesiasticus 14:9.

23. The Hours are prayers to be read or recited during the different canonical hours of the day (Matins, Lauds, Terce, Sext, None, Vespers, Compline); for each day, the prayers reflect the holy events of the Christian calendar. Many noble men and women owned Books of Hours, which were sometimes beautifully illuminated.

24. "Pechié de gueule," literally the sin of the gullet.

25. Philippians 3:19.

26. 1 Peter 2:11.

27. Otaka compares Proverbs 6:16, "There are six things that Yahweh hates . . ."

28. Psalm 30:7 in the Latin Vulgate. Corresponds to Psalm 31:6 in the New Jerusalem Bible

29. The Decretals refer to collections of pontifical letters involving papal rulings and decisions as well as other canon law. References for the legal statutes in this section, from the *Corpus iuris canonici* and the *Corpus iuris civilis,* are provided by Otaka, *Jehan de Saintré,* pp. 344–45.

30. Cf. Deuteronomy 6:16. "Do not put Yahweh your God to the test . . ."

31. This same incident is mentioned by Christine de Pizan, *Book of Deeds of Arms and Chivalry,* pp. 197–98.

32. Eusebi says that these citations are from Lombard law, the legal codes of the Lombard kings who ruled Italy in the early Middle Ages, as conserved in the *Monumenta Germaniae Historica, Legum,* volume IV; Eusebi, p. 60, note 162. Otaka says the references are too imprecise to allow for exact identification, "Citations," p. 345. The Lombard laws have been translated by Drew, *The Lombard Laws.*

33. This section is taken from the *Ordonnance sur les gages de bataille* of Philip the Fair, which is included in its entirety in *La Salade,* pp. 208-23. The *Ordonnance* is from 1306; see Lefèvre, p. 137. For an edition of the complete *Gages de bataille* with facsimile prints of the eleven illustrations, see *Cérémonies.* King Philip IV outlawed private warfare, duels, and tournaments during the war in Gascony in 1296; later, he imposed restrictions on private warfare at any time; see Kaeuper, *War, Justice,* pp. 235–47, and Jager, *The Last Duel,* pp. 82–83. The 1306 decree permits duels in certain instances: (1) following evident capital crimes: murder, treason, rape; (2) in cases where the death penalty would be invoked, theft excluded; (3) where no other legal remedies are possible; and (4) incontrovertible evidence.

34. MF "espee de giet," a sword that uses only the point, like a rapier (although technically the term "rapier" does not appear until the sixteenth century).

35. Vegetius's fifth-century *De Re Militari* (On Military Matters) remained a popular military guide throughout the Middle Ages; it was translated and adapted into MF by Christine de Pizan in her *Deeds of Arms and of Chivalry.*

36. Cited earlier, *Saintré,* p. 16, attributed to the Philosopher (Aristotle).

37. In this context, "enemies" (MF *nos ennemis*) may refer to devils, enemies of the Lord.

38. The precepts known as the Ten Commandments appear, in versions somewhat different from those given here, in Exodus 20:1–17 and Deuteronomy 5:6–21.

39. The twelve articles of faith are contained in the Apostle's Creed, a statement of Catholic belief that dates to late antiquity; its tenets remain part of Catholic doctrine today and are used in some Protestant congregations.

40. Hebrews 11:6.

41. The Seven Gifts originate in Isaiah 11:2–3.

42. The Beatitudes originate in Matthew 5:1–12, from Christ's Sermon on the Mount, where they are different in order and substance.

43. The Divine and Moral Virtues are often referred to as the theological and cardinal virtues; the cardinal virtues originate in classical ethics of ancient Greek philosophy; the theological virtues are Christian additions, following St. Paul, 1 Corinthians 13:13, where "Faith," "Hope," and "Love" (or "Charity") are key. For a history of the incorporation of classical virtues into Christian thought, see Bejczy.

44. In Thomas Aquinas, *Summa theologiae,* 3a, 45, 1, the qualities of the glorified body are "impassibilitas, agilitas, subtilitas, and claritas," translated by Parson and Pinheiro as "impassibility, agility, subtlety, and splendor," see Aquinas, *Summa theologiae,* vol. 53, pp. 148–49.

45. The Corporal Works of Mercy have biblical roots in Matthew 25:31 46.

46. Cited earlier, *Saintré*, p. 17.

47. The Eucharist.

48. MF "la saincte unction," now Extreme Unction, or "Anointing of the Sick."

49. Madame has of course already sermonized at length on these [*Saintré* 17–28].

50. MF "impugnier verité," contesting the truth.

51. Sometimes called Obstinacy.

52. This is one of the rare instances in which La Sale does not translate the Latin, perhaps because this prayer was well known. "May Yahweh bless you and keep you. May Yahweh let his face shine on you and be gracious to you. May Yahweh uncover his face to you and bring you peace." This is known as the Aaronic blessing, or priestly blessing, from Numbers 6:24–26.

53. A transposition of the previous prayer into the first person. "May Yahweh bless me and keep me. May Yahweh let his face shine on me and be gracious to me. May Yahweh uncover his face to me and give me peace."

54. Genesis 9:6. "He who sheds man's blood, / Shall have his blood shed by man." La Sale erroneously cites Deuteronomy as his source.

55. Matthew 26:52, "for all who draw the sword will die by the sword."

56. 1 Chronicles 22:8, "it is not for you to build a house in my name, since you have shed so much blood on earth in my presence."

57. Psalm 55:23.

58. Psalm 5:6.

59. Psalm 139:19. La Sale appears to have made an error in transcription and translation of the original verse, as Dubuis notes. The biblical verse reads: "God, if only you would kill the wicked! Men of blood, away from me!" La Sale's transcriptions, and translations, biblical and other, are often faulty, as Dubuis asserts: see for instance below, on

p. 54 of our text, his mistreatment of the quotation from Claudian (see Dubuis, p. 295, notes 65, 66).

60. Blanchard and Quereuil observe that La Sale's translation is incorrect, since "ygnosco" means "to pardon" and not "to be ignorant"; Blanchard, ed. *Jehan de Saintré,* pp. 100–101. Otaka refers us to Seneca, *Moral Essays* I, "De Clementia" I, 7, 1, p. 374, for comparison.

61. Matthew 6:33.

62. Cf. Aristotle's *Nicomachean Ethics,* II, v–ix (pp. 86–114), as suggested by Otaka, *Jehan de Saintré,* 347.

63. Cited earlier *Saintré* [25].

64. 2 Esdras 3 does not appear to contain this rather commonplace saying.

65. Otaka cites for comparison Job 21:26 and Luke 16:23–25.

66. Otaka refers us to Aristotle, *Politics,* V, ix, 6–7, pp. 462–63.

67. This is the correct form in which, today, to address Queen Elizabeth II.

68. Refers to the eastern Roman Empire, or Byzantium.

69. The feast of *Toussaint,* All Saints' Day, November 1.

70. The same reading list, drawn from Simon de Hesdin's translation of Valerius Maximus's *Memorable Doings and Sayings,* appears in *La Salade,* chapter II, p. 22.

71. May 1 (May Day) was the first of the major summer festivals, and therefore a good moment for Saintré to make his mark.

72. The uncles Madame mentions are the sons of King John: Louis, Duke of Anjou (1339–84), Jean, Duke of Berry (1340–1416), and Philippe le Hardi, Duke of Burgundy (1342–1404). Madame seems to be claiming them as uncles, which would make her the daughter of one of their three surviving sisters Jeanne, Marie, or Isabelle. Antoine seems to have the royal family confused: he makes the three dukes the King's brothers, whereas King John had only one living brother (Louis d'Orléans).

73. This refers to Jacques de Longuyon's *Vows of the Peacock* (c. 1312), which tells how Alexander the Great and his courtiers swore courtly oaths, of service to ladies and to chivalry, on a dressed peacock; in 1454, Philip, Duke of Burgundy had given a spectacular banquet known as the Vows of the Pheasant, at which the participants swore oaths vowing to retake Constantinople (captured by the Turks in 1453).

74. Patron saint of travelers.

75. It is worth noting the importance of formalities and ceremony at the French royal court, for royal permission to depart the court, for leave-taking.

76. Madame has already, of course, taught Jean this prayer; see pp. 29–30 above, with translation, notes 52, 53.

77. That is, the shield is quartered—divided into four parts—showing the arms of each of the families from which the holder is (usually paternally) descended.

78. MF "seigneurs conseillers": these are older and more experienced men, of noble birth, who might act as "safe hands," curb excesses, and act as judges.

79. Note a confusion here: La Sale describes only three destriers, instead of the promised four. None of the manuscripts appears to offer a different reading.

80. What the king of arms is wearing here is an escutcheon that is a badge of office; the blazons in the four quarters are "presumably those of Aragon, insular Sicily, peninsular Sicily (or Naples), and Jerusalem" (our thanks to Jonathan d'Arcy Boulton for this).

81. That is, the front half of the animal, in gold, rising from a *fesse* in the center of the shield; see the Glossary.

82. In MF, here and below, *piece*: that is, a solid plate installed to protect the heart and upper chest.

83. Note a discrepancy here: on p. [80], Madame had specified that three lances should be broken; here, victory accrues from five.

84. MF "lance des dames": final deciding bout after the end of the prescribed combats.

85. Note that even La Sale, here, is conscious—although also admiring—of the complexities of chivalric etiquette.

86. Covered, because hand-produced weapons cannot be guaranteed identical; for fairness, they must be covered, and the knights must choose blind.

87. What La Sale is stressing, here, is that this joust is not a judicial duel—from which the term "appellant" would derive. Saintré is, in MF terms, the *entrepreneur*, the challenger, in a sporting contest; this contrasts with p. 79 where, on the contrary, La Sale calls the hero the *appellant*.

88. Suggests—rather intriguingly—that he is warming up.

89. This is MF "aulne": a variable measure for cloth (c. 1.18 m).

90. Reims cloth had a reputation for fine quality, until the seventeenth century.

91. Perhaps a Murgese breed, taking name from Murge, a village in Apulia: it is all black, much favored as a cavalry horse in the fifteenth century.

92. Sumptuary laws, for instance—laws relating to habits of consumption—seem to say that squires were allowed to wear silver (but not gold); see Frances Baldwin, "Sumptuary Legislation and Personal Regulation" (unpublished dissertation, Johns Hopkins University,1926; online), p. 114.

93. These gifts look disconcertingly like slavery, or at least the sort of indentured servitude under which a craftsman might be contracted to work for a specific period in exchange for subsistence only: see M. Bloch, *Slavery and Serfdom in the Middle Ages*, trans. William R. Beer (Berkeley: University of California Press, 1975).

94. The sentence is ambiguous: it could also read: "I'll say no more about the questions the Queen and her ladies asked."

95. This is Jean I le Meingre, known as Boucicaut (c. 1317–68), Marshal of France, whose dates coincide neatly with those of the King of France, John II, who is at the centre of *Saintré*. La Sale however, perhaps deliberately (see Szkilnik, *Jean de Saintré: Une carrière*), seems frequently to confuse him with his son, Jean II le Meingre, also known as Boucicaut (c. 1366–1421), who is the subject of an important chivalric biography, *Livre des faits,* ed. D. Lalande (Geneva, 1985); he too was Marshal of France, participated in the great crusade of Nicopolis in 1396, and died in England as a prisoner after Agincourt; it was he who took part in the single combat with Galeazzo described below pp.121–24, and

it is his chivalric career—the *pas d'armes*, the tournaments – which most resembles Sain-tré's and which therefore makes him the more convincing model.

96. The *chamberlain* holds a trusted position as the King's confidant, as the officer who controls access to the King: initially designated someone who was in charge of the King's chamber and his wardrobe, but by now had a more ceremonial function.

97. This tag was quoted by Madame, p. 32, as was the poem that follows; it shows how careful La Sale is to show Saintré remembering her teachings.

98. See above, p. 33.

99. "Jest," because this is a nickname deriving from an obscure fishing term, suggest-ing Boucicaut's ability to "net" fame and fortune (see Lalande, *Jean II le Meingre*, pp. 5–6).

100. These are lances armed as for war; this combat therefore is more brutal than Saintré's previous adventures.

101. "Prince," here, designates the person in charge of the conduct of the tourna-ment—not necessarily, in other words, the King.

102. The need to police these complicated arrangements explains (figs 3 and 4) the close supervision of the judges and supporters.

103. Chief herald and King of Arms of France.

104. Statue said to have been brought back from Egypt during the Crusades; object of particular pilgrimage for Charles VI and Charles VII.

105. Also "cut-pile velvet" (MF "velours velluté"): a luxury finish for velvet, with a high luster.

106. For an image from a fifteenth-century manuscript, see detail of a miniature of the tournament of Inglevert, southern Netherlands (Bruges), at http://www.bl.uk/cata logues/illuminatedmanuscripts/ILLUMIN.ASP?Size = mid&IllID = 28394.

107. MF *toise*: nearly two meters.

108. Note that Boucicaut himself (that is, Jean II le Meingre) also organized in 1390 the *pas d'armes* between Calais and Boulogne, known as the "Joutes de Saint-Inglevert," in 1390.

109. MF "duc des Normans": there is no such rank. La Sale must be thinking of Norroy King of Arms, royal herald designate for the north of England.

110. From 1347 (under Edward III of England) to 1558, Calais was in English hands; to declare a truce around Calais would obviate the need for safe-conducts.

111. This would have involved erecting a timber frame faced with more elaborate materials—to be built by the carpenters who constructed the stands and the lists.

112. La Sale lists both *escabeaux* and *escabelles*, both meaning stool; "cracket" is an old synonym for "stool."

113. La Sale calls all the English dignitaries *counts*, a rank that does not exist in England; we replace with the appropriate title.

114. Senior King of Arms for England, having jurisdiction over the whole body of heralds.

115. La Sale is sometimes shaky as to identities and blazons; we are especially grateful to Jonathan d'Arcy Boulton for his help.

116. His blazon would identify him as Sir Thomas Dagworth.

117. MF "Seigneur de Brues"—but the arms are those of the Burghersh family.

118. Niccolò and Galeazzo were authentically visitors to the French court, and in consequence conducted jousts in Padua in 1395 with Jean le Meingre II, known as Boucicaut; La Sale is adroitly mixing fact and fiction.

119. The Porte Baudet is now the Porte Saint-Antoine.

120. The House of Malatesta took Ancona in 1348, and held it until 1383.

121. This time again, Jean le Meingre II dit Boucicaut (1366–1421), the son of the Boucicaut who as we saw above (note 95), and who, if the dates are a guide, figures in this romance. Jean II took part in a single combat with Galeazzo shortly before the capture of Padua by the Venetians in 1405.

122. Venice took Padua in 1405 and held it until the fall of the Republic in 1797.

123. No doubt to do with the complex politics of the Italies and their warring city-states in the fourteenth and fifteenth centuries.

124. Unidentifiable, in the absence of any detail or blazon.

125. See the Introduction, pp. xxi–xxii; note that the term *voiage* is commonly used for a crusade (as in "voiage de Iherusalem").

126. What is meant, here, is a *lance garnie,* or *fournie*—that is, a combat unit consisting of a knight or knights but also of men at arms and archers. Its size varied; see Contamine *Guerre,* p. 278, and Prestwich, *Armies and Warfare.*

127. MF "saige," which is ambiguous: "clever" or "good."

128. This list of names and blazons is almost certainly transcribed from an existing roll of arms, possibly from one related to the so-called Armorial d'Urfé: see Vaivre. As before, La Sale's heraldry can be faulty; names have been given modern spelling when possible.

129. The transcription by Misrahi and Knudson is faulty here and we amend accordingly: see Lecoy's 1969 review.

130. The transcription by Misrahi and Knudson is faulty: see Lecoy's 1969 review; the MS. reads *clefs,* not *cerfs.*

131. France Ancient: *azure semé-de-lis Or*; France Modern: *azure, three fleurs-de-lis Or.*

132. Mentioned by Froissart, who places it in North Africa, and by Chaucer. No one seems able to locate it.

133. Once again, this list must surely have been copied from an existing roll of arms, perhaps one listing participants in the Prussian crusades, like the Bellenville armorial: see Werner Paravicini, *Die Preussenreisen des Europäischen Adels,* 2 vols. (Sigmaringen, 1989–94). It seems more likely, however, that La Sale had access to a general armorial (not, that is, one relating to the Prussian crusades). We are grateful to Dr. Godfried Croenen (Liverpool University) for his help here, and for his help in identifying, from the *Armorial de Gelre,* some of the names, from the Low Countries, listed by La Sale; where possible, the names are modernized. Where no secure identification is possible, we retain La Sale's orthography, and his (sometimes faulty) titles.

134. Both at this date part of the diocese of Liège.

135. Note that in the Middle Ages, Brabant and Holland, Zeeland, Hainault, Liège, Namur, Luxembourg, etc., were all part of the German Empire; it is normal for Brabanters of that date to be called Germans. Again, we are grateful to Dr. Croenen for help with Low Country names.

136. Hoorn in North Holland?

137. A crusading military order, formed at the end of the twelfth century; after the fall of the crusading kingdoms in the Middle East, the Order reestablished itself in Eastern Europe, and launched the Prussian crusades as from 1230.

138. It has proved impossible to locate a source for all this geographical information, some accurate, some fantastical; again, we have modernized where possible.

139. Misrahi and Knudson misread *mescreans* here as *mesureans*: see Lecoy's 1969 review.

140. Saint Catherine is indeed buried in Saint Catherine's Monastery in Sinai. Her remains were "found" by the monks in c. 800. "Rubo" is mysterious.

141. We are grateful to Professor Matthew Strickland (Glasgow University), who explains in a private letter: "There are two distinct events happening here: 1) the dubbing of young men to knighthood, and 2) the elevation of certain chosen knights to the status of banneret. A banneret was a superior rank, denoting a knight of sufficient wealth and status to retain his own knights, in a troop which was identified by his banner (from 'ban',command/ authority). The ceremony for creating a banneret was that the knight presented his pennon, which had two or more V-shaped points, to the lord. The lord elevating the knight would then cut off these points, leaving a distinctive square/rectangular banner."

142. Is La Sale borrowing his account of the battle from an existing source relating to a crusade? Or combining existing sources? If so, the source(s) are unidentifiable: see Knudson, "Prussian Expedition."

143. Who was earlier, of course (p. 145), referred to as Abzin.

144. Blanchard and Quereuil, in their edition, read in their MS. *marais de Lascan* (by the marshes of Lascun)—which actually sounds more plausible: see Lecoy's 1969 review.

145. Saint Denis, saint and Christian martyr, is of course the patron saint of Paris.

146. One of the three royal residences in Paris (the others were the Palais Royal and the Château de Vincennes).

147. The adjective La Sale uses is "nouvelle," a word used increasingly in the latter part of the romance.

148. Presumably, these attach the spurs to the feet.

149. Marriage to a cousin would be forbidden by church rules against consanguinity. The King's analogy underscores the severity of Jean's transgression in having conceived of an *emprise* without prior royal sanction.

150. The papal curia.

151. This elaborate Lenten meal resembles those suggested in the cookbook included in the didactic treatise *Le Ménagier de Paris*. For a translation see Greco and Rose, trans., *The Good Wife's Guide*. The dishes are of fish, and thus appropriate for Lent, but the fare is hardly meager.

152. Although we might rather say that the time passed gaily or merrily, the word "joie" in MF has sexual connotations that are probably not lost on La Sale, who uses the adverb "joieusement."

153. Literally, a justification of authenticity. This is the concluding formula read by the messenger to certify that the letter has indeed been sent by its stated author. Madame is well aware that she has overstayed her leave. Later, after she has written a response, she will listen to the formal letter of credence.

154. The Church of Saint Cosmas and Saint Damian in Luzarches, located about fifteen miles to the north of Saint-Denis, is dedicated to twin brothers Cosmas and Damian, early Christian martyrs and patron saints of physicians.

155. The colorful expression La Sale uses is *pissié en son jaque de soye,* or "pissed in her silken jacket"; Madame has offended the Queen in a way she will not pardon. The crudeness of language here perhaps anticipates the vulgarity of upcoming events and certainly plays on the tension between courtly and uncourtly behavior in this section of the romance.

156. Speaking in one voice, in unanimous agreement.

157. The Abbot is presumably referring to his monk's habit.

158. This passage repeats almost verbatim advice about avoiding vengeance and cruelty that Saintré has received previously from Madame (p. 30).

159. The MF here is "faulse langue," which means literally both "treacherous speech" and "wicked tongue." The double entendre of "langue" makes clear that Jean sees the ensuing punishment of the pierced tongue as just retribution.

160. "Here lies lord Jean de Saintré, knight, seneschal of Anjou and of Maine, and chamberlain of the Lord Duke of Anjou, who died in the year of Our Lord 1368, the 25th day of October. May his soul rest in peace. Amen."

GLOSSARY

We do not gloss the translations of La Sale's heraldic terms (which are italicized in the text); refer to the standard *Boutell's Heraldry*, or Stephen Friar's *New Dictionary of Heraldry* (1987). For definitions and illustrations, see also http://www.heraldsnet.org/saitou/parker/Jpframe.htm. Note that blazoning is not an exact science: La Sale's own blazons are sometimes incomplete, or faulty.

First instances of each term are asterisked in the text; MF refers to Middle French.

accoutred: equipped, dressed, esp. of decorative items.

accoutrements: decorative elements for armor.

appellant: challenger, in a tournament or a *pas d'armes*.

arming points: slits in the doublet to which to attach plate armor

arming sword: tournament sword, designed for thrusting and slicing.

array: *n.* full ceremonial equipment or dress.

articles (of the joust): detailed document setting out the terms of a joust or *pas d'armes*.

Balas rubies: imported from Afghanistan (Badakhshan). Not as valuable as normal rubies, violet rather than true red.

banneret: commanded troops in war under own banner; ranked higher than a knight, but lower than, e.g., a count.

barding: full horse armor, in two sections for fore-and hindquarters.

bascinet: open-faced rounded or pointed helmet; see fig. 4.

basse-danse: stately dance (ancestor of the minuet), by contrast with *morisque* (q.v.) which involved leaping.

baton: white rod used by a king or other authority (see figs. 3, 4) to start and stop a tournament.

beaver: lower part of helmet, attached to the neck armor to protect chin and throat.

beaver flap: hinged metal flap on helmet that protects mouth; can be raised and closed.

besagew: circular reinforcing piece designed to protect armpit (which is especially vulnerable).

blazon: *n.* coat of arms; *v.* to describe a coat of arms in technically correct terms.

Book of Hours: devotional book, containing the breviary and prayers; often magnificently decorated.

bracer: armor for forearm (see fig. 4).

brigandine: sleeveless jerkin with integral overlapping plates fastened between layers of stout fabric by a series of rivets (see fig. 4); cf. *jack.*

brunet from Saint-Lô: fine, dark-colored wool cloth, from town celebrated for weaving.

canopy (MF *ciel*): decorative tent, providing privacy, with roof of tapestry, curtained around.

caparison: *n.* cloth covering for horse, displaying coat of arms; *v.* to cover (with a *caparison* or *trapper,* q.v.).

charnel (MF *charniere*): hinged hasp attaching helmet to breastplate.

chausses: leg armor (see figs. 3, 4).

clarion: medieval trumpet, with a shrill, clear tone.

cloth of silver or gold: cloth woven with silver or gold weft.

coat of arms: 1. emblazoned surcoat, or tabard; 2. the blazon itself.

commissary: official delegated to execute a duty or office.

couch: *v.* 1. lower and aim the lance at the opponent, tucking it under the arm and against the *lance rest* (q.v.) (see fig. 3); 2. embroider with e.g. gold thread.

course [of arms]: each individual bout or joust at a tournament or *pas d'armes.*

courser: horse bred for speed, in war or in a tournament; see also *destrier.*

couter: heavy reinforcing piece attached over the elbow for added protection (see fig. 4).

cracket: small stool.

culverin: a musket or cannon designed to bombard targets from a distance.

demission: abdication, from a formal engagement.

destrier: heavy horse bred for combat, in war or in tournament.

device: pictorial badge, or motto.

dishelm: to remove the helmet.

doublet: man's close-fitting buttoned jacket.

écu: high denomination gold coin stamped with a coat of arms.

emprise: 1. object or token (ring or a bracelet), given to a knight or squire to carry into battle with another knight as a sign of favor and as a prize; 2. contest conducted according to a set of rules devised by the challenger and conveyed to an opponent by a king of arms or herald.

entremets: entertainment dish, often dramatically flavored, colored, and modeled.

entrepreneur: challenger, in joust.

Florence taffeta: Florentine silks and taffetas: highly prized as fine and beautifully dyed.

florin (Aragonese): gold coin (weighing 3.35 g) first minted 1346.

fluke: head of a battle-axe, which consists of the blade proper, and a spike (fluke) (see fig. 4).

forager: officer charged with organizing accommodation and provisions for army, or chivalric enterprise.

franc: franc a cheval, gold coin (3.88 g) showing king armed and on horseback.

gage: item presented in a *pas d'armes* (q.v.) to signify willingness to take up challenge.

gardbrace: plate armor to cover the upper arm (see fig. 4). *Double g:* reinforced.

goodwife: literally, "townswoman"; title of respect for a woman not of noble birth living in a town.

gown: french *robe*: short garment (for a man), worn over a coublet.

greaves: armor for the lower leg.

grooms of the chamber: well-born young men acting as attendants to a king.

hackney: docile, well-trained horse, especially for a lady.

haft: handle or hilt of a weapon.

helmet crest: object—often model of a figure or animal—fastened to the helmet (see fig. 3).

herald: court official charged with conveying ceremonial messages, and marshaling combatants in tournaments and warfare.

hypocras: drink made from spiced, sugared wine.

jack (MF *jaquecte*): padded doublet often worn by archers and foot soldiers: made of small iron plates sewn between layers of felt and canvas; lighter than mail or armor (cf. *brigandine*, where plates are riveted).

jennet (Andalusian): specific breed of light riding horse noted for smooth gait and good disposition.

journeyman: a craftsman who has completed an apprenticeship but is not yet a master.

king of arms: senior rank of an officer of arms, having authority to grant armorial bearings; referred to by honorific titles.

lames: jointed plates of armor making up the *fauld* covering lower body (see figs. 3, 4).

lance aux dames: during a tournament, final joust in honor of the ladies.

lance rest: metal flange or stop on right side of the breastplate under the armpit; serves to absorb some of the backward shock of the lance.

lawn: fine gauzy linen cloth used (among other things) for the veil on a headdress.

league: variable distance, between 3.25 and 4.68 km.

letter of challenge: letter issued by challenger inviting all comers to a *pas d'armes* (q.v.).

levée: ceremonial rising of the Queen, attended by a few trusted ladies.

list (often plural): field set up for jousting.

livery (pl. liveries): uniform dress adorning the members of a household.

mantling: protective cloth attached to the back of the helmet to protect the knight from elements (see fig. 3).

mark: gold or silver coinage valued by weight.

marten: pine marten, whose pelts were highly valued.

Mass of the Holy Spirit: Mass said at the beginning of an enterprise (also known as Invocation Mass).

mêlée: general tournament fight where knights are divided into two sides and come together in a charge.

morisque: energetic, leaping dance imported from Moorish Spain.

musk: class of aromatic substances used as base notes in perfumery.

nobles: high-value gold coins.

obeisance: attitude or gesture conveying deference.

outrance, a: using war weapons and armor, at risk of death—as opposed to a combat *a plaisir*.

parting cup: traditional nightcap of wine and spices.

pas d'armes: a knight establishes himself at a landmark (bridge, ford, tournament field . . .) and offers to take on all comers.

pattens: protective outer shoes, elevated like clogs, designed to be worn over indoor shoes or slippers.

pauldron: reinforced armor protecting shoulder and upper arm (see fig. 4).

pavilion: ornate tent used in tournaments and ceremonial occasions.

pavise: tall shield used by crossbowmen to protect themselves while reloading.

petition of arms: request for permission to undertake a joust or *pas d'armes* (q.v.).

Plaisance linen: Plaisance (Piacenza) was center of weaving in the Middle Ages.

plastron: reinforcing plate, double thickness, covering the belly and lower body.

poleaxe: axe designed for tournaments, rather than battle; consists of a hammerhead balanced by a fluke (q.v.), with the head of the haft a spike (see fig. 4).

pomander (MF *oiselet de Chypre*): ball made of perfumes to protect against bad smells or infections.

poudre de duc: mixture of powdered ginger, cinnamon, nutmeg, galingale, and sugar, thought to have aphrodisiac qualities (perhaps a corruption of *poudre doux,* "sweet powder"); see *Le Ménagier de Paris*.

presence chamber: large room in the monarch's (or Queen's) private apartments used to receive, and hear addresses.

pursuivant: junior officer of arms, assistant to king of arms.

rere-banquet: sumptuous meal taken after dinner or supper: "a banket where men syt downe to drynke and eate agayne after their meate" (attested 1530; see OED).

rest: lance is *in rest* when fitted to the *lance rest* (q.v.).

robing room: room in the monarch's private apartments where courtiers witnessed ceremonial robing.

rouncey: (MF *roncin*): ordinary, all-purpose riding horse.

roundel: 1. circular reinforcing plate fixed to the back of the gauntlet; 2. circular or conical plate fixed in front of lance grip to prevent hand sliding up the shaft on impact; also known as a vamplate (q.v.) (see fig. 3); 3. brooch or medallion.

roundel dagger: stiff-bladed dagger, taking its name from a round hand guard; standard sidearm, designed for warfare (see fig. 4).

Ruyers: inhabitants of the region between the Meuse and Rhine Rivers; that is, from the west of the Empire, and principally from the Low Countries.

sabatons: plate armor for the foot, consisting of overlapping plates ending in a toe cap (see figs. 3, 4).

saddlebow: the raised front part of a saddle (also known today as the pommel) (see fig. 3).

saddletree: framework of saddle, designed to balance the rider's weight away from horse's spine.

salad helmet: lightweight helmet with a brim flaring in the back, sometimes with a visor.

sans reproche: (of a knight) having a blameless bloodline and reputation.

shaffron: armored head defense for a horse, often richly decorated (see fig. 3).

simples: potions or herbal medicines deriving from a single herb.

sou: a *livre* (pound) consisted of twenty *sous.*

station: area on the tournament field where each combatant would have his seconds, and his spare equipment, spare horses, and weapons.

subtlety: highly ornamental dish, largely made of sugar.

supporters: each combatant in a joust or *pas d'armes* (q.v.) would have two or more supporters, whose role it was to ensure fair play and to bring the joust to an end if one of the combatants was seriously wounded (see figs. 3, 4).

swag: feathers, fabrics, etc., bound together and used to decorate fabrics or armor (see fig. 3).

tabard: sleeveless cloth tunic worn by a king of arms or a herald, when on his lord's business; decorated with the coat of arms of the house to which he is attached (see fig. 3).

table-cut (of diamond): ground down to form a square facet; technique developed in the fourteenth century, still rare (and precious) in the fifteenth.

targe: escutcheon worn by a herald as a badge of office.

tennis (MF *jeu de paume*): the original sport from which modern tennis derives, played without a racket in an indoor court; players struck the ball with the palm of the hand.

thrusting lance: shorter lance intended for combat at barriers or tilt barriers (q.v.); intended for thrusting (see fig. 4).

tilt barrier: partition (of wood or canvas) designed to separate combatants and avoid injury to horses (see fig. 3).

tilting helmet: elaborate full helmet, also known as a *great helm* (see fig. 3).

trapper: richly embroidered cloth that covered horse armor in a tournament (see fig. 3).

trundle bed: small bed that slides under a larger one (Brit. *truckle-bed*).

usher: gentleman u.: staff member who controlled access to the noble lord and his family.

vamplate: circular or conical plate fixed in front of lance grip to prevent hand sliding up the shaft on impact; sometimes known as *roundel* (*q. v.*) (see fig. 3).

varlet-tranchant: most prestigious of squire positions: attends personally to the king at table, and carves his meat.

visor: hinged piece of steel protecting eyes and nose while permitting breathing and vision; also known as *beaver* (q.v.) (see fig. 4).

war saddle: high-backed, so rider can brace himself against the shock of encounter ("high-cantled") (see fig. 3).

whiteware: fine-glazed pottery manufactured in France and elsewhere, made from white-fired clay, usually in shades of buff: see Alan Vince and Richard Jones, "Normandy Whitewares from Ronaldsons Wharf, Leith, Scotland," *Medieval Ceramics* 29 (2005): 25–30, and for illustrations, see www.museumoflondon.org.uk.

withdrawing room: private apartment of monarch or lord.

wrapper: plate(s) used to reinforce the *beaver* (q.v.) across the mouth and cheeks (see fig. 4).

SELECTED BIBLIOGRAPHY

EDITIONS

Antoine de La Sale. *Le Petit Jehan de Saintré*, ed. Pierre Champion and Fernand Desonay. Paris: Éditions du Trianon, 1926.

———. *Jehan de Saintré*, ed. Jean Misrahi and Charles A. Knudson. Geneva: Droz, 1965 (repr. 1978). (Note review by Félix Lecoy, *Romania* 90 [1969]: 411–19).

———. *Jehan de Saintré, suivi de l'Adicion extraicte des croniques de Flandres,* ed. Yorio Otaka. Tokyo: Librairie Takeuchi, 1967.

———. *Jean de Saintré*, ed. Mario Eusebi. Paris: Champion, 1993–94.

———. *Jehan de Saintré*, ed. Joël Blanchard, trans. Michel Quereuil. Paris: Le Livre de Poche, 1995.

TRANSLATIONS

Antoine de La Sale. *The History and Pleasant Chronicle of Little Jehan de Saintré, and of the Lady of the Fair Cousins, together with the book of the Knight of the Tower Landry, which he made for the instruction of his daughters,* trans. Alexander Vance. London: Chapman and Hall, 1862.

———. *Little John of Saintré,* trans. Irvine Egerton Gray. London: G. Routledge, 1931.

———. *Saintré, roman du quinzième siècle,* trans. Roger Dubuis. Paris: Champion, 1995.

———. *Jehan de Saintré,* trans. Quereuil: see *Jehan de Saintré,* ed. Joël Blanchard (1995).

OTHER WORKS BY LA SALE

Antoine de La Sale. *Œuvres complètes d'Antoine de La Sale,* ed. Fernand Desonay. 2 vols. I: *La Salade*; II: *La Sale.* Liège: Faculté de philosophie et lettres and Paris: Droz, 1935, 1941.

———. *Le Paradis de la reine Sibylle,* ed. Fernand Desonay. Paris: Droz, 1930; trans. Francine Mora-Lebrun. Paris: Stock, 1983.

————. *Le Réconfort de Madame de Fresne*, ed. Ian Hill. Exeter: University of Exeter Press, 1979.

————. *Traité des anciens et des nouveaux tournois*, ed. Lefèvre, in her *Antoine de La Sale* (see below).

PRIMARY SOURCES

La Sale may have drawn from versions of these works or from collections of quotations (florilegia) that include passages from these works, or he may have been indirectly influenced by these or similar works. La Sale's precise source is usually impossible to pinpoint. We provide English or French translations when possible.

Aquinas, Thomas. *Summa theologica*. Volume 5. *The Life of Christ*, trans. Samuel Parsons and Albert Pinheiro. New York: McGraw-Hill, 1971.

Aristotle. *The Nicomachean Ethics,* trans. H. Rackham. Loeb. Cambridge, MA: Harvard University Press, 1934.

————. *The Politics of Aristotle,* trans. Ernest Barker. Oxford: Oxford University Press, 1962.

Bible: *The New Jerusalem Bible*. Garden City, NY: Doubleday, 1985.

Cato. *The Distichs of Cato*, ed. and trans. J. Wight Duff and Arnold M. Duff. In *Minor Latin Poets*. Loeb. Cambridge, MA: Harvard University Press, 1934. Pp. 585–639.

Cérémonies des gages de batailles selon les constitutions du bon roi Philippe de France: représentées en onze figures [. . .], ed. G.-A. Crapelet. Paris: Imprimerie de Crapelet, 1830. (Online: BnF GALLICA.)

Chrétien de Troyes. *The Story of the Grail, or Perceval,* ed. Rupert T. Pickens, trans. William W. Kibler. New York: Garland, 1990.

Christine de Pizan. *The Book of Deeds of Arms and of Chivalry,* ed. Charity Cannon Willard, trans. Sumner Willard. University Park: Pennsylvania State University Press, 1999.

Diogenes Laertius. *Lives of Eminent Philosophers*, trans. Robert D. Hicks. 2 vols. New York: G. P. Putnam, 1925.

Froissart, Jean. *Chronicles,* selected, ed., and trans. Geoffrey Brereton. Harmondsworth: Penguin, 1978.

Geoffroi de Charny. *The Book of Chivalry of Geoffroi de Charny: Text, Context, and Translation,* trans. Richard W. Kaeuper and Elspeth Kennedy. Philadelphia: University of Pennsylvania Press, 1996.

Geoffroy de la Tour Landry. *The Book of the Knight of the Tower,* trans. William Caxton, ed. M. Y. Offord. Early English Text Society, SS2. Oxford: Oxford University Press, 1971.

Jacques de Lalaing: Livre des faits de Jacques de Lalaing, ed. Denis Lalande. Geneva: Droz, 1985; trans. C. Beaune. In *Splendeurs de la cour de Bourgogne,* ed. Danielle Régnier-Bohler. Paris: Laffont, 1995. Pp. 1193–1409.

Jehan d'Avennes: L'istoire de tres vaillans princez monseigneur Jehan d'Avennes, ed. Danielle
    Quéruel. Villeneuve-d'Ascq: Presses Universitaires de Septentrion, 1997.

Jerome, Saint. "Against Jovinian." In *Jankyn's Book of Wikked Wives,* ed. and trans. Ralph
    Hanna III, Traugott Lawler, et al. Athens: University of Georgia Press, 1997.
    Pp. 157–94.

Le Livre du Chevalier de la Tour Landry pour l'enseignement de ses filles, ed. Anatole de
    Montaiglon. Paris: P. Jannet, 1854. (Online: BnF GALLICA); see also above, Geof-
    froy de la Tour Landry.

The Lombard Laws, trans. Katherine Fisher Drew. Philadelphia: University of Pennsylva-
    nia Press, 1973.

Llull, Ramon. *Livre de l'enseignement des enfants (Doctrine pueril),* trans. Bernard Jolibert.
    Paris: Klincksieck, 2005.

———. *The Book of the Ordre of Chiualrye and Knighthood,* trans. William Caxton, ed.
    Alfred T. P. Byles. London: Early English Text Society, 1926.

———. *Livre de l'ordre de chevalerie,* ed. Patrick Gifreu. Paris: Editions La Différence,
    1991.

*Le Ménagier de Paris. The Good Wife's Guide: "Le Ménagier de Paris": A Medieval Household
    Book,* trans. Gina L. Greco and Christine M. Rose. Ithaca, NY: Cornell University
    Press, 2009.

Pierre de La Cépède, ed. Toberet Kaltenbacher. "Der altfranzösischer Roman *Paris et
    Vienne.*" *Romanische Forschungen* 15 (1904): 391–629.

Ponthus et Sidoine: Le Roman de Ponthus et Sidoine, ed. Marie-Claude de Crécy. Geneva:
    Droz, 1997.

Raoul de Houdenc. *Le Roman des eles, followed by The Anonymous Ordene de Chevalerie,*
    ed. Keith Busby. Amsterdam: J. Benjamins, 1983.

Rasse de Brunhamel, *"Floridan et Elvide,"* ed. H. P. Clive. *Medium Aevum* 26 (1957):
    154–85.

Robert de Blois. *Biaudouz,* ed. and trans. Jacques Lemaire. Liège: Éditions de l'Université
    de Liège, 2008.

Seneca. "De beneficiis." In Seneca, *Moral Essays,* trans. John W. Basore. Loeb. Vol. 3.
    New York: G. P. Putnam's Sons, 1928.

Valerius Maximus. *Memorable Doings and Sayings,* trans. D. R. Shackleton Bailey. Cam-
    bridge, MA: Harvard University Press, 2000.

Vegetius Renatus, Flavius. *De re militari: Epitome of Military Science,* trans. N. P. Milner.
    Liverpool: Liverpool University Press, 1993.

Virgil. *The Aeneid,* trans. Robert Fitzgerald. New York: Random House, 1983.

STUDIES OF ANTOINE DE LA SALE AND *JEAN DE SAINTRÉ*

For a regularly updated bibliography for La Sale and Jean de Saintré, see the
ARLIMA [Archives de littérature du Moyen Âge] website: http://www.arlima.net/ad/
antoine_de_la_sale.html

Bénet, Jacques. *Jean d'Anjou: Duc de Calabre et de Lorraine, 1426–1470.* Nancy: Société Thierry Alix, 1997.

Brown-Grant, Rosalind. *French Romance of the Later Middle Ages: Gender, Morality, and Desire.* Oxford: Oxford University Press, 2008.

Champion, Pierre. *Le Manuscrit d'auteur du "Petit Jehan de Saintré," avec des notes autographes d'Antoine de La Sale.* Paris: Champion, 1926.

Cholakian, Patricia Frances. "The Two Narrative Styles of Antoine de La Sale." *Romance Notes* 10 (1969): 362–72.

Delogu, Daisy. "Desire, Deception and Display: Linguistic Performance in *Jehan de Saintré.*" In *Visualizing Medieval Performance,* ed. Elina Gertsman. Aldershot: Ashgate, 2008. Pp. 193–206.

Desonay, Fernand. *Antoine de la Sale, aventureux et pédagogue.* Liège: Bibliothèque de la Faculté de philosophie et lettres de l'Université de Liège; paris: Droz, 1940.

Dubuis, Roger. *Les Cent Nouvelles nouvelles et la tradition de la nouvelle en France au Moyen Âge.* Grenoble: Presses Universitaires de Grenoble, 1973.

Dufournet, Jean, ed. *Saintré d'Antoine de la Sale: "Entre tradition et modernité."* Sp. issue *Revue des langues romanes* 105 (2001).

Emerson, Catherine. "No Way to Treat Your Mother: Understanding Petit Jehan de Saintré's Rage." *French Studies* 65 (2011): 429–43.

Jeay, Madeleine. "Les éléments didactiques et descriptifs de *Jehan de Saintré*: Des lourdeurs à reconsidérer." *Fifteenth-Century Studies* 19 (1992): 85–100.

———. "Une théorie du roman: Le manuscrit autographe de *Jehan de Saintré.*" *Romance Philology* 47 (1994): 287–307.

———. "*La Salade* d'Antoine de La Sale: Les leçons d'un loyal serviteur à un 'futur roi.'" In *Quant l'ung amy pour l'autre veille: Mélanges . . . Claude Thiry,* ed. Tania Van Hemelryck and Maria Colombo Timelli. Turnhout: Brepols, 2008. Pp. 123–31.

Johan, Frédérique. "Quelques accents uniques: Pour une autre lecture du *Petit Jehan de Saintré*: L'apport des images du Bruxellensis 9547." *Le Moyen Français* 57–58 (2005–6): 177–93.

Keen, Maurice. "Huizinga, Kilgour and the Decline of Chivalry." *Medievalia et Humanistica,* n.s., 8 (1977): 1–20.

Knudson, Charles A. "The Prussian Expedition in *Jehan de Saintré.*" In *Études offertes à Félix Lecoy.* Paris: Champion, 1973. Pp. 271–77.

Kristeva, Julia. *Le Texte du roman: Approche sémiologique d'une structure discursive transformationelle.* The Hague: Mouton, 1970.

Labère, Nelly. "*Du pied sous la table au croc en jambe*: Lecture gastronomique de l'itinéraire amoureux et chevaleresque dans *Jehan de Saintré* d'Antoine de La Sale." In *Quant l'ung amy pour l'autre veille: Mélanges . . . Claude Thiry,* ed. Tania Van Hemelryck and Maria Colombo Timelli. Turnhout: Brepols, 2008. Pp. 133–46.

Lalande, Denis. "Le couple Saintré-Boucicaut dans le roman de *Jehan de Saintré.*" *Romania* 111 (1990): 481–94.

Lazard, Madeleine. "Le costume dans *Jehan de Saintré*: Valeur sociale et symbolique." *Studi Francesi* 78 (1982): 457–64.

Lecourt, Marcel, "Une source d'Antoine de La Sale: Simon de Hesdin." *Romania* 76 (1955): 39–83, 183–211.

Lecoy, Félix. Review of Antoine de La Sale, *Jehan de Saintré*, ed. Jean Misrahi and Charles A. Knudson. *Romania* 90 (1969): 411–19.

Lefèvre, Sylvie. *Antoine de La Sale: La fabrique de l'œuvre et de l'écrivain (suivi de l'édition critique du Traité des anciens et des nouveaux tournois).* Geneva: Droz, 2006.

Léglu, Catherine. "Between Hell and a Fiery Mountain: Antoine de La Sale's Ascent of Vulcano." *Studies in Travel Writing* 11 (2007): 109–26.

Mora, Francine. *Voyages en Sibyllie: Antoine de La Sale: les hommes, le paradis et l'enfer.* Paris: Riveneuve Éditions, 2009.

Speer, Mary. "The Literary Fortune of the *Petit Jehan de Saintré*." *Kentucky Romance Quarterly* 22 (1975): 385–411.

Szkilnik, Michèle. "Nourriture et blasons dans *Jehan de Saintré* d'Antoine de La Sale." *Fifteenth-Century Studies* 26 (2001): 183–99.

———. *Jean de Saintré: Une carrière chevaleresque au XVe siècle.* Geneva: Droz, 2003.

———. "*Jean de Saintré* ou le rêve d'une internationale chevaleresque." In *La novel·la de Joanot Martorell i l'Europa del segle XV,* ed. Ricard Bellveser et al. Special issue of *Tirant* 14 (2011): 385–401.

Taylor, Jane H. M. "The Pattern of Perfection: *Jehan de Saintré* and the Chivalric Ideal," *Medium Aevum* 53 (1984): 254–62.

———. "Image as Reception: Antoine de la Sale's *Le petit Jehan de Saintré*." In *Literary Aspects of Courtly Culture*, ed. D. Maddox and S. Sturm-Maddox. Cambridge: D. S. Brewer, 1994. Pp. 265–79.

———. "La fonction de la croisade dans *Jehan de Saintré*." *Cahiers de recherches médiévales* 1 (1996): 193–204.

Uitti, Karl D. "Renewing and Undermining of Old French Romance: *Jehan de Saintré*" In *Romance: Generic Transformation from Chrétien de Troyes to Cervantes,* ed. Kevin Brownlee and Marina Scordilis Brownlee. Hanover, NH: University Press of New England, 1985. Pp. 135–54.

Vaivre, Jean-Bernard de, "L'héraldique dans le roman du *Petit Jehan de Saintré* d'Antoine de La Sale." *Cahiers d'héraldique* 3 (1977): 67–83.

OTHER READING

Anglo, Sydney. "L'Arbre de chevalerie et le perron dans les tournois." In *Les Fêtes de la Renaissance*, ed. Jean Jacquot and Elie Konigson. Paris: Editions du CNRS, 1975. Pp. 283–98.

Barber, Richard W., and Juliet R. V. Barker. *Tournaments: Jousts, Chivalry and Pageants in the Middle Ages.* Woodbridge, UK: Boydell, 1989.

Barker, Juliet R. V. *The Tournament in England, 1100–1400.* Woodbridge, UK: Boydell, 1986.

Bejczy, István. *The Cardinal Virtues in the Middle Ages: A Study in Moral Thought from the Fourth to the Fourteenth Century.* Leiden: Brill, 2011.

Bianciotto, Gabriel. "Le *pas d'armes de Saumur* (1446) et la vie chevaleresque à la cour de René d'Anjou." In *Le roi René: René, duc d'Anjou, de Bar et de Lorraine . . . : Actes du colloque international, Avignon 13, 14, 15 juin 1981: Annales universitaires d'Avignon,* no. sp. 1 and 2 (1986): 1–16.

Christiansen, Eric. *The Northern Crusades.* London: Penguin, 1980.

Contamine, Philippe. "Les tournois en France à la fin du Moyen Âge." In *Das ritterliche Turnier im Mittelalter,* ed. Joseph Fleckenstein. Göttingen: Vandenhoeck und Ruprecht, 1986. Pp. 425–49.

———. *Guerre, état et société à la fin du Moyen Âge.* Paris: Mouton, 1972.

Cooper, Helen. "Good Advice on Leaving Home in the Romances." In *Youth in the Middle Ages,* ed. P. J. P. Goldberg and Felicity Riddy. Woodbridge, UK: York Medieval Press, 2004. Pp. 101–21.

Edge, David, and John Miles Paddock. *Arms and Armor of the Medieval Knight: An Illustrated History of Weaponry in the Middle Ages.* New York: Crescent Books, 1988.

Gaucher, Elisabeth. *La Biographie chevaleresque: Typologie d'un genre (XIIIe–XVe siècle).* Paris: Champion, 1994.

Glixelli, Stefan. "Les contenances de table." *Romania* 47 (1921): 1–40.

Heers, Jacques. *Fêtes, jeux et joutes dans les sociétés d'occident à la fin du moyen âge.* Montreal: Institut d'études médiévales and Paris: Vrin, 1971.

Huizinga, Johan. *Homo Ludens: A Study of the Play Element in Culture.* London: Routledge and Kegan Paul, 1948.

———. *The Waning of the Middle Ages,* trans. Frederik Jan Hopman. Hardmondsworth: Penguin Books, 1955. (Also published as *The Autumn of the Middle Ages.*)

Jager, Eric. *The Last Duel: A True Story of Crime, Scandal, and Trial by Combat in Medieval France.* New York: Broadway Books, 2004.

Jeay, Madeleine. *Le commerce des mots: L'usage des listes dans la littérature médiévale (XIIe–XVe siècles).* Geneva: Droz, 2006.

Johnston, Mark D., ed. *Medieval Conduct Literature: An Anthology of Vernacular Guides to Behaviour for Youths, with English Translations.* Toronto: University of Toronto Press, 2009.

Jones, Robert W. *Bloodied Banners: Martial Display on the Medieval Battlefield.* Woodbridge, UK: Boydell and Breuler, 2010.

Jourdan, Jean-Pierre. "Le symbolisme politique du *pas* dans le royaume de France (Bourgogne et Anjou) à la fin du Moyen Âge." *Journal of Medieval History* 18 (1992): 161–81.

Kaeuper, Richard W. *Chivalry and Violence in Medieval Europe.* Oxford: Oxford University Press, 1999.

———. *War, Justice and Public Order: England and France in the Later Middle Ages.* Oxford: Clarendon Press, 1988.

———, ed. *Violence in Medieval Society.* Woodbridge, UK: Boydell, 2000.

Keen, Maurice. *Chivalry.* New Haven: Yale University Press, 1984.

————. *Nobles, Knights and Men-at-Arms in the Middle Ages.* London: Hambledon Press, 1996.

Krueger, Roberta L., ed. *The Cambridge Companion to Medieval Romance.* Cambridge: Cambridge University Press, 2000.

————. "Teach Your Children Well: Medieval Conduct Guides for Youths." In Johnston, ed., *Medieval Conduct Literature*, ix–xxxiii (see above).

Lalande, Denis. *Jean II le Meingre, dit Boucicaut (1366–1421): Étude d'une biographie héroïque.* Geneva: Droz, 1988.

Mérindol, Christian de. *Les fêtes de chevalerie à la cour du roi René.* Paris: Éditions du Comité des travaux historiques et scientifiques, 1993.

Pastoureau, Michel. *Heraldry: Its Origins and Meaning,* trans. Francisca Garvie. London: Thames and Hudson, 1997.

Piponnier, Françoise. *Costume et vie sociale: La cour d'Anjou, XIVe et XVe siècles.* Paris and The Hague: Mouton, 1970.

Planche, Alice. "Du tournoi au théâtre en Bourgogne: Le Pas de la Fontaine des Pleurs à Châlon-sur-Sâone (1449–1450)." *Le Moyen Âge* 8 (1975): 97–128.

Poirion, Daniel. "Écriture et réécriture au Moyen Âge." *Littérature* 41 (1981): 109–18.

Prestwich, Michael. *Armies and Warfare in the Middle Ages: The English Experience.* New Haven: Yale University Press, 1996.

Riley-Smith, Jonathan. *The Crusades: A Short History.* New Haven: Yale University Press, 1987.

Robin, Françoise. *La Cour d'Anjou-Provence: La vie artistique sous le règne de René.* Paris: Picard, 1985.

Stanesco, Michel. *Jeux d'errance du chevalier médiéval: Aspects ludiques de la fonction guerrière dans la littérature du moyen âge flamboyant.* Leiden: Brill, 1988.

Strubel, Arman. "Le *pas d'armes:* Le tournoi entre le romanesque et le théâtral." In *Théâtre et spectacle hier et aujourd'hui. Moyen Âge et Renaissance.* Paris: Éditions du Comité des travaux historiques et scientifiques, 1991. Pp. 273–84.

Das Turnierbuch für René d'Anjou (Le Pas de Saumur), ed. N. Elagina et al. Graz: Akademische Druck-und Verlangsanstalt/Moscow: Verlag Naslediga, 1998.

Vale, Malcolm. *The Princely Court: Medieval Courts and Culture in North-West Europe, 1270–1380.* Oxford: Oxford University Press, 2001.

————. *War and Chivalry: Warfare and Aristocratic Culture in England, France, and Burgundy at the End of the Middle Ages.* London: Duckworth, 1981.

DICTIONARIES

Dictionnaire du moyen français. Online only, see http://www.atilf.fr/dmf.

Godefroy, Frédéric. *Dictionnaire de l'ancienne langue française et de tous ses dialectes du 9e au 15e siècle.* 10 vols. Paris: Vieweg, 1881–1902. (Online: BnF GALLICA.)

New Oxford American Dictionary. Oxford: Oxford University Press, 2001.

ACKNOWLEDGMENTS

Part of the attraction of *Jean de Saintré* is that it is written by an authority in different specialties—chivalry and tournaments, heraldry and dress—and one of the great pleasures of this project, for us, has been exploring these different, and demanding, fields. Translating required us to consult a number of specialists in the United States and the United Kingdom, and we are extremely grateful for their expertise, patience, and commitment. Jonathan D'Arcy Boulton, Professor of History at the University of Notre Dame, has been an invaluable informant on the vocabulary and formalities of heraldry: not just the blazons themselves, but also in identifying their holders and pointing out La Sale's errors. Dr. Ralph Moffat, Curator of European Arms and Armour at Kelvingrove Art Gallery and Museum in Glasgow, has been a mine of information on arms and armor and tournament practice: his guidance has been essential, and like Professor D'Arcy Boulton, he has guarded us from a multitude of misunderstandings. On medieval dress, we have been helped by two authorities: Dr. Rebecca Dixon, Lecturer in French at Liverpool University, and Professor Sarah-Jane Heller, of the Department of French and Italian at Ohio State University. Both of them were able to identify items of clothing, and to suggest appropriate translations. On warfare and crusading, and on the participants in Saintré's crusade, we received considerable help from Michael Prestwich, Emeritus Professor of History at Durham University; from Dr. Len Scales, also of the History Department at Durham University; from Dr. Godfried Croenen of the School of Cultures, Languages and Area Studies at the University of Liverpool. Richard W. Kaeuper, Professor of History at the University of Rochester, advised us on the regulation of chivalric violence in *Saintré*, and Barbara Gold, Edward North Professor of Classics at Hamilton College, was most helpful in clarifying La Sale's Latin translations and paraphrases. It has been a pleasure to work with them, and we are deeply grateful for their help; any remaining errors are entirely our responsibility.

We are also very grateful to the Burgess Chair at Hamilton College for generously subsidizing the cost of manuscript reproductions.